A STUDY OF DIALECTIC IN PLATO'S *PARMENIDES*

SERIES EDITOR

John Russon

REREADING ANCIENT PHILOSOPHY

A STUDY OF DIALECTIC IN PLATO'S *PARMENIDES*

ERIC SANDAY

NORTHWESTERN UNIVERSITY PRESS • EVANSTON, ILLINOIS

Northwestern University Press
www.nupress.northwestern.edu

Copyright © 2015 by Northwestern University Press.
Published 2015. All rights reserved.

ISBN 978-0-8101-3485-0

The Library of Congress has cataloged the original, hardcover edition as follows:
Sanday, Eric, author.
A study of dialectic in Plato's Parmenides / Eric Sanday.
pages cm. — (Rereading ancient philosophy)
ISBN 978-0-8101-3007-4 (cloth : alk. paper) — ISBN 978-0-8101-6791-9 (ebook)
1. Plato. Parmenides. 2. Form (Philosophy) 3. Reasoning—Early works to 1800. 4. Zeno, of Elea. I. Title. II. Series: Rereading ancient philosophy.
BS1415.52.H36 2014
184—dc23

2014036194

For Eve

CONTENTS

ACKNOWLEDGMENTS

I owe credit for the writing and realization of this book to those who have accompanied me in thought, friendship, and life. I am most indebted to Eve Rabinoff for her wisdom and kindness, without which all my familiar points of reference in the world and many in philosophy would be lost. I am deeply grateful for Mitchell Miller's extraordinary generosity, uniquely powerful insight into Platonic philosophy, and steadfast attention to nuance, which drew the Parmenides out of darkness and into a chartable region; his presence can be felt throughout this book. For his constant friendship and astonishing commitment to philosophy, I thank John Russon. For the care in his reading and reverence for the artistry of Plato, I thank John Sallis. I have aspired in this book to be sufficient to the friends with whom I have grown in dialogue, Ömer Aygün, David Ciavatta, Greg Recco, and Patricia Fagan. I am thankful to the seminar participants at the University of Kentucky, especially Michael Wiitala and Paul DiRado, for sustaining an environment of serious reflection and conversation through the very personal contribution of their time and care. I thank I-Kai Jeng for his assistance editing and thinking about the Greek translations. I also thank the Department of Philosophy at the University of Kentucky for its unflagging support. And in a most basic sense I want to acknowledge my mother and father, Peggy Reeves Sanday and Carlos Sanday, and my sister, Julie Sanday, for being the lenses through which I learned to see.

A STUDY OF DIALECTIC IN PLATO'S *PARMENIDES*

INTRODUCTION

Dialectic and Philosophical Method

This book is a close reading of Plato's *Parmenides*, which is notoriously one of the great mysteries of the Western philosophical tradition. The difficulty and hubris of wading into the complexities of this text should not be underestimated, and a book-length study of its arguments will strike many as as much a thrilling enterprise as it is a risky one. The dialogue holds singular importance for understanding Platonic philosophy, and, through Plato, it grants entry into an ancient and contested philosophical tradition. As Parmenides says in the dialogue, philosophy will not "seize hold of you" until you make your way through these arguments.

The *Parmenides* opens with a discussion between a very young Socrates and two visiting Eleatic philosophers, Zeno and Parmenides, focusing on various metaphysical claims concerning the nature of the intelligibility of things, especially what it means to be "one" and what it means "to be." Zeno, a friend and companion of Parmenides, begins the conversation with an argument reflecting on some apparent contradictions in the way we conceive the world to be "many," i.e., composed of a multiplicity of things. Socrates responds by introducing his so-called theory of forms (εἴδη), which he uses as a basis on which to address and resolve the apparent contradictions in our ways of thinking about multiplicity. Parmenides then puts Socrates' theory to the test with a series of objections; in the end, these objections leave Socrates speechless and without a clear sense of how to proceed. Parmenides announces his belief that Socrates' account is true, and that everything hinges on its being true: the very possibility of serious dialogue hangs in the balance. But the truth of the account is not yet held by Socrates as a secure possession, and it will not be until Socrates undergoes a series of exercises provided by Parmenides, in which he will begin to develop the ability to answer a host of objections and the ability to teach the account of forms to someone who doubts their existence or their accessibility to human knowing. The tools for this transformation are given to Socrates in the form of the dialogue's long second section, which is introduced as an example of serious philosophical training. This training will enable Socrates and all budding dialecticians to fulfill their potential to overcome the ordinary attitude toward the world and become the sort of knower and teacher that is required.

The basic aim of this book is intended to be bold: to show that Plato's "theory of forms" is true and relatively intuitive once we have done the hard work of clearing away misconceptions about the nature of "is." There is perhaps no single idea in the history of philosophy that has been subject to such a wide range of conflicting interpretations, and in some notable cases it has been considered simply implausible. I will argue that the chief obstacle standing in the way of the theory of forms is the distorting effect that our everyday privileging of individual things has on understanding. Furthermore, I will claim that this privileging of what we can own, produce, and exchange, and through which we gain mastery of our surroundings, is understood in Platonic philosophy and the *Parmenides* in particular to be a significant obstacle to philosophical education. The chief philosophical work in the dialogue, in my view then, is to destabilize the false privileging of individual things that stands at the core of our everyday attitude. Once we do this, some version of the "theory of forms" will become relatively intuitive and easily understood.

My approach begins from the assumption that the tacit metaphysical privileging of individual things is unavoidable and in some sense necessary. Things, treated as the ultimate building blocks of what-is, are indeed the basis of an important connection we have to the world, one by which our mastery over things and environments is established. But this attitude, which sees no intelligible source prior to things, fits neatly into the larger attitude according to which human subjectivity imposes meaning on things, a stance that achieves mastery at the cost of subjecting us to a potentially destructive and vicious forgetfulness of the ultimate sources and principles governing our residence in this world, inviting the view that the ultimate "reality" hinges on technical exploitation of available resources.

In order to free the soul from its subjection to the paradigm of human mastery of meaning, I contend that we must first break a bond of trust in the independent integrity of things, which is difficult. The bond we have with things is difficult to break because it is on the basis of this facilitating bond that we establish an identity for ourselves. The stable object, among other things, offers itself as a basis on which to develop the power of thinking critically about people, things, and values by discovering points of view other than our own on the objects we all share. Without the object on which to attempt different perspectives and interpretive angles, we would not be able to access the possibility of thinking anew. As important as the bond with ordinary things is for the process of the maturation of thought, so important and difficult is this bond to break. And yet, unless this bond on which our initial maturation depends can be broken, the gap between ourselves and the world will fuel the skeptical suspicion that we are placeless in this world. This skepticism invites a response of technical mastery of things and exploitation of resources, feeding into a vicious cycle that increases by alternating between alienation and skepticism. In the end, the suspicion that all meaning is invented, and that invented meanings are mere semblance, or self-assertiveness, gives rise to the view that all norms are either instrumentally valuable or meaningless; this despair is in its different forms sometimes called sophistry and rhetoric, and it is represented by figures such as Callicles in Plato's *Gorgias*.

I believe that it is the work of the *Parmenides* to set the foundation on which to reveal a higher source of meaning in even the most mundane things and to secure an appropriately receptive stance toward the intelligibility of the determinateness of things in the world. The *Parmenides* was written, in my view, with an awareness of the danger human mastery poses to the core of human identity, and was written out of a desire to turn the attitude of mastery into an attitude of receptivity. The dialogue thus provides the context in which the philosopher's attention, at a very specific stage of philosophical education, might be turned toward the basic structures of intelligibility. The first part of the dialogue exposes limitations in the way we imagine the distinction between forms and participants, and the second part of the dialogue follows through with a rehabilitating initiation into the priority of forms. In this process the hard-working reader is weaned from tacit but habitual reliance on the presence of things and initiated into the metaphysical perspective from which serious thinking and conversation are rooted. By way of dialectic and an introduction to scientific philosophy, the dialogue reveals the priority of the sources of intelligibility over individual things.

The primary target of this critical enterprise is the network of metaphysical presuppositions that support and sustain the things that appear metaphysically primary to us. Key to the project of the dialogue is to demonstrate not only that things owe their being to the forms but also to show that there is a basic layer of intelligibility that does not shift back and forth with changes in time and perspective. This basic layer of intelligibility must be satisfied for anything that will, so to speak, pass through the gates of spatio-temporal existence. A study of the core eidetic structure of spatio-temporal individuals reveals to us the conditions of thinghood, which include aspects of being one and many, like and unlike other things, same and other in relation to themselves and others, having shape, being in some things and capable of containing others, etc. The focus of my study is to isolate and understand these conditions and their eidetic structure and to analyze the ways in which these structures demand to be discussed. I use the expression "constitutive participation" to refer to participatory relations out of which the spatio-temporal individual is eidetically composed or, alternatively, the complex of forms that any substantial form requires for its instantiation in space and time. I draw a technical distinction between being "subject to forms," which refers to the efficacy non-spatio-temporal ones have in spatio-temporal things, and "participation," which refers more broadly to any type of participation, whether of spatio-temporal individuals in their causal source (constitutive or otherwise) or of these prior causes participating in sources of their own. It is on the basis of "participating in" and being "subject to" constitutive causes that we will draw out what I will call the "categories" of magnitude, quality, substance, etc. Once the categorial structure of things is revealed to reflection, we will be in a position to re-orient ourselves toward the givenness of the intelligibility of those things.

In the end of this book I conclude that the gap between ourselves and the world, which I will argue is both a threat to and a well-spring of philosophy, should be approached in the attitude of receptivity, which is the stance in which intelligibility is recognized as a gift.[1] In the attitude of wonder, the philosopher is able to see intelligibility as given in abundance, and she is able to attune herself to that giving. The courage of the philosophical attitude is one closely tied up with the non-possessive receptivity in which intelligibility is not put to use for the sake of provisioning and securing a future but is instead allowed to remain in its abundance and generosity. Thus I will show that the *Parmenides* creates the space within which we can exercise away our dependencies on the spatio-temporal object and actively cultivate receptivity to the giftedness of intelligibility. Although the completion of this Platonic project lies outside the scope of the present study, the work accomplished in the *Parmenides* prepares a basis on which the philosopher can adopt a new stance toward the study of Goodness, Justice, and Beauty. The present volume is meant to be an invitation to practice different approaches to the sources of being.

The Platonic Context

The basic approach taken to forms in this book amplifies and extends methods and problems running throughout many of the most familiar Platonic dialogues, where the philosophical concern is often to examine the terms guiding and governing intelligibility and to attend to the way these terms present themselves. As Socrates urges us to notice in these dialogues, our experience of being is constituted by forms, but our ways of formulating an understanding of these governing sources have a decisive impact on the way we are guided in life. Forms exceed and challenge their formulations, and in the Platonic dialogues we often find Socrates working in concert with others to re-determine the just, the pious, the friendly, the courageous, the virtuous, etc., in a way that is responsive to the excessive intelligibility of those forms, i.e., the way those forms exceed the limited and one-sided interpretation of them that we cleave to in our lived experience of the world. Philosophical conversation creates openness to the possibility of reorientation within the horizon of meanings by which our lives are guided. Our very distance from the sources of intelligibility is also the space in which we can articulate to ourselves and others who and what we are and reformulate the structure of terms guiding us. Socratic conversations in other dialogues are preparatory for the metaphysical analysis undertaken in the *Parmenides*.

We wrestle with the metaphysical sources of intelligibility that inform and constitute our relation to things most explicitly in those moments when we are challenged to clarify meaning and revisit our guiding principles. As Socrates indicates in several places, such as the *Euthyphro*, human beings struggle with themselves and each other over how best to construe the basic terms of which our experience of things consists, for example the just and unjust (τό τε δίκαιον καὶ τὸ ἄδικον), the noble and the base (καὶ καλὸν καὶ αἰσχρόν), and the good and the bad (καὶ ἀγαθὸν καὶ κακόν) (*Euthyphro*, 7d1–2).[2] These forms, much more than the empirically verifiable and quantitatively measured objects, are the primary constituents of our reality that guide us and call on us to revisit them. When we refuse to acknowledge the ambiguity to which our familiar ways of thinking about the world are subject, as does Euthyphro, we fail to appreciate the inexhaustible richness of the causal sources by which determinate intelligibility is given to us. That is, we fail to do justice to the forms when we ignore the challenge to specify their intelligibility through our receptive articulation of the sources governing our discursive knowing. Plato's project in the *Parmenides* is to undermine the ignorance of our own ignorance by dismantling the deeply rooted but deceptive primacy we grant individual things, and the refusal of explanatory incompleteness in our basic relationship to meaning, so as to make room for an attitude of active receptivity. In the attitude of active receptivity, we are able to acknowledge and respond to the forms as the higher sources of intelligibility by which things and discursive knowledge are determined.

I contend that the *Parmenides* links to these other Platonic dialogues primarily through the *Republic*, specifically through Socrates' comments about the "longer road" of philosophical education.[3] I identify the longer road with what Socrates describes as "dialectic" in Books 6 and 7 of the *Republic*, and

I interpret dialectic to be the project of breaking down basic assumptions in order to recapture the animating source that lives at their core.[4] Dialectic is the process of transforming the metaphysical distinctions sketched in images by Socrates in those central books of the *Republic*, most importantly the images of the Sun and Cave, in which Socrates presents the metaphysical division between forms and things. I take it that the *Republic* brings this division to our attention through images, and then identifies dialectic as the work of articulating this division in rigorously discursive terms. In this book I argue that we find the preliminary execution of this program in the *Parmenides*.

The interesting philosophical turn we discover in the *Parmenides* is that key metaphysical insights can, even once they have achieved an initial break from the metaphysical primacy of individual things, still find themselves governed by that metaphysical bias. Old habits die hard, as it were. For example, I take Socrates in the *Parmenides* to represent not only someone who has grasped the basic distinction between the attitude of the cave and the causes by which individual things are explained but someone, moreover, who has grasped this distinction with conceptual rigor. The thrilling and surprising thing about the *Parmenides* is that here especially, albeit not uniquely, in the Platonic corpus we witness certain kinds of insight subject to a higher-order error. Indeed, not only do our ways of reflecting on scientific insight contain errors, they do so more intractably, for such insight considers itself to have moved thoroughly beyond ignorance. We have, thus, a version of what Socrates in the *Apology* calls "ignorance of one's own ignorance"—those who take themselves to know will lack sufficient motivation to wonder about their knowledge and therefore to inquire more deeply. Having read the *Apology*, we already think of this as a prevalent condition affecting most, if not all, non-philosophical attitudes. The innovation of the *Parmenides* is to show that this condition plagues even those who consider themselves philosophical, and is a problem in particular for people with a certain kind of theoretical understanding. This attitude of apparent wisdom, I take it, is what Socrates in the *Republic* calls "mathematical," and it is something he contrasts to dialectical wisdom.

The *Parmenides* thus belongs to the broader context of Platonic dialogues as the place where purportedly philosophical insight into the distinction between forms and things is put to the test in a sustained and thorough-going cross-examination. What is at stake in this process for the soul of the philosopher is to develop the "awareness of one's own ignorance" in a way that is rooted in the nature and principles of intelligibility. What Socrates has not yet accomplished at the outset of the dialogue is the hard work of freeing his insights from the way metaphysical presuppositions re-assert themselves in theoretical environments. Socrates, with his theory of forms and his theoretical commitment to their explanatory power, has what we might characterize as a theoretical "true belief." We are asked to accept that the belief is true when Parmenides embraces Socrates' hypothesis of forms in principle and enjoins Socrates to pursue a deeper understanding of their causal priority over things. But belief is not knowledge (ἐπιστήμη, i.e., scientific knowledge in the Greek sense); Socrates has not yet put his theoretical commitment thoroughly to the test in such a way as to transform and elevate his true belief to the status of knowledge. Most importantly, Socrates has underestimated the length to which thinking will go to preserve its faith in the ultimacy of individual, denumerable things, which it understands ultimately on the basis of its experience of spatio-temporal individuals. Socrates has, in other words, not yet perceived the sophistry of the assumptions that support and facilitate theoretical understanding.

In a direct address to the habit of thinking that privileges the type of presence that spatio-temporal things seem to have, each of Parmenides' challenges to Socrates' insight into the nature of forms and participation in the first section of the *Parmenides* exaggerates and makes more decisive the privileged role Socrates inadvertently grants in his thinking to spatio-temporal individuals.[5] Coupled with these objections, each of the hypotheses in the dialogue's second section addresses the constitutive limits of spatio-temporal presence, encouraging a shift of view from things to categories. In this process, we find that thinking presumes, as if by habit, that all being, whether form or participant, must be subject to the categories of spatio-temporal presence. What we slowly come to realize, however, is that spatio-temporal presence is structured by forms, and that forms are radically distinct from participants. Spatio-temporal presence rests on a specific sense of what it means to be "one" characterized by complexity (i.e., the divisibility of a spatio-temporal presence) and individuality (i.e., the spatio-temporal duplication of things of a similar or identical kind).[6] As we study the eidetic structure of spatio-temporal presence, we will discover ways of re-thinking the terms "being" and being "one" as they apply to forms, which will help Socrates deepen and clarify his insight into participation.

Thus, in the Platonic dialogues, broadly speaking our attention is drawn to the basic terms guiding us in thinking, and the *Parmenides* in particular challenges the would-be philosopher to examine the self-concealing sophistry that the presence proper to things is proper to the forms. Even the philosopher, such as young Socrates in the *Parmenides*, who has seen the ontological priority of forms and the secondary status of spatio-temporal things, has not necessarily overcome the habits of thinking and is vulnerable to repeating the same mistake at a higher level. By fixing intently on the impasses that we find in our study of the fundamental eidetic structures of things as such, metaphysical inquiry gains for itself an important, dialectical opportunity for re-habituation and new ways of practicing wisdom, extending the educational program that was first launched in the *Republic*.

Commentary on Method

I take philosophy to be the shared search for truth within a broader context of received opinion and everyday practices. Philosophy, in my view, begins in wonder. It works to reveal things as they are in their being, and it has as one of its primary aims the goal of setting aside the constraints of pride and the desire to avoid embarrassment, so as to release human potential for the possibility of virtue. We might perhaps consider Aristotle to take philosophy in one sense to be like what I have described: in Aristotelian practical work, philosophy is necessarily communal and educative, aiming not only at one's own virtue but also at that of others, both friends and others in community. However, we might wonder whether the interpersonal dimension of philosophical wisdom is of great importance to Aristotle's conception of theoretical philosophy and the contemplative virtues, given that these virtues seem consistent with a relatively isolated life. Be that as it may, I think we are compelled to see the interpersonal dimension of philosophy as central to the way scientific insight is construed in the Platonic corpus. We find in the dialogues a clear emphasis on the interpersonal dimension of philosophical epiphany. Furthermore, the very nature of the Platonic text appears to demand of the reader that she become a participant in the genesis of meaning through engagement in the difficult and risk-laden activity of making philosophical decisions about the evidence and inquiry that is presented in the Platonic text. I find in Plato a persistent demand that we be transparent about our own founding assumptions and the role they play in guiding our inquiry.

In reading the Platonic text I am not trying to determine what position Plato did or did not hold in relation to a set of historically defined subject matters. Rather, I am trying to ascertain what it is that the text is calling on us to ask ourselves and what insights our engagement with the text invites us to entertain. I think the dialogical form lends itself to this type of reading because it presents insight always and only as something said by a particular character in certain concrete situations with important but diverse issues at stake in conversational exchange. Whenever possible, I take my lead from what the context of the dialogue seems to warrant or require. A related implication of this principle is that I do not rest any part of my argument on a supposed chronology of the composition of the dialogues in Plato's career. I think it will never be decided in what order Plato wrote the dialogues, and even if it were, nothing would follow from that order about the quality or character of the thought Plato would be obligated to have. However, I do think that we can share with Plato the things he invites us to notice, and I think that Platonic writing is especially designed to draw attention to certain indications that, while less than explicit, are aimed at a careful reader and reward care and attention. Furthermore, I believe that Platonic writing is designed to draw us into dialogue with our own shared and received assumptions, and the text often provides one with the tools to engage in dialogue with received wisdom. My main reason for adopting this stance is found in the Platonic text itself, where the letter of the text does not stand on its own. The text is effectively incomplete in such a way that it will not allow itself to remain unanswered. In the way a good conversation opens by inviting, sometimes demanding, a reply, the dialogues at various levels of depth and scope present themselves as not having said enough, requiring supplement, addition, or recapituation. In this book I take the stance that the Platonic text will show us how it demands to be read. The truth that emerges from this dialogical reading practice will come as a slowly growing harmony arising between oneself, other people, the text, and the world around us.

For these very reasons, however, we must remain aware of the dangers of subjectivism. If we feel called on by the apparent incompleteness of the text to supplement its surface content or raise questions of our own, there is the very real and obvious danger that we are seeing only what we want to see and "learning" what we already believe. The result of such a reading is that anything can be true because nothing is true, for there would be nothing there to say "no" to us. The risk I see in philosophy is also a risk of self-indulgence and tyranny over the text. I believe, however, that the Platonic dialogues are structured in such a way as to capture the importantly subjective aspect of philosophical truth at the same time as they invoke the constraints that govern and sustain conversation. The dialogues are unique for the way they are able to bring these two aspects of truth into relation: responsiveness to what has been said *and* recognition of the open-endedness of meaning.

Platonic dialogue captures the subjective aspect of philosophical insight by demanding that reading and thinking begin from our received ways of understanding. The text never provides us with an account complete enough to dispense with our own ways of understanding, so we cannot excuse ourselves from the responsibility for our contribution to the ways the text speaks to us. That is to say, we cannot talk about Platonic dialogues or draw meaning from them without revealing our own commitments and limitations in, for example, the way we understand piety, justice, and beauty, but also the way we understand one, same, other, and the theoretically abstract terms we will be studying in the *Parmenides*. Taking responsibility for our commitments and their limitations, so as to be able to work through our conception of the good and arrive at a grasp of truth: this is what Plato calls "philosophy." The process by which we gain insight into what is at stake for us and the key decisions that life would have us make is what we might call a process of reading philosophically. The Platonic text teaches us how to read philosophically.

At the same time as the dialogues address us at an intimately personal level, they also capture the impersonal aspect of truth by drawing attention to a level of intelligibility that is just as constitutive of our ability to begin to think and act as it is constitutive of the ability of things to be. The dialogues often focus on the constitutive conditions on which an entire horizon of meaning is based, such as the argument Socrates offers to Thrasymachus in Book 1 of the *Republic*, where Socrates points out that no action would be possible without the form of justice to secure agreement, with oneself and others. The notion of a constitutive condition is central to the thinking that is demanded of us in the dialogues, and it is deeply indifferent to the individually contingent conditions from which we all begin to think and act.

The *Parmenides* specifically requires the active reader to take personal responsibility for the errors and omissions they witness being made, particularly by Aristoteles, in order that she may better explore the impersonal structures by which the spatio-temporal individual is constituted. There are many contradictions in the dialogue, some merely apparent and some purposefully calling for correction or emendation, all of which are in service of deeper understanding. If these contradictions are let stand on the surface, they reject insight and result in a merely formal exercise.[7] Were we not active in our engagement with these apparent contradictions in the text, the dialogue would yield exclusively negative results. However, if we move beyond the surface content of the text to take responsibility for the insight that is offered to us through those contradictions in the dialogue, I claim that we will discover within ourselves the impersonal truth to which Parmenides is pointing. I urge us to take the necessary risks in the practice of active reading that responsibly answers the unavoidable dangers of subjectivism and skepticism.

Outline of the Chapters

This book deals with the entirety of Plato's *Parmenides*, addressing each of the arguments in turn and seeking to establish a unified interpretation of the whole that will organize each of its sections and draw from them a coherent picture of dialectical education. The book has two parts. In the first I analyze the dramatic setting of the dialogue's narration, and then the discussion between Socrates, Zeno, and Parmenides (Chapter 1). Parmenides then raises a series of objections to Socrates' metaphysical claims, which I use as an opportunity to lay out the basic contours of the metaphysical puzzles and challenges (Chapter 2). In the second section I analyze the Eight Hypotheses and the addendum on the "instant" (ἐξαίφνης), which as a group Parmenides offers as an example of philosophical training that will enable Socrates (and us) to answer the skeptic who rejects the notion that there are forms. The second part of the book has three chapters, one for each of the First and Second Hypotheses (Chapters 3 and 4, respectively) and one for the discussion of the instant, the Third, Fifth, and Seventh Hypotheses (Chapter 5).

Chapter 1: After a consideration of the metaphysical themes that are implicitly brought to our attention by the dramatic opening of the dialogue, I introduce what I identify as the dialogue's thematic concern with the stance of "technical mastery," and I relate this stance to a certain set of metaphysical assumptions. Explaining Socrates' "theory of participation," I claim that the dialogue is a critique of everyday metaphysical assumptions in order to make room for "scientific" philosophy and force to one side "normative" philosophy (i.e., what Parmenides attributes to Socrates' youthful concern with honor and dishonor). In this chapter I attempt to show that the style of rhetoric and disputation (eristic) bears an important resemblance to philosophical method insofar as it strips away norms and allows us to see the invariant structure of intelligibility in the objects of our concern.

Chapter 2: In this chapter I attempt to deliver on my promise to explain "scientific" philosophy by examining Parmenides' first two sets of objection to Socrates' account of the forms and participation. I show that if we read Parmenides' objections carefully, we can see that he is slowly constructing a metaphysical account of spatio-temporal objectivity, in the first set of objections focusing on the object as an aggregate "one" and in the second set of objections treating the object as an individual "one." I argue that there is a reciprocal relation between "aggregate" and "individual" aspects of the spatio-temporal "one," i.e., the intelligibility of each of these aspects of the object would not be possible without the intelligibility of the other. By showing that the determinate intelligibility of the spatio-temporal object depends on the aspects of "aggregate" and "individual" intelligibility, and that these two aspects depend on each other, I assert for the first time in the book that the true object of knowledge is not the spatio-temporal thing but the eidetic structure by which that thing is constituted. This is the first concerted attempt to illustrate what is meant by "constitutive participation," and it is meant to be read in light of the analysis of the various kinds of "one" we encounter in the hypotheses of the dialogue's second section. I ask the reader to consider the asymmetrical relation that must obtain between forms and things, and I attempt to show how Parmenides' "greatest difficulty" objection outlines the difficulty of being precise about the nature of the separation (χωρισμός) between forms and things. I conclude this chapter (and the first part of the book) with a discussion of what it would mean for Socrates to hold his account of participation dialectically.

Chapter 3: The first of three chapters in the second part deals exclusively with the First Hypothesis, "if one is," and begins with a review of the various candidates we might have thought correspond to the "one" hypothesized. I go through the arguments of the First Hypothesis (which I refer to as H1) with the intention of showing that (a) the many exclusions listed in that hypothesis suggest that the subject of H1 is a one that is simple and unique, but one that cannot be identified with either form or participant, and (b) that the order and organization of the arguments point to a coherent set of metaphysical categories that prepare us to think through the eidetic structure of the spatio-temporal one. I argue that Aristoteles constrains "is" to refer exclusively to spatio-temporal things, but that he does so in a way that demonstrates a commitment to a conception of being that is not subject to space and time.[8]

Chapter 4: The second chapter in Part II deals exclusively with the Second Hypothesis (H2), and it contains the most extensive and painstaking analysis of the eidetic structure of which spatio-temporal objects consist. The key to this chapter is the initial attempt Parmenides makes to show that the hypothesis "if one is" entails an unlimited multiplicity, which conclusion he draws on the basis of (a) the divisibility of the one, and then (b) the individuality of the one. The entire chapter is spent showing that the many arguments of the extremely dense and difficult, but rewarding, Second Hypothesis are designed to reveal the eidetic structure already in place as soon as there is a spatio-temporal object that is complex and individual: that it have shape, be in place, that it be capable of motion and rest, that it be same and other in relation to itself and others, etc. Here we begin to get a well-defined sense of what an a-spatial and atemporal "is" would mean in general, and how that sort of being applies in particular to the eidetic structures of spatio-temporal objects. I conclude this chapter with the observation that the intelligibility of the "one" of H1 presupposes the intelligibility of the "one" of H2, and vice versa, and I offer this as a preliminary solution to the problem of the separation of forms and things from the first part of the dialogue.

Chapter 5: In this concluding chapter I tie together the lessons learned from Chapters 3 and 4, showing that the instant (Hypothesis 2a, the "addendum" to H2), the idea of limit and the unlimited (H3), the idea of "veridical predication" (H5), and the idea of appearance (H7) are the necessary consequences stemming from the transformed understanding of the spatio-temporal "one" arising from the dialectical study in which we have been engaged.

Conclusion: The conclusion I draw from this study is that the *Parmenides* reveals that there must be a sense of appearance that is fundamentally distinct from spatio-temporal objectivity, and that in spite of the way we routinely imagine being in terms proper to spatio-temporal things, the primary objects are forms (or, at least, what we might call immanent or substantial forms). The world of appearance is governed by the forms in the sense that it does not consist primarily of individual things but of normative limits demanded by the forms for their instantiation. Once we clarify the nature of intelligibility, we put ourselves in a position to suspend the metaphysical assumption that all presence is of the sort that spatio-temporal things seem to have (and suspend the attitude of human mastery that depends on it). Having accomplished this turn from spatio-temporal things to the higher intelligibility that governs those things, we become capable of adopting the attitude in which intelligibility may be received as a gift rather than as a resource at our disposal.

PART I

Scientific Philosophy

CHAPTER 1

Zenonian Method

The opening third of the *Parmenides* consists primarily of an exchange between Parmenides and the young Socrates in which they discuss the nature of the intelligibility of things. Their overarching concern is to determine whether Socrates' account of *eidē* (forms) is a plausible way of understanding what we encounter and experience in the world. Their conversation is prefaced by a preliminary critique of what is the most self-evident of all metaphysical views: that the individual things we encounter in the world are the most basic elements of what-is. In Socrates' exchange with Zeno, which precedes the longer discussion with Parmenides, we are offered a brief review of the evidence that our trust in things is not well founded. First, Zeno identifies an ambiguity in the intelligibility of the "many," and although the puzzle Zeno identifies is merely provisional, the puzzle he will propose defines the horizon within which the remainder of the dialogue proceeds. Zeno's challenge invites Socrates to wonder about what "is" means and about what it means to be "one." By abstracting from the "thisness" of individual things and turning toward their determinate intelligibility, Socrates and Zeno interrogate what we mean whenever we talk about things. The ambiguities that we uncover as soon as we attempt to be explicit about the commitments implied by this everyday stance can of course be exploited for the sake of disputation and games of one-upmanship, and the Platonic dialogues contain many examples of such abuse under the headings of rhetoric and sophistry. But these same ambiguities can be used by the philosopher to interrupt our familiar connection with things and draw out a deeper understanding of being. The path to philosophy leads through the sort of ambiguities Zeno sets up in the opening exchange with Socrates.

Before we scrutinize the arguments in which Zeno, Socrates, and Parmenides introduce the core philosophical work of the *Parmenides*, let us first examine the narrative framework in which the discussion between Socrates and his Eleatic friends is placed, after which we will turn to take a closer look at the metaphysical issues that arise in that discussion.

Reception

In this section I discuss two sets of ideas. On the one hand, the opening scene of the *Parmenides* flags key metaphysical themes of place, time, unity, and multiplicity in relation to the contingencies of age, desire, and location, and these framing themes point to the extent to which knowledge transcends contingency and yet depends on the contingencies of embodied life. The introduction of these themes also reminds us that the abstract metaphysical concerns studied in the *Parmenides* are the very terms on which our most familiar experiences stand. On the other hand, the image of the blacksmith, bridle, and master horseman raises the issue of technical mastery over our surroundings, the basic unit of which is the object. The dialogue will show us that whereas we take the things in our world to belong to us and our projects, in truth the object and the norms governing their being and use belong to the forms.

The dialogue is narrated by Cephalus, an Ionian, to an unidentified audience, presumably an audience of fellow Ionians. He is recounting to them a journey taken with other Clazomenaen citizens (πολῖται, 126b8) across the Aegean Sea to Athens. Once there, they happened to run into (ἐντυγχάνω, 126a2) Glaucon and Adeimantus, who took them to the house of Antiphon in *Melitē* to hear a recitation of a conversation held long ago between Socrates, Zeno, and Parmenides.[1] Antiphon heard from Pythodorus, who witnessed the conversation firsthand. At first Antiphon resists the request but finally he is persuaded and starts the recitation in full. Thus, we see an unmistakable stress placed on the chain of witnesses who have transmitted the original conversation down from its inception to its recitation. If someone were reading the dialogue to us aloud, we could not fail to notice that we have access to the dialogue through yet another link in this chain of transmission; our easy access to writing obscures this aspect of the dramatic enactment.

The first metaphysical theme pointed out by the dialogue itself is that the conversation and its insights are never simply present in the way that a thing appears to be but must be heard, remembered, narrated, and, through exchanges between historically specific persons, transmitted to its auditors. The events recounted in the *Parmenides* did not simply take place a long time ago. In order to continue having taken place in the meaningful sense of being remembered and preserved, the text must be taken care of, and this caretaking is the work of particular individuals who preserve the event for others. Only in the context of ongoing care can we join in the dialogue's movement of thought. The dialogue flags the themes of time and remembrance by underlining the manifold layers of "when" (ἐπειδὴ) that make not only the occurrence but also the telling of the dialogue possible; indeed, "when" is the dialogue's first word.

We are also reminded that the transmission of the dialogue occurs along lines of family relation. When Cephalus arrives in the Athenian agora, he runs into Glaucon and Adeimantus by chance. Failing to remember the name of the person from whom he hopes to hear the dialogue narrated (Antiphon), he is forced to pick out that person through his qualities within a web of natural relations: Cephalus is, he says, looking for Glaucon's half-brother on his mother's side, someone who was a child when Cephalus was in Athens a long time before and whose father's name is Pyrilampes. The emphasis here is on the natural context in which the dialogue is being passed along, in a place, at a time, and on the basis of familial relations. It should also be noted that these familial relations are Plato's family history. All of these details point suggestively to the contingencies and dependencies that make up the context in which something (the narrative of the *Parmenides*) can be made present.

Behind the contingencies of time and place and the familial relations that create the context for the transmission of the dialogue, there is also a reference to the political as part of the context in which philosophical tradition is possible. The conversation recounted between Parmenides and the others took place during Parmenides' visit to Athens on the occasion of a quadrennial ("Great") celebration of the Panathenaea, a celebration honoring Athena and consisting of rituals in which Athens acknowledged the divine source from which it drew its political identity. At some point in the 6th Century BCE the lesser, annual Panathenaea festival became a celebration of the birth of Athena and was opened to both citizens of Attica and other Hellenes generally.[2] The end of that new festival was marked by a large procession carrying a woven robe (πέπλος) from the *Kerameikos* through the agora to the acropolis, where it was presented to the statue of Athena.[3] The "Great" Panathenaea was held every four years and featured additional athletic and poetry competitions, and scholars have associated it with Athens's growth as a center of power and culture. Thus, in the background of the metaphysical study of the dialogue we might see a subtle recognition of the gift of political unity. If this point is well taken, it indicates that not only are the contingencies of time, place, and natural relations themes of the dialogue, but, more distantly, political organization and the relationship to origins are also operative concerns in the Platonic engagement with forms and participation.

Lastly, in addition to the themes of the past, family, political unity, and divinity, the dramatic framing of the *Parmenides* points to the theme of bodily desire and age. Antiphon begins his recitation by pointing out that Parmenides was sixty-five years old with a "beautiful and good countenance" (καλὸν δὲ κἀγαθὸν τὴν ὄψιν, 127b2–3).[4] Zeno was forty years old and described as being "tall and graceful" (εὐμήκη δὲ καὶ χαρίεντα ἰδεῖν, 127b4–5). Zeno and Parmenides are described as lovers, which Socrates obliquely references in his comments to Zeno. Furthermore, Socrates is described as being young and, like the Ionian visitors in the dialogue's narrative outer layer, he comes "desiring to hear" (ἐπιθυμοῦντας ἀκοῦσαι, 127c3) the arguments Zeno brought with him to Athens. Desire moves us toward knowledge, and it is part of who we are as philosophers; it is yet another condition without which there would be no dialogue.

Thus, the possibility of joining in the conversation of the *Parmenides* rests on the contingency of particular people desiring to take care of that conversation who are in the right place working to receive and maintain insights. Inquiry happens on a particular day; it comes at a certain cost, sometimes involving risk, which the dialogue flags in the themes of reception, hosting, and friendship. The early sections of the *Parmenides* contain multiple references to the fragile collaboration that makes philosophy possible. At the same time, the dialogue itself is singularly focused on the turn away from the contingencies of circumstance toward the source of insight and the structures of intelligibility, which are causally prior to these situational aspects of meaning.

The Ionian visitors have not come simply to memorize the conversation and pass it on as a list of empty claims. They have come to Athens for the sake of understanding, and in the context of seeking and gaining knowledge, the dependencies of circumstance are only a necessary condition. Even with those conditions in place, no claim is truly received until it has been understood (i.e., owned) and the explanatory principle has been grasped. The Ionians have traveled to Athens seeking knowledge (ἐπιστήμη) distinct from the conditions in which mortal beings come to know. This implies that philosophical dialogue is a continuation of a past handed down to us and subject to the vulnerabilities of context, but that dialogue is also something that must be seen "for oneself," as it were, in a way that is detached from context.

The *Parmenides* thus reminds us that the insights we seek as readers are dependent upon the work of individuals passing down a tradition, and yet those insights are not properly received until their truth is broken from received wisdom and seen directly for oneself. In a sense we readers of the *Parmenides* stand with the unidentified Ionians who are receiving the text offered to them in Antiphon's recitation. We, like them, are privy to a conversation that is made possible by others working to shepherd philosophical accomplishment over a gap of time and space. We, like them, are the contingent basis upon which the truth of the text depends. And yet, the truth of the text will not reach safe harbor until and unless it is actively studied and its insights gathered anew by us, who must earn the right to own them. As the image of the silent Socrates in the hypotheses of the dialogue's second section indicates, what is said cannot simply be heard but must actively be taken up and restored to its proper place if the power of dialogue is to be maintained.

The stance of active receptivity in which dialogue is taken up contrasts with the stance of technical mastery in which things are manipulated and controlled, as introduced by the image of Antiphon and the blacksmith. When Glaucon and Adeimantus arrive with Cephalus and the Ionian visitors in *Melitē* to hear the dialogue, they find Antiphon no longer working on philosophy but on horses, like his grandfather. Formerly Antiphon had practiced philosophy seriously, but he has by now taken the family profession of horse care. When they find him, Antiphon is busy giving instructions to a blacksmith regarding the construction of a bridle. The familiar world in which we dwell, the world in which horses and horsemanship have their place, is a world in which philosophy can be preserved but not necessarily one in which philosophy will come alive. The basic attitude of mastery invoked here assumes a very particular model in which one thing is ruled by another, and two things are joined together by a yoke to form larger systems of organized activity. In this case the bridle yokes horse and rider, and this particular image points to the joints by which things generally are artificially combined into larger wholes in which one part, such as the rider, has a controlling position over the others. The efficacy of the rider is enhanced by being brought into a relationship of domination over the horse, which is transformed by its partial and subordinate position in relation to the rider.[5] Physical mastery operates by identifying the dependencies of bodies for the sake of managing them and fulfilling aims that do not always stem from those bodies, aims that often stem from the nature of the political community to which that mastery is subordinate. Thus, insofar as the *Parmenides* is taking on the assumption of the primacy of objects, it is thereby taking on the stance of mastery and the momentum of social and economic practices built on that foundation, and in some sense it is challenging the very attitudes on which it relies.[6]

Looking ahead, we will have occasion to consider how the critique of the primacy of things and the challenge to the attitude of mastery help to liberate thinking for self-awareness and fulfill, rather than undermine, the promise of life in the city. I will make the argument that it is only in the displacement of the attitude of human mastery of objects that we can free ourselves from the things we possess and, thereby, gain access to the sources and ultimate terms of what-is, which possess us more than we possess them. That is, although we seem to gain mastery over things through our mastering techniques, the dialogue shows us that our mastery belongs to the forms that constitute things and the norms according to which things are used. Although the critique of mastery extends across many Platonic dialogues and includes diverse aspects of the things held in honor by Athenian society, we are going to focus on the assumption of thinghood, the assumption on which the technical attitude depends. Our goal will be to undermine the perceived ontological ultimacy of the "thing" on which technical mastery operates—as well as the norm toward which it looks—and see thinghood as derivative of sources of being (the *eidē*) that are not at our disposal.

Participation

Before turning to the conversation between Socrates and Zeno with which the body of the *Parmenides* begins, let us consider briefly the nature of what Socrates in other dialogues calls "participation" and the distinction he draws between "forms" and "participants." I will use this distinction to set up an account of the higher order "ignorance of one's own ignorance" in which one takes a likeness of form as surrogate for the form itself, an error of substitution difficult to correct and one which Parmenides targets in the discussion with Socrates. But first we should consider the basic parameters of the account of participation.

In Platonic and Aristotelian texts generally, the primary sense of being is per se being, i.e., *kath' hauto*, being "as such" or "by itself." This sense of being is contrasted with an account of what only happens to be the case; in Aristotelian parlance this is being *kata sumbebēkos*. The *kath' hauto* sense of being refers to what is the most intelligible of all objects of study, virtually identical to the intelligibility of truth itself by which all other senses of being and appearing are measured. For the historical Parmenides, being, properly speaking, refers to the "[it] is" that lets stand the contrasts by which the determinate intelligibility of the world is articulated.[7] Mortals wander two-headed failing to grasp being, which they overlook in favor of the individual things that "is" lets stand. In Parmenides' sense, being is absolute, and any of our discriminations that would oppose it to something other, so as to let it stand forth as something determinate, only miss the "[it] is" or, worse, distort it by construing it in terms proper to particular somethings. All of the specified modalities of being invoked in any instance of determinate intelligibility (e.g., it is now not day but night, or it is hot but not cold) are subordinate to their source insofar as these instances rely on a contrast with what each "is not" and is therefore tacitly co-constitutive of what it "is." This source of all intelligibly determinate being corresponds to Parmenidean "being as such."

Against this sketch of the historical Parmenides, Plato's account of being is clearly innovative. The forms are the *per se* (*kath' hauto*) dimension of being of specific kinds, rather than being in the absolute sense. Furthermore, Plato's Parmenides focuses on individual participants that partake in the *kath' hauto* being of the forms rather than focusing on the intelligible oppositions into which the determinacy of things is generally articulated. In Platonic language, the forms are what-is "truly" or "really," and the participants by contrast happen to be as they are or are "accidentally." Insofar as the forms are the *per se* dimension of what-is without being subject to their own causal efficacy, they possess no attributes or aspects other than what they are, and strictly speaking they cannot be opposites, sames, others, likes, or unlikes (although Socrates has a hard time with this particular point in the dialogue). Therefore, the forms share the character of the Parmenidean "[it] is," i.e., they are prior to the determinacy of the objects of determinate intelligibility. However, unlike the Parmenidean "[it] is," Plato's forms are not the unique and simple absolute source that shows itself through all determinate intelligibility. Rather, forms are the unique and simple terms by which all determinate being is governed. Our interpretation of the account of being with which Socrates operates in the *Parmenides* and which introduces what I am here calling a transformed Parmenidean account of being will take its lead from Socrates' discussion of forms in the *Republic*.

In the *Republic*, Socrates identifies the distinguishing mark of the philosopher as an orientation toward the forms. In the concluding sections of Book 5, Socrates, in the face of real and imagined laughter, describes the nature of the philosophical soul that the perfectly just city would require as its leader. The philosophers would belong to one group within the broader class of lovers of spectacle (οἱ . . . φιλοθεάμονες, 475d2), distinguished from the others by being lovers of the spectacle of truth (τοὺς τῆς ἀληθείας . . . φιλοθεάμονας 475e4). All lovers of spectacle, he tells Glaucon, are implicitly lovers of learning who take pleasure in beholding the beautiful and who in truth desire the beautiful itself. However, the non-philosophers fail to notice about themselves that they are in love with what is unique and simple, i.e., the cause of beauty in all beautiful things, and as a result they unknowingly split beauty up into many beautiful sensory experiences of sounds and colors

(476b). This metaphysical error concerning the source and true object of their desire prevents them from seeing beauty itself or even being able to appreciate that the things they love point beyond themselves to something else. The non-philosopher is caught up in *doxa* while hungering for knowledge.

The distinction Socrates there draws between the *doxa* of the non-philosopher and the knowledge of the philosopher corresponds to the metaphysical distinction between things and forms, which, although problematic in the *Republic*, serves as the basis on which to begin reading the *Parmenides*. Spatio-temporal things both "are" and "are not" in the sense that their characters are revealed only in relation to the character of other things, and they shift accordingly.[8] We say "the finger is large," "Simmias is tall," or "the Doryphoros status is beautiful" because they "are such" in relation to some things, but in relation to others they are "small," "short," and "ugly." Thus spatio-temporal things both are and are not, and thereby they are many in their being rather than one. The forms themselves, e.g., the form of the beautiful, simply are, i.e., what is beautiful, and the forms are one rather than many. In brief, spatio-temporal things both are and are not, and both one and many, whereas forms simply are and are simply one.

The non-philosophers are bound to reality through accidental being, and, consequently, their bond is fickle. For the non-philosophers, what-is presents itself as both being and not being. Tied to the determinate character of individual sights and sounds, non-philosophers are tied to an "is" that also "is not," for example, tied to things that are beautiful, are large, or are like others, and which simultaneously thereby also are not beautiful (ugly), are not large (small), are not like (unlike). The beings toward which the non-philosopher is oriented is both one and many in the sense that they are each one thing, but that one only shows itself to be in many distinct facets. When we say that something both is and is not "beautiful," for example, and thereby we say of it that it is subject to becoming, what we have in mind is that it has the character of being beautiful in relation to a character possessed (or participated in) by something else. The double, the large, the heavy in things, Socrates says, "will no more be addressed as these [i.e., double, large, heavy] than their opposites" (*Republic* 479b6–7), i.e., no more double or large than half or small. Thus focused on the inherently shifting world of appearance, the non-philosopher operates in the element of what Socrates calls opinion (*doxa*). The philosophers, by contrast, are oriented toward what simply is and is simply one.

The person caught up in *doxa* is not only wrapped up in an untenable bond to being, she is in a bind from which she sees no escape. The non-philosophical "lover of sights" is unfamiliar with the form truth takes and does not know how to seek truth. Socrates suggests that such people are aware at some level of a lack and a loss, one that propels them from spectacle to spectacle with breathless abandon; Socrates says that they would rend out their ears and eyes if only by doing so they were able to see and hear more and newer sights. As though they were confusing the shine of newness and diversity with the shine of the beautiful, these lovers seem to fall in love with every beautiful thing they see, instantly dispensing with the old so as to be transported to the new.[9] For them there is no center, no point of rest inside the sound and fury of their passion.

Socrates compares this stance to a dream in which we take what we see to be primary. The beautiful person, house, display, are all original and ultimate elements of reality. In truth, from the philosophical perspective, this stance is mistaken. Each of these objects is speaking of a reality that exceeds and challenges the soul, a reality that cannot itself be owned or exchanged. Rather than making room for the "beautiful itself" beyond these beautiful things encountered, people in the dream insist on reducing the beautiful to the particularity of beautiful things on a human scale, and therefore its availability for possession. Socrates asks:

> The one believing (νομίζων) that there are beautiful things (καλὰ . . . πράγματα), but neither believing that there is a beautiful itself nor, even if someone directs him toward knowledge (γνῶσιν) of it, is able to follow, does it seem to you that he lives in a dream or awake? Consider this. Isn't this dreaming: whether waking or sleeping someone thinks the likeness (τὸ ὅμοιον) of something to be (εἶναι) not a likeness but that (αὐτό) of which it is the likeness (ᾧ ἔοικεν)?
>
> I, for one, he said, would claim dreaming to be this sort of thing.
>
> What of this? The one who, on the contrary, thinks there is a beautiful itself (τι αὐτὸ καλόν) and is able to see clearly it and the things partaking (μετέχοντα) in it, and does not think the things participating are it, nor that it is the things participating in it, does it seem to you in turn that he lives in a dream or awake?
>
> He is very much awake, he said.

ὁ οὖν καλὰ μὲν πράγματα νομίζων, αὐτὸ δὲ κάλλος μήτε νομίζων μήτε, ἄν τις ἡγῆται ἐπὶ τὴν γνῶσιν αὐτοῦ, δυνάμενος ἕπεσθαι, ὄναρ ἢ ὕπαρ δοκεῖ σοι ζῆν; σκόπει δέ. τὸ ὀνειρώττειν ἆρα οὐ τόδε ἐστίν, ἐάντε ἐν ὕπνῳ τις ἐάντ᾽ ἐγρηγορὼς τὸ ὅμοιόν τῳ μὴ ὅμοιον ἀλλ᾽ αὐτὸ ἡγῆται εἶναι ᾧ ἔοικεν;

> ἐγὼ γοῦν ἄν, ἦ δ' ὅς, φαίην ὀνειρώττειν τὸν τοιοῦτον.
> τί δέ; ὁ τἀναντία τούτων ἡγούμενός τέ τι αὐτὸ καλὸν καὶ δυνάμενος καθορᾶν καὶ αὐτὸ καὶ τὰ ἐκείνου μετέχοντα, καὶ οὔτε τὰ μετέχοντα αὐτὸ οὔτε αὐτὸ τὰ μετέχοντα ἡγούμενος, ὕπαρ ἢ ὄναρ αὖ καὶ οὗτος δοκεῖ σοι ζῆν;
> καὶ μάλα, ἔφη, ὕπαρ.[10] (476c2–d4)

The dreaming person is constitutively unable to exhaust the beautiful in her enjoyment of beautiful things and yet is insistent that beauty is complete in beautiful things. The soul is gorged but still undernourished. The individual thing points to a completeness that the lover of sights pursues in multiple unsuccessful iterations of the same experience. The lover of sights is unable to focus these many instances into a complete presence (or into the awareness of a singular absence), and each object becomes merely the first note of a song that is not sung, or the first stroke of a painting that is never finished. The beautiful always presents itself piecemeal, promising other respects and different relations in other circumstances where the complete presentation is made. The lover of sights senses this inexhaustibility, but bound by her own desire for beauty and deceived by the expectation of a complete experience of the beautiful in bodies, she is driven out of every place she finds. She cannot achieve possession of the beautiful, and she fails to wonder about what is being pointed out to her, even growing angry at any attempt to draw attention away from individual sights and sounds back to their source. Like a sleeper who is not aware of being asleep, her insistence on the wholeness of beauty in experience splinters beauty into a series that prevents her from gathering herself toward its source. The search for more beauty reveals the deprivation that lives in appearances.[11]

The analogy of the unphilosophical soul and the sleeper suggests, falsely, that people would find awakening as easy and natural as returning from a good night's sleep. But the sleeper is not just dozing; she is also in some sense unhealthy. *Doxa* is a kind of sleeping that imagines itself awake and thereby cannot awaken "by nature" but must struggle through the process of awakening. The philosopher can see that the beauty appearing to her in things is never beauty itself; those things are beautiful in one respect but not beautiful in another, and in some respects they are ugly. All nonetheless give expression to a norm in light of which they are beautiful, and that norm is apparent through the derivative character, or secondness, of things. The secondness of things implies the firstness of beauty. Initially the philosopher's awareness of the source is just an empty placeholder in need of a method for interrogating that source and drawing it out. In *Republic* 5, Socrates lays the ground for the struggle of "waking up" philosophically by inviting his friends to set aside the presumed authority of individual things and understand the perceptual presence in light of its source.

With these programmatic remarks concerning the basic orientation of Socratic inquiry, we are in a position to turn to opening exchange between Socrates and Zeno in the *Parmenides*. Zeno's puzzle incites Socrates to offer a basic version of the theory of participation that includes the account of things as embodying contrary characters and the priority of the forms on which those characters depend. Socrates' account is a brilliant but undigested inheritance of Parmenidean wisdom, and it will fall to Parmenides in the dialogue to help Socrates to deepen and mature his insight.

The Conversation between Zeno and Socrates

The body of the *Parmenides* begins when Pythodorus, who is the host and original source of the account, returns home from a walk with Parmenides. As Pythodorus and Parmenides enter, Zeno is just finishing up reading aloud from a book Zeno wrote in his youth and brought with him to Athens. The opening conversation among Socrates, Zeno, and Parmenides offers an especially pointed attack on the assumption that what-is can be coherently said to consist of a plurality of individual things. The conversation begins once Pythodorus returns and inserts himself into the flow of conversation.

In this section we are going to learn about Socrates' account of participation in the *Parmenides* and get an initial sense of the shortcomings of that account. Specifically we will learn that Socrates believes that "forms" are the principle that can account for the determinate intelligibility of spatio-temporal objects, and that this is particularly clear in the case of relational qualities (e.g., large/small, like/unlike). We will see, at the end of this section, that Socrates does not distinguish as carefully as he should between forms and participants, if he wants forms to have the explanatory power and ontologically distinct character that he believes they do. It will turn out that the best way to address Socrates' flawed understanding of participation is to focus on the intelligible (eidetic) structure of the subject of participation, i.e., the individual spatio-temporal thing as such, or what in an Aristotelian context we might call the "categories."[12] To be clear, the subclass of forms that are responsible for the intelligibility of any spatio-temporal thing just as such are of special interest to us; I am referring to these forms as the categorial structure of spatio-temporal individuals. Socrates begins the conversation in the *Parmenides* by singling out the first hypothesis in Zeno's book, clarifying its meaning, challenging its motivations, and finally offering an alternative account.

Zeno's hypothesis reads as follows: "If beings are many" (εἰ πολλά ἐστι τὰ ὄντα, 127e1–2), "it is necessary that they be like and unlike" (ἄρα δεῖ αὐτὰ ὅμοιά τε εἶναι καὶ ἀνόμοια, 127e2). Zeno abstracts from the context of relationships in which individual spatio-temporal things stand to focus on the intelligibility of the "many" he hypothesizes. If beings are many, they *are* like and are unlike. However, this is impossible, Zeno says in the next step of the argument, "for neither are unlikes able to be likes nor are likes able to be unlikes" (οὔτε γὰρ τὰ ἀνόμοια ὅμοια οὔτε τὰ ὅμοια ἀνόμοια οἷόν τε εἶναι, 127e3–4).[13] Zeno is abstracting from concrete context, looking at the being of each of the many hypothesized in his argument, and he is noticing that they would each embody a contradiction. It is impossible for the likes (i.e., likeness) to be "unlike," or for the unlikes (i.e., unlikeness) to be like, with the result that beings are not many. Zeno leaves it open whether this implies that all is one, but the affinity of his argument with a certain interpretation of the historical Parmenides is apparent. The incoherence of the hypothesis of many beings points to a sense of "is" that is prior to the negation implicit in the contrary (or contradictory) characters of individual things. Zeno confirms that Socrates has followed the arguments as well as a Spartan hound tracking down its quarry.[14]

Socrates replies to the Zenonian hypothesis with an assertion of a kind of being, the forms, that would save the phenomena from self-contradiction. Socrates hypothesizes that the things we see and handle are "participants," and that these participants depend on and derive their determinate intelligibility from forms. Forms, by contrast, are simply and exclusively what it is to be a certain way, for example simply what it is to be "many," etc.[15] Socrates says that there is a form of likeness "itself by itself" (αὐτὸ καθ' αὑτό, 128e6–129a1) and some other [form that is] opposite (ἄλλο τι ἐναντίον, 129a1–2), i.e., what unlike is (ὃ ἔστιν ἀνόμοιον, 129a2). Forms are simply and uniquely what they are. Things can be like and unlike because likeness and unlikeness occupy an ontological level distinct from particulars. Things can be both like and unlike because there is a "being" that transcends things, with the result that the likeness and unlikeness in things is not intrinsic to them. Socrates says "the others that we call many" (τἆλλα ἃ δὴ πολλὰ καλοῦμεν) participate (μεταλαμβάνειν) in these two beings (τούτοιν δὲ δυοῖν ὄντοιν) (129a2–5), i.e., in the forms of likeness and unlikeness. Some of the others become like(s) (ὅμοια γίγνεσθαι) by partaking in likeness, to the extent that they participate in likeness, and others become unlikes; those that partake in both become both like and unlike. Thus the many "are" like and unlike in the sense that they "partake in" likeness and unlikeness, not in the sense that they are identical with like and unlike.

Socrates' reply to Zeno rests on two important foundations. The first is the premise that form is "itself by itself," which entails that forms are separate from each other and, insofar as they are separate, there is nothing preventing something's being subject to contrary properties.[16] The second is that each individual is one among many others to which it is related in various ways. Using himself as an example, Socrates points out that spatio-temporal things are divided into a right side, left side, front, back, top, and bottom, for they partake in multitude (πλήθους γὰρ οἶμαι μετέχω).[17] Similarly, Socrates is "one human being among the seven" of them (ἑπτὰ ἡμῶν ὄντων εἷς . . . ἄνθρωπος, 129d1) "by partaking in the one" (μετέχων καὶ τοῦ ἑνός). Participants, including human beings and "sticks and stones and things of that sort" (λίθους καὶ ξύλα καὶ τὰ τοιαῦτα, 129d3–4), each show themselves to be something that can be subject to contradictory characters.

Socrates' sense of the limitations of his account extend only as far as the first of these two premises, i.e., that forms are themselves by themselves. Socrates says that if someone were "dividing forms themselves by themselves separately" (διαιρῆται χωρὶς αὐτὰ καθ' αὑτὰ τὰ εἴδη, 129d7–8), such as likeness and unlikeness, one and many, motion and rest, and then were to show that forms combined and divided, he would be amazed. Socrates is explicitly relying on the second premise that "something" participates in the forms (129a3–6)—"something" is one and many, like and unlike. The real wonder, he says, would be if someone were to demonstrate that the likes themselves (αὐτὰ τὰ ὅμοιά) were unlikes (ἀνόμοια) or the unlikes themselves were likes (129b1–3).[18] If Zeno could demonstrate the "form of one" (ὃ ἔστιν ἕν) to be "many and, in turn, the many (τὰ πολλά) one" (129b7–c1), there would be cause for wonder. If Zeno could show "the kinds and forms in themselves undergoing these opposite passions" (129c2–3), Socrates would indeed be amazed.[19] Thus Socrates' account resolves Zeno's puzzle by positing a kind of being in the primary sense: the forms, which are not subject to contradictories and cannot be subject to being "mixed and discerned" (συγκεράννυσθαι καὶ διακρίνεσθαι, 129e2–3), in distinction from the "visibles" (ὁρώμενα).

But Socrates, in spite of himself, speaks of the forms as "somethings" that have at least some of the same characteristics as things. For example, the form of "one," i.e., "what *is* one (ὃ ἔστιν ἕν)," cannot be "many" because it does not have any aspect other than being "one." Conversely, the form "many" cannot have any other aspect than being "many." Forms must have one and only one character. However, Socrates switches from referring to the idea of "likeness" (ὁμοιότητος, 129a1, 129a4) as one to many, referring to "the likes themselves" (αὐτὰ τὰ ὅμοιά, 129b1) as if "it" were many. This shows that Socrates is not rigorous in the way he maintains the view that each form has only one aspect. Similarly, Socrates shows that he thinks of "what is many" as numerically multiple, i.e., as subject to multiplicity. He says that it would be a wonder if someone were to demonstrate "what is many [to be] one" (ὅ ἔστιν τὰ πολλὰ . . . ἕν, 129b6–c1) just after having referred to the "many" in the singular (*plēthos*) as that in which things participate (τῷ πλήθους αὖ μετέχειν, 129b6). Thus, Socrates treats forms as simply what they are but also as having certain abstract or uniform characteristics *qua* forms. In a related example, Socrates calls likeness and unlikeness "opposites" (ἐναντία, 129a1–2) and refers to likeness and unlikeness as "these two beings" (τούτοιν δὲ δυοῖν ὄντοιν, 129a2). However, if forms were genuinely above, or prior to, combination and division, then it would be unclear in what sense they can be counted as many or even as two, or both, or opposites. These abstract characteristics held by forms generally do not follow from what each is in its essence, but Socrates has not yet fully grasped the fundamental dissimilarity between forms and things. It is necessary, and yet Socrates is not yet able, to treat forms in some sense as subject to general (and sometimes contradictory) characteristics.

At the same time as Socrates subjects forms to the same categories as things, he elevates things to the level of forms. Socrates avails himself of the premise that "something" participates in the forms and, thereby, is the subject of the contrary characters derived from participation in the forms. However, Socrates makes no effort to explain the relationship between the "something" and the parts or aspects that are derived from participatory relations, and he makes no effort to explain the ontological status of a "one" that is the subject of participation.[20] This subject, the spatio-temporal "one," is an unexplained given of the same sort as the forms.

What is needed, therefore, is to differentiate more clearly between forms and participants. Socrates must learn to account for the characteristics that forms share with particulars and the aspects that particulars share with forms. Forms are denumerable and, in some cases, opposed to and therefore paired with other forms. Things are "one" in a way that allows them to be the subject of contrary (sometimes contradictory) characters. One way to approach the challenge to differentiate between forms and things more clearly is to become clear about the eidetic structure of particulars. In order to understand the complexity of forms or the eidetic character of particulars, we can begin by clarifying the necessary and universal structure of things.

It is quite natural, then, that Parmenides begins interrogating Socrates by challenging the separation between things and forms. If we can understand the constitutive participatory relation—the basis on which any spatio-temporal "one" is subject to space and time—we might be able to distinguish from that the types of participatory relation by which a "one" is subject to number and relation. Doing so would allow us to disambiguate the relationship between forms and things, first by seeing that the forms are subject to the character of being "something" (τί, cf. 129d4), and second by seeing that things have necessary eidetic structures.

Rhetoric, Eristic, and Scientific Philosophy

In this section we will step to one side of our reading of the *Parmenides* in order to understand the nature of the philosophical method employed by Zeno and Socrates and to consider what this method can tell us about the breakthrough it seems Socrates is being enjoined in the *Parmenides* to attempt. The key point I want to make is that scientific thinking about the nature of intelligibility requires that we detach ourselves from particular perspectives and subject the premises of our thinking to a refutative *reductio* (as eristic does), in order that we may strike a new foundation for thinking and action (as rhetoric does). I will argue in this digression that Socrates must travel down the road of rhetoric and eristic to detach himself from the assumption of the fundamentality of thinghood in order to overcome his description of forms as subject to the characters of things. My basic point is that Zeno's style of argumentation is an example of the sort of philosophical method that Socrates, in striving to grasp the incommensurability of forms and things, requires.

Versions of the Zenonian style of argumentation, both its abstraction and its focus on the self-contradictory character of basic framing assumptions, can be seen at work in a variety of places throughout the Platonic dialogues. The style bears a certain obvious affinity, for instance, with the way Socrates characterizes rhetoric and sophistry, most notably in the *Phaedrus* where Socrates refers to the Eleatic Palamedes (who is generally taken to be Zeno). Socrates describes the art of contention (ἀντιλογική), when used in the courtroom, as capable of making the same thing appear just at one time and unjust at another to the same person (ποιήσει φανῆναι τὸ αὐτό τοῖς αὐτοῖς τοτὲ μὲν δίκαιον, ὅταν δὲ βούληται, ἄδικον 261c10–d1). When used by the Eleatic Palamedes, this art, if an art it really is, can make the same thing appear (φαίνεσθαι) both like and unlike, one and many, moving and at rest (261d6–8). Strictly speaking, courtroom disputation and its philosophical cousin, dialectic, do not make anything. Rather, they draw on the multivalence of appearance and the multiplicity of perspectives that can be accommodated by appearances. The same contentiousness that serves destructive purposes in the courtroom can be put in service of the dialectical study of forms.

In the *Parmenides*, the way Zeno characterizes his aim shows something of the value of Zenonian method for eristic, and it will help us understand what value eristic methods can have for philosophy. Just after Socrates reviews the first hypothesis in Zeno's book and before the introduction of the account of participation, Zeno describes the purposes for which he originally designed his treatise. Zeno says that the book was written to discredit people who ridiculed Parmenides' hypothesis "if one is" (εἰ ἕν ἐστι, 128d1), but the book was not written to be published, and it was never intended as a search for truth.[21] The treatise was simply an attack on the perceived opponents of Parmenides, and it was intended to undermine the force of their attack by showing the self-contradictory absurdities that follow from what they implicitly must believe. Zeno's intention was to contend against (ἀντιλέγει) their laughing claims and pay them back "with interest" (πλείω), he tells Socrates, by showing that their hypothesis "if many are" (εἰ πολλά ἐστιν) results in more laughable (γελοιότερα) conclusions than Parmenides' hypothesis of the one (128c6–d6). From this perspective, the methods Zeno employs in his book can and did belong to a person in his youth writing in a spirit of competition and love of victory (φιλονικίαν, 128d7). Zeno did not employ a standard of truth to which everyone would be subject. Rather, he used a standard of relative absurdity, showing his opponents' thesis to be more laughable than the one he was defending. Zeno clearly believes that his methods can be used in a spirit of competition, but their competitive aim of their composition does not imply that the arguments themselves are invalid, nor does it explain why a much older Zeno saw fit to bring the book with him to Athens.[22] It demonstrates only that in Zeno's eyes, Zenonian method has a merely eristic aspect, but it leaves us to wonder what the philosophical aspect of that method might be.

We can gather clues from similar methods used by Socrates elsewhere when, for example, he examines the opposed characters manifest in one and the same action, event, thing, or person to disrupt received opinions and clear the way for new insight. Zeno's argumentative approach in the *Parmenides* seems to follow Socrates' general approach insofar as it does not offer positive conclusions but simply draws attention to the limitations in the way we talk about things.[23] The apparent lack of a definitive conclusion to Zeno's hypothesis demands that the reader decide the purpose to which his critique should or can be put, and as such it encourages the same critical reflection on the intelligibility of things.[24]

The destructive moment of Zenonian method is then accompanied by the potential for a certain kind of positive moment that we might associate with rhetoric. As described in Plato's *Gorgias*, rhetoric is wildly free from external standards as a quasi-revolutionary power to re-found and reorient perspectives. For instance, in the *Gorgias*, when Polus injects himself into the conversation, the others ask him why he believes himself better at giving answers than Gorgias, whom he replaces. Polus says it only matters that his responses seem good enough to his audience. Giving no more than the appearance of truth, rhetoric becomes a power (δύναμις, 456a5) above all types of externally measured types of knowledge, on which basis it makes the craftsmen, doctors, trainers, and moneymakers its "slaves" (δοῦλοι, 452e5).[25] It seems that rhetoric's power depends on (or exploits) the audience's willingness to forget themselves, to ignore their belonging to external standards, and to participate in the quasi-divine moment of carving out a starting point.

Zeno's book is an example of eristic and rhetoric that is at least potentially philosophical insofar as it is destructive of received ways of speaking and encouraging of new beginnings of the path of thinking. Zeno's book seems to have been written to attack the absurdity of the thesis "that there are many" without bothering to defend the thesis "that there is one." It is in this regard an example of eristic, and if there is a lasting philosophical value to this method, we should be able to locate that value within a broader context of self-contradiction.

I propose that Zeno's method is, at least potentially, a philosophical appropriation of eristic and rhetoric insofar as it is opens up a non-normative, or extra-normative, attitude in the way we speak of things. A philosophically serious person, free from the authority of borrowed norms and able to break with the presumed authority of individual things, can use this method to re-found the paths along which their thinking runs. The special value of Zeno's method is to reveal the explanatory inadequacy of our received ways of speaking of one and many. By helping us to challenge the perceived authority of things, Zeno will provide the context in which we and Socrates can begin to rethink the difference in kind between forms and things. Understanding the way Socrates in the *Parmenides* conflates forms and things will help us to extricate ourselves from the perspective that treats "thinghood" as self-evident and questions only the different ways things can be taken up.[26]

Parmenidean Intervention [130a3–130e3]

After Socrates completes his presentation of the nature of the participatory relation, Parmenides and Zeno are described as silently smiling at each other.[27] Parmenides first turns to ask Socrates about the causal priority of forms, focusing on the separation (*chōrismos*) between forms and things. Parmenides' aim is to establish with greater precision the sense in which forms differ from things and, specifically, what if any characters are proper to forms and what characters are proper to things. The main thrust of the questioning interrogates the sort of entities that forms are, so as to differentiate forms from things. We might begin by wondering whether certain categories, such as magnitude, number, relation, etc., are exclusive to one or the other type of entity, or shared by both.

As we began to see above, Socrates does not have a clear idea of the specific forms that constitute the necessary and universal aspects of spatio-temporal things. Nor does Socrates perceive the depth of the problem created once we find ourselves obligated to say that forms participate in other forms and, thereby, are subject to combination and division. In order to access these questions properly, we will need (a) to get a glimpse of what it is necessary for an object to be insofar as it is subject to spatio-temporal determinacy, and (b) to see that the spatio-temporal object owes its determinate intelligibility to the forms. On the basis of distinguishing between forms and participants and, at the same time, determining the eidetic structure of spatio-temporal individuals through the analysis of Parmenides' objections, we will be in a position to move toward a positive account of the relationship between forms and participants in the hypotheses.

Parmenides begins by refocusing the discussion in the following way. He asks whether Socrates divides (διῄρησαι) forms themselves as separate (χωρίς) from those things that partake of them, and whether he also divides as separate (χωρίς), again, the things that partake of the forms (130b1–2). Parmenides organizes the discussion of this question into four parts, dealing in turn with forms of abstract determinacy (e.g., one, many, likeness), forms of value (e.g., justice, beauty, goodness), forms of concrete determinacy (e.g., human being, fire, water), and forms of things that seem beneath determinate structure (e.g., hair, mud, filth). By considering each of these groups in turn, we will be able to understand the distinction Parmenides will go on to draw between the things we hold in honor and the objects of science.

Parmenides asks whether it seems to Socrates that there is a form of "likeness itself" (αὐτὴ ὁμοιότης) separate from the likeness we have, and if there are forms of one (ἕν) and many (πολλά) themselves (130b3–5).[28] Socrates is willing to grant these forms. The next group of forms seems drawn from the ethical and political context of the *Republic*, where the primary concern is with virtue and the life in which virtue is housed.[29] Parmenides asks whether there is some form itself by itself (αὐτὸ καθ' αὑτό) of justice (δίκαιον), beauty (καλόν), goodness (ἀγαθόν), and these sorts of things; Socrates easily agrees (130b7–9). These forms have a normative and ordering efficacy in things, making the internally differentiated soul virtuous, the coordinated action of a group of individuals efficacious, and the *polis* happy. In their ethical and political context, these forms lend themselves to being called "value" forms, since at least part of their work requires that human beings have a relatively explicit formulation of them and use that formulation to guide action and belief. However, this need not rule out a constitutive aspect of, for instance, justice, which renders possible any action as such by virtue of constituting self-agreement. Insofar as these forms are in a certain respect the forms that come first to mind in the context of honoring and dishonoring, they are forms responsible for certain kinds of value; insofar as action would not be efficacious without justice, however, these are constitutive forms.

The third group is a set of forms that govern the concrete determinacy of individuals, such as human being (ἄνθρωπος), and qualitatively determinate bodies, such as fire (πῦρ) and water (ὕδωρ) (130c2). Socrates says that he has been thinking of the question often and has been at a loss (ἀπορία) about whether these naturally occurring bodies are to be counted with the others as subject to a separate form or whether, perhaps, the form they have is inseparable from the qualitatively or numerically determinate bodies they are.

The fourth and final set of things, hair, mud, and filth, Parmenides describes as seemingly laughable (γελοῖα), most lacking in honor (ἀτιμότατον), and most base (φαυλότατον) (130c5–7). The question is whether they have any form that is separate from them, which is suggestive of a norm by which they are measured. Socrates replies that "these are just what we see" (ταῦτα μέν γε ἅπερ ὁρῶμεν); there is nothing separate from them that explains what they are. At this point, Socrates says that he has often wondered about what would be implied if he were to say that such things have forms. When he thinks along these lines, he finds himself cast into "an abyss of nonsense" (βυθὸν φλυαρίας) (130d3–8). Socrates can see what is at stake, that "there is some same account concerning all" (τι ᾖ περὶ πάντων ταὐτόν, 130d5–6), but he fails to see how there can be something that is "what is filth" or "what is hair."[30]

According to Parmenides' diagnosis, Socrates excuses himself from answering these questions because Socrates is young and philosophy (φιλοσοφία, 130e2) has not yet seized him as it one day will. The youthfulness Parmenides identifies in Socrates pertains to Socrates' inability to detach himself from the particularity of perspective, attached to shame and pride, which is connected to the ability to subject each premise to refutative *reductio*. I believe that Parmenides is saying to Socrates that it takes time and patience to develop the view that everything has its own specific share of intelligibility, and that the scientific philosopher will not refuse to examine and consider intelligibility in all its forms. That is to say, Socrates' orientation toward intelligibility is trapped by his guiding intuitions. Socrates has not differentiated the distinct kinds of determinate intelligibility to see that there are categories to which forms are subject *qua* form, and there are eidetic structures by which participants are constituted *qua* participant. Such a clarification of types would allow Socrates to see that forms are not things but nonetheless do share some of the characters possessed by things. According to Parmenides, the reason Socrates has not allowed the limitations of the account of participation to rise to the level of honest perplexity, lead where it may, is a fear of being made laughable.

Maturing into Scientific Philosophy

Parmenides has said that Socrates is too "young" to let philosophy seize hold of him. We want to know in particular how it is that youthfulness, which is characterized as being overly tied to the normative web of honor and dishonor, prevents us from gaining access to the intelligibility of participants *qua* participant. I will frame this question using the discussions of recollection in the *Phaedo* and philosophical method in Book 7 of the *Republic*, to which Socrates refers as the "study of the one" (ἡ περὶ τὸ ἓν μάθησις, 525a2). I will argue that the basic thrust of these two discussions is to help the soul of the would-be philosopher move beyond the imagistic thinking of the "lovers of sights" toward a rigorous account of forms and participation.

In the *Phaedo*, Socrates helps us to see beyond appearances by pointing toward the relationship of relative magnitude in which any two spatial objects can stand. Sticks, for instance, can be picked out according to the character of equality they have in relation to each other. The sticks, however, are not simply equal to each other; as spatial particulars, they are equal to each other at the same time as they are *unequal* to other things.

> Look at it this way. Don't the sticks and stones, although being the same, appear equal in some respects and unequal in other respects?
>
> Entirely so.
>
> What about this? Is there ever a time when the equals themselves sometimes appear to you unequal, or equality inequality?
>
> No, never, Socrates. (74b7–c3)

σκόπει δὲ καὶ τῇδε. ἆρ᾽ οὐ λίθοι μὲν ἴσοι καὶ ξύλα ἐνίοτε ταὐτὰ ὄντα τῷ μὲν ἴσα φαίνεται, τῷ δ᾽ οὔ;

πάνυ μὲν οὖν.

τί δέ; αὐτὰ τὰ ἴσα ἔστιν ὅτε ἄνισά σοι ἐφάνη, ἢ ἡ ἰσότης ἀνισότης;

οὐδεπώποτέ γε, ὦ Σώκρατες.

Once we distinguish the form of equality, which cannot be unequal, from the equality in the sticks, we will have effectively adopted the stance of the lover of learning (lover of the spectacle of truth) in the *Republic*. The sticks are capable of being taken up in many different respects; the sticks appear both equal and in many ways unequal. As things, they both *are* (equal) and *are not* (equal). If the equality were identical to equality *in things*, then equality would be no more equal than its opposite, which is clearly impossible. Thus we find two conditions required by the appearance of equality in things: (1) there must be a respect in which things can be compared with one another, for example, magnitude, and (2) there must be a norm toward which the sticks, taken up in respect of magnitude, point. The discovery of the respect in which individual things can be compared and the normative limits ordering their comparison demands that we acknowledge a distinct metaphysical reality prior to individual things.[31]

Socrates characterizes participants as falling short of the distinct metaphysical reality on which they depend. Equal things, for instance, "fall short" (ἐνδέω, 74d6) of the perfection of equality insofar as things, such as sticks, are equal but also are not equal, i.e., they are larger or are smaller. Things aim at (βούλεται, 74d9–10) being equal, but they fall short of the being of equality and are unable to be such (τοιοῦτον, 74e1). Socrates uses this point to argue that we must have known those perfect beings beforehand (πρόοιδα, 74e2), so that we can now be in a position to see that individual beings resemble (προσεοικέναι, 74e2) them. We have prior knowledge of the forms, Socrates concludes, and things strive for (ὀρέγεται, 75a2) the forms.[32] Socrates' language almost invites the assumption that the forms and participants are in the same sense, but participants also are not in addition. It seems that forms are paradigm instances of participants that have no other contrary aspect of their being.

A problem arises when we use this language of falling short and striving for the forms, a problem that presages the rejection of conceiving participation as a relationship of likeness and conceiving form as a paradigm in nature in the *Parmenides*. Only insofar as a stick is large or is small is it possible for the stick to "not be" equal. That is, in order to fall short of one form, the stick must "be" according to another form. The stick must fully embody being-large and not fall short of that if it is going to fall short of equality, for what is not-equal must be either larger or smaller. Socrates thus clarifies a distinction between forms and participants only on the basis of holding "being" constant and unquestioned. What he ignores, at least in the context of the *Phaedo* conversation, is that spatio-temporal objects are subject to magnitude, and they participate in the ideas of "large," "small," and "equal" as a condition of their being in place.[33] Conversely, Socrates needs to give an account of the being that is proper to forms.

Before moving on to how the "study of the one" in *Republic* 7 can help clarify the being proper to forms and participants, allow me clarify the terms with which I will draw that distinction. When I refer to things that participate in forms and are also spatio-temporally present, I say they *both* participate in *and* are subject to forms. Thus, for something that is present in space and time and is both large and small, I say that it *participates in* the large and, additionally, *is subject to* the large. It is possible, for instance, for a spatio-temporal individual to relate to a form as something unequal insofar as the form participates in inequality; however, this does not imply that the form is subject to relative magnitude because the form is not also subject to inequality. To be present in space and time implies the causation of the forms of size, which place the individual thing in spatial relation to other things and grant them their characters as, e.g., equals. For this reason, I refer to magnitude and other specific aspects of spatio-temporal individuals as their "categorial" aspects, which are proper to spatio-temporal individuals through participation in the forms. In this case, the category is magnitude, according to which any object in space and time can be compared, and the spatio-temporal object is present in space and time by constitutive participation in the large, small, and equal.

In *Republic* 7, Socrates addresses shortcomings in his account of participation in the *Phaedo* by focusing on the necessarily implied structure of a one that is placed into spatio-temporal relation to others through constitutive participation. Socrates holds up three fingers for comparison. Insofar as each one is a finger, it invites no insight. The finger's position, color, and size are distinct from its unity as a numerically distinct particular, and unlike these other properties the unity of the finger as a countable one does not imply its own opposite; as Socrates says, the finger (*qua* one) does not imply its opposite in the way that large implies small.[34] But when the finger is placed next to others and considered in terms of magnitude, it shows itself as subject to multiple relations at the same time; it is hard and is soft, is thick and thin, and long and short. When the soul sees that hard and soft, long and short, are both commingled in the finger, and thereby sees something lacking (ἐνδεῶς), the soul is at a loss and calls on intellect to distinguish between the one itself, i.e., the finger *qua* one, and the two commingled characters in the finger, i.e., long and short. The soul must strike an interrogatory pose and wonder what this thing is that can be at once hard and soft, heavy and light, long and short.

Socrates says that in this stance of inquiry, the soul "first invites calculation (λογισμόν) and understanding (νόησιν) to examine whether each of the things announced is (ἐστίν) one or two" (*Republic* 524b3–5).[35] Sight reports large and small as "mixed up," but understanding separates large and small into distinct ones, asks what the large and small are (τί . . . ποτ᾽ ἐστὶ τὸ μέγα αὖ καὶ τὸ σμικρόν, 524c11–12), and takes these "whats" as objects of understanding (νοητά, 524c13), which "the soul, summoning thought and calculation, attempts to see whether each of the things brought forth [by sensation] is one or two."[36] The soul is drawn toward these characters and made to look beyond the perceptual given to the determinate intelligibility that explains appearances, i.e., toward being (*ousia*). Contradiction stirs the soul to "make a decision" (ἐπικρίνω, 524e4), requiring it to be at a loss, "the thought within him being moved to ask whatever is the one itself' (κινοῦσα ἐν ἑαυτῇ τὴν ἔννοιαν, καὶ ἀνερωτᾶν τί ποτέ ἐστιν αὐτὸ τὸ ἕν, 524e4–6).[37] The soul distinguishes the contraries mixed together in our perception of the one itself. In this way, the study of the one would refer to the study of the way in which various ones, or determinately intelligible aspects of the things we see and judge, can co-relate in the self-same object.

The *Republic* discussion can thus be used to address the shortcomings we identified in the language of falling short of and striving in the *Phaedo*, for here we are focused on the basic constitution of a spatio-temporal particular as something that is one (what it is) and many (the various ways it is).[38] The study of mathematics is designed to lead the would-be philosopher to a mature stance by turning the soul from becoming to being, upward on an ascent to what-is (τοῦ ὄντος οὖσαν ἐπάνοδον, 521c7). The journey begins with a turn away from the self-contradictory face of things toward a synoptic view predicated on a sense of the immanent and pure characters of which the determinate intelligibility of things consist. Starting with number, we are looking specifically at the grasp we have of things *qua* intelligible.

The study of the one, which I have argued is a study of the distinct characters present but commingled in our perception of the perceptual "one itself," helps the soul turn away from the empirical particularities of objects and toward their intelligibility.[39] As we saw in the case of the three-fingers example, the point of these mathematical studies is to allow contradictories to summon thought. But notice that this study does not pick out value forms, e.g., the just and the unjust, pious and impious, or of beautiful and ugly appearance, but the abstract intelligible character of bodies stripped of their value and specific natural organization. It picks out all bodies insofar as they are intelligible and are therefore subject to spatio-temporal determinacy as being of a certain magnitude, having certain qualities, being one in the sense of composite and countable, being in a place, at a time, being subject to relation, doing and undergoing, etc. In short, the mathematical turn picks out the categorial determinacy of any spatio-temporal one and subjects that abstract character to systematic interrogation.

In sum, the discussion in the *Phaedo* helps us to see that perceptual individuals are unable to explain their own characters as, for example, equal. The sticks "are" equal only insofar as they are in principle also "not equal," which distinguishes them in their being from forms. Forms and participants are ontologically distinct. However, we noted a deficiency in this regard in the *Phaedo* account, which characterized individuals as "falling short," and in the *Republic* 5 account, which treated the being-X of things in a certain respect the same as the being of forms. Participants are subject to categories, such as relation and magnitude. The categorial aspects of forms and participants allow us to see that participants have a necessary and universal eidetic structure, and that forms, at least in a certain respect, are subject to certain of these categories. The study of the one begins to address these deficiencies by distinguishing the aspects of the perceptual one commingled in our perception. The result is that we can begin to see that prior to participation, "the one itself" is not subject to spatio-temporal determinacy, and that spatio-temporal determinacy itself is rooted in an atemporal and a-spatial cause. This important insight is the beginning of the turn from becoming to the priority of being, i.e., what simply "is."

Conclusion of First Chapter

After the initial clarification of Socrates' account of participation, Parmenides begins the long process of drawing Socrates into the abyss where, according to Parmenides, philosophy will take hold of him and Socrates will not "disdain" (ἀτιμάζω) anything. The hinge of the turn toward the abyss is the suspension of received authority and the sense of shared concern of which that authority consists.[40] The suspension of the norm that governs bodies and the turn toward aggregates that are "one" by accident, which have neither the determinacy and vitality of fire and water, nor a proper place of the parts within the organized whole, allow us to raise the question of the genesis of order in the following chapter.

Stepping back from the *Parmenides* momentarily, the dialogue has presented itself as a philosophical diagnosis of, and response to, the danger that in learning to think for ourselves we lose sight of the dependencies of thinking and unknowingly give absolute priority to the project of technical mastery. By presuming to know ourselves and to know the limits of thinking, we mistake our limited perspective for one that is complete. In the *Parmenides*, Parmenides presents the hypotheses as an initiation that frees thinking from its inherited momentum without growing all the more catastrophically dependent upon assumptions that it cannot, or will not, acknowledge. We have been pursuing the hypothesis that the abstract character of Zeno's puzzle opens the Socratic account of participation onto a crucial new vista in which the efficacy of forms is seen as constituting the categorial structure of things in some sense "behind" complex individuals. What is at stake in the examination of the constitutive categories of spatio-temporal things is the recognition that thinking and being are dependent on forms.

As indicated already, the questions of fundamental ontology are anathema to Socrates, and he tends to avoid them, apparently because he is committed to the questions and disputes about what is most valuable. However, I believe that scientific philosophy, which travels the same road as *eristic* practices, holds value for ethics and politics. What is required is a demonstration of the dependencies of thinking and, therefore, the absolute nature of the normative constraints under which thinking, virtue, and the human way of being are erected and by which they are called. Specifically in the context of the *Parmenides*, we are able to study the first step of the scientific journey that will lead, later in the day so to speak, to the ethical and political concerns of the *Statesman*, *Philebus*, *Timaeus*, and other dialogues. That journey begins with the problem of the constitution of bodies out of a sheer mass, and the precise way in which bodies are aggregates and are subject to a range of categories. All bodies, including living things, rest on a constitutive basis of indefinite, aggregate stuff (πλῆθος) in which organization and qualitative determinacy rest. It is to that level of determinacy, the first order, that we turn with Parmenides in the discussion of sharing by parts and whole.

CHAPTER 2

Putting Participation to the Test

In this chapter we are going to take a look at each argument in the conversation between Socrates and Parmenides consecutively and develop a way to think through them as a group. At the end of the discussion we will discover that our basic understanding of the most common and familiar phenomena contains important ontological interpretations. As Parmenides will ask us to notice, we are at each moment intimately familiar with the determinate intelligibility of spatio-temporal individuals. That is to say, in every object with which we have dealings, we tacitly understand the necessary aspects of complexity and individuality: part/whole relations, inside/outside relations, contact, shape, magnitude, multiplicity, likeness, unlikeness, number, etc. These aspects of the intelligibility of spatio-temporal individuals are so pervasive that we cannot have an intelligible experience of objects without drawing on them, and yet our ways of understanding this intelligibility are unsophisticated and rarely scrutinized. If we are going to make a start at achieving the "good passage" that Socrates mentions in the *Philebus*, we will first have to overturn the misleading obviousness in the intelligibility of ordinary things.

We will be dealing with the section of the dialogue in which Parmenides attempts to impress on Socrates that there is insufficient justification for adopting the theoretical commitment to forms that Socrates has just introduced in his response to Zeno. It is important to notice, as we proceed through the objections, that Parmenides will acknowledge the truth of Socrates' account.[1] Parmenides says that if there were no forms and no idea that is always the same (τὴν αὐτὴν ἀεί, 135c1) for each of the things that are, thought would have nowhere to turn, which would "completely destroy the power of dialectic" (τὴν τοῦ διαλέγεσθαι δύναμιν παντάπασι διαφθερεῖ, 135c1–2). Thus, in our reading we should understand Parmenides to be challenging the account of participation in order to strengthen it. His objections have a pedagogical purpose: to transform Socrates' account from a matter of correct opinion into a truth that is grasped "authoritatively" (κυρίως).

Parmenides sees in Socrates "a noble and divine impulse that drives toward arguments" (ἡ ὁρμὴ ἣν ὁρμᾷς ἐπὶ τοὺς λόγους, 135d3) but one without merit until Socrates can become the "more astonishing" person capable not only of discovering the forms but also of teaching them to another who has carefully gone through all the difficulties. In order to become a serious person and to hold an account seriously implies, on the terms provided by Socrates in the *Republic*, that the person holding the account must fight through all attempted refutations, "strenuously desiring to test [his account] according to being rather than according to opinion" (κατ' οὐσίαν προθυμούμενος ἐλέγχειν, 534c2–3), becoming "synoptic" (537c7) in the process. In the *Parmenides*, Parmenides instructs the young dialectician to "draw" (ἕλκυσον) himself through what most people consider to be of no value, idle talk (ἀδολεσχία) (135d5). Once again, what I want to keep in mind is that the objections Parmenides raises to Socrates' account of participation are not meant to disprove the account but to provoke a deeper insight into the truth toward which that account points.

The string of objections that Parmenides levels at Socrates are designed to provoke Socrates (and the reader) into doing the work of justifying the account of forms and participation, work primarily accomplished by attacking two key assumptions. The assumptions that will be exposed to critique in the course of Parmenides' objections are (1) that the forms are complex wholes subject to divisibility, and (2) that the forms are individuals subject to number. These objections stem from the governing assumption that forms can be treated in the same terms that constitute spatio-temporal objects. Spatio-temporal things are at a basic level characterized by divisibility and multiplicity—they are aggregates subject to division, and they are individuals subject to relation (to other individuals). The leading edge of the critique will thus be asking about the proper way to construe the nature of the forms. More specifically, if we cannot understand forms on the paradigm of complex individuals (i.e., spatio-temporal objects), as it will seem that we cannot, then precisely how are forms to be understood?

Parmenides' objections specifically address the conditions that must obtain if forms are to have a causal relation to things and, conversely, things are to partake in forms. The strategy of this series of objections is to use the paradigm of complex individuals as a basis for understanding the participatory relation. In each case the relation between forms and things is construed in terms of one or another aspect of the nature of complex individuals (i.e., their complexity or their individuality). In the first set of objections, Parmenides will treat the form as a divisible aggregate, and in the second set of objections he will treat the form as a spatio-temporal individual. These two sets of puzzles are implications of the ontological difference Socrates has inserted into being between the "is" of forms and the "is" of participants, which Parmenides has singled out by asking about the separation between the two. Insofar as Socrates still has not purified his thinking of the governing model of spatio-temporal individuals, he finds himself still committed, in spite of his best intentions, to the view that if forms are separate from participants but *related* to participants through participation, the forms will be individuals of the same kind and therefore subject to indefinite divisibility. Likewise, if forms are related to participants and *separate* from them, the forms will be individuals of the same kind and therefore subject to indefinite reiteration. By forcing Socrates to establish a more rigorous ontological difference between forms and things, Parmenides is inviting Socrates to mature philosophically.

One in Quantity: Part/Whole Complexity

In this section we will look at the portion of the dialogue in which Parmenides offers the first two challenges to Socrates' metaphysical claims. Socrates has just responded to Zeno's puzzle with an account of form and participation. Parmenides will ask Socrates to agree that there is a separation between forms and things, and on that basis Parmenides will challenge participation on the basis of its implied consequences.[2] We will begin by analyzing in turn each of Parmenides' two challenges. The thrust of these objections is that forms can either be "one," as Socrates has asserted, or they can share themselves with participants, but they cannot do both.

Parmenides understands Socrates' account in the following terms: "these other things" (τάδε τὰ ἄλλα, 130e5–6)[3] "have their names" (τὰς ἐπωνυμίας αὐτῶν ἴσχειν, 130e6) and, therefore, their qualitative determinacy "by getting a share" (μεταλαμβάνοντα, 131a1) of the forms. Parmenides compels us to interpret "getting a share" in terms of a symmetrical relationship between two complex individuals, i.e., form and participant. That is to say, a form is a "one" as spatial whole of spatial parts, it relates to participants by "sharing" itself with them either as a whole (ὅλου τοῦ εἴδους, 131a4) or by parts (μέρους, 131a4), and it is present in its participants.[4] However, Parmenides argues, if the form were to share itself as a whole simultaneously in many things that are separate from each other, the form would be separate from itself in spite of being one (ἓν ὄν, 131a9). Thus, sharing by wholes implies that forms will not be one, for they will be divided into numerically distinct wholes. However, if the forms remain one, there can be no sharing.

Socrates has a powerful response to this objection. Socrates objects that the form could share itself as a whole with many individuals without being separate from itself if it were "similar to" (οἷον, 131b3) a day, which is one (μία, 131b3) and the same at the same time (ἅμα, 131b4) in many places but not separate from itself. I take Socrates to mean that daylight is in many places simultaneously at any single time of day. If the form were one in the same sense as a day is one, each of the forms could be one (ἕν, 131b5) and the same (αὐτή, 131b6) at the same time as it is in many (ἐν πᾶσιν, 131b5–6).[5] Parmenides declares how "sweetly" (ἡδέως, 131b7) Socrates makes one and the same being in many places at the same time (ἅμα πολλαχοῦ, 131b7), and Parmenides proceeds to translate Socrates' image of a day into the image of a sail. A day is simultaneously present as a whole in many places in the way a sail spread over many people is, as a whole, present to each of them. A part of the sail is over each person, and the sail is thereby divided into parts.[6] One part of the sail is over one person, and another part over another, and on this model the forms would be "divisible" (μερίζεσθαι) (131c10). Socrates agrees to the conclusion that he cannot say the "one form" (τὸ ἓν εἶδος, 131c9) is one at the same time as it is "in truth divisible" (τῇ ἀληθείᾳ μερίζεσθαι, 131c10).

Parmenides' reply to the "day" example seems almost brutally unresponsive to Socrates' image of the day and the spirit of Socrates' account of participation.[7] When Parmenides translates Socrates' example of a day into the example of a sail, his interpretation of the "day" as a "sail" placed overtop many people seems to represent a willful misinterpretation of the image. But that is precisely the point. Socrates goes along with the translation of "day" into "sail" because, I contend, Socrates does not see any better way of articulating the meaning of his image in discursively rigorous terms, i.e., non-imagistically, and Parmenides insists that he do attempt to do so. Thus, Parmenides presses a one-sided construal of the image of the day in order to impress on Socrates the necessity of articulating the type of "one" a form is with rigor and precision.

There does seem to be something wrong with Socrates' way of articulating the truth of his image; at least there is more that he could go on to say. The image of the day is insightful, and it responds in a sense to Parmenides' objection.[8] When Socrates offers the image of the day, he seems to be relying on the sense that "day" is a context for things, and the "day" is thereby not "in" the context and subject to the requirements of that context. We have to be cautious with this interpretation for the same reason that the image is unsatisfactory as a basis for understanding: images are imprecise. Our reading of the "day" image could be picking out some aspect of the image that is unintended and due to the multifaceted, uncontrolled nature of any image. However, if we read the "day" as an image for the category of place, we can see that the day is one in the sense that it is what gives things the context in which to encounter and be present to other things (or, at the level of lighting up our surroundings, it gives perceiving beings access to their situation). At the same time as the day gives the context for many things, it is not one of the things "in" the day, and it is not subject to the relationships to which it gives rise. If day were one of the things in the day, it would not have the power to open up their relations; that is, none of the things in the day could do anything or have any power unless it were already in the day. Socrates therefore seems to have a sense of the categorial dimension of things, and a sense of ontological priority at least as it pertains to categories, but Socrates does not have the vocabulary and the set of habits firmly ingrained that would allow him to parse out the very differences to which he gestures. We cannot know what Socrates thinks because he has not laid it out with precision. Parmenides' set of challenges here is focused explicitly on the mechanisms by which (ᾧ) participation happens, rehearsing as he goes the categories to which a spatio-temporal one is subject. Parmenides is challenging Socrates to articulate himself in more precise terms.

Parmenides extends and amplifies the sail analogy by proposing that participation happens when a form shares part of itself with things. Parmenides picks the large, small, and equal as his examples and shows that if the forms shared themselves by adding a part of the form to something, (a) larges would become "large" by partaking in something smaller than the large itself, (b) equals would become "equal" by getting a part smaller than the equal itself, and (c) the "small itself" would become larger relative to its part, and the participant would become smaller by having something more added to it. Parmenides is here encouraging the view that if Socrates agrees that all three results are absurd, then the *logos* of sharing by parts annuls itself in the style of Zeno's first hypothesis.

Parmenides' challenge attacks the manner in which Socrates conceives the forms by visualizing them rather than thinking in a rigorously discursive manner about their essential characteristics. The "being" of the form is twofold insofar as the form is (a) "itself" (i.e., it "is" what is large), and the form is (b) subject to size (i.e., the "large itself" "is" a spatial whole of spatial parts). The absurd (ἄλογον, 131d2) conclusions follow as a consequence of treating the cause of greatness as something subject to magnitude and, therefore, as subject to the large, small, and equal, similar in a way to treating the "day" as a thing that appears in the context of a day.

In response to these two objections, Socrates concedes that it will be very difficult to determine how "the others" (τὰ ἄλλα, 131e4) get a share of the forms if they are able to do so neither by whole nor part. Having seen this, Socrates rules out one important avenue by which visualizing the forms will serve as a reliable guide for thinking about their nature and the participatory relation. Whereas Parmenides uses these aspects of spatio-temporal being as a framework for satisfying the primary objective of correcting Socrates' style of allowing visualization to guide thinking of forms and participation, we can also see Parmenides establishing a general account of spatio-temporal being. We can begin to see that spatio-temporal particulars just as such are subject to quantity and quality.

Parmenides is juxtaposing qualitative and quantitative identity in these arguments. At first Parmenides clearly identifies forms and things as something like extensive magnitudes, as ones to which and from which some amount can be added or subtracted. For instance, he suggests that part of the large itself can be taken away and added to "the things in our world."[9] The idea of "magnitude" appears here in the *Parmenides* only insofar as it is possible to add or subtract an indefinite amount, so the emphasis must be placed on the indefinite addition and subtraction rather than indefinite magnitude as such, which is not yet clearly hypothesized. In the determination of addition and subtraction of an indefinite amount, the part is a magnitude added to something to make it larger. The part is conceived as carrying an intrinsic, qualitative identity, and it is conceived as simply "more," i.e., more stuff to be added to some aggregate. This is what Parmenides has in mind when he asks whether it makes any sense that something will become smaller by addition, i.e., by adding an indefinite amount of the "small itself" to the smalls by us. At the same time, Parmenides understands identity qualitatively, in terms of relative measure, saying that "what" something is will be decided in relation to what it is not, such that a part of the large itself will be smaller than the large itself. It is with this account of identity in view that Parmenides asks whether something can become large by addition of something smaller than the large itself, i.e., a part that is relatively smaller than the whole from which it is taken. Qualitative identity based on relative measure is determined by the context in which something stands,[10] and when it is juxtaposed to quantitative identity in these arguments, we find ourselves compelled to wonder at the metaphysical relationship between aggregate and relative identity.

We are now in a position to reinterpret Socrates' "day" example in metaphysically precise terms. The main point of the objection the dialectician would want to raise to Socrates' characterization of the unity of form as a day is that forms and things are incommensurate with one another. Socrates seems to have intended to say that as day is intimately close to the things that are in the day, as perhaps the element of water or air is intimately close to fish and birds as they move through their element, so too the form is close, as it were, to the things that participate in them. On this reading, Socrates is trying to conceptualize the relation between a thing and the source that constitutes that thing as a thing.

But this reading of participation as closeness undermines rather than elucidates the incommensurability of forms and things and stops short of metaphysical explanation. The ideas of large, small, equal, one, part, and whole are not close to the things that partake in them, they are logically prior to and incommensurate with participants. When Parmenides imagines the "large itself" as something divisible, he imagines it as something already participating in the forms large, small, equal. Parmenides' objection in a sense comes too late, and we are reminded of his original question of the separation. That is, the work of conceptualizing the forms requires that we think of separation in such a way that the forms can be without being spatio-temporally present in the way things are.

Parmenides' objection to the account of participation underscores the problem with our opening concept of separation between incommensurate terms, and the problem if not also the inevitability of construing this relation in inappropriate terms. The perspective of mastery, which takes individual things to be the primary building blocks of reality, is a metaphysical perspective deeply ingrained and tacitly operative in our everyday dealings. Parmenides' pedagogical purpose in this exchange with Socrates, which we can now better understand, seems to be the attempt to show Socrates that although the account of participation is not false, Socrates holds that account in a false way by trusting in the presence of things and letting pre-philosophical dogma in the way of his own deeper insight.

We should at this point be suspicious of the way Socrates earlier in the dialogue declared his ease and comfort with ordinary things, saying that he understood well enough that they could be like and unlike, large and small, one and many, and a host of other differences at the same time. In fact, Parmenides is trying to show Socrates precisely that the eidetic structure of ordinary things stands in need of being questioned and understood anew. Parmenides is urging Socrates to take a closer look at the determinate intelligibility of the things with which Socrates is most comfortable, so that by so doing Socrates might be able to approach the "abyss of nonsense" from which he flees when he tries to develop a unified account of participation.

Thus far we have considered only the objection to Socrates' so-called theory of participation that Parmenides launches from the perspective of the divisibility of aggregates and the intelligibility of aggregation. I take these objections to correlate to the complexity of spatio-temporal particulars. In the next section we will turn to Parmenides' objection often referred to as the "third man regress" with the intention of examining the metaphysical puzzles pertaining to the other chief aspect of spatio-temporal intelligibility: being individual, i.e., being one of many.

One of Many: Individuality

The objections raised by Parmenides have helped us to step back from Socrates' habit of visualizing the forms and allowing, thereby, the structure of spatio-temporal individuals to guide his thinking about participation. Consistent with the sort of "is" to which the historical Parmenides drew attention, Parmenides here is attacking the unexplained and dependent nature of what Socrates holds up as ultimate and explanatory. What Parmenides' objections show us is that an aggregate, such as the one described in the sharing by parts challenge, is intelligible only insofar as it is already subject to and participating in certain forms. In order to operate with an aggregate presence, we must presuppose participation in and subjection to the ideas of "being," "one," "large," "small," and so on. These are the terms on which anything subject to space and time must rely in order to have causal power, and the source by which these terms are explained will be unable to draw on the assumption of an already constituted spatio-temporal presence. Thus, Parmenides has encouraged us to ask what makes spatio-temporal presence possible.

In this section, as we turn to the greatness regress, we are considering the sense in which a "one" has an identity as one of many other individuals, and we are considering the eidetic complexion of this aspect of spatio-temporal individuals. In the following objection, Parmenides enjoins the perspective from which to be "one" implies being subject to number, subject to "appearing" (φαίνεσθαι), and being able to "seem" (δοκεῖν) to a certain point of view. What we discover through the analysis in this section of the dialogue is that being one in number draws on a source prior also to denumerability, just as being one in quantity showed itself to draw on a source prior to divisibility.

Parmenides begins by asking Socrates about the reasons for thinking that each form is "one." Parmenides suggests to Socrates that the reason he believes each form to be "one" is that to someone looking (ἰδόντι, 132a3) over many things that are the same, e.g., many "larges," some one "look" (μία τις . . . ἰδέα, 132a2–3) announces itself to that person as the same in all. From that evidence, Parmenides suggests, you might gather "the large" to be one (ἓν τὸ μέγα ἡγῇ εἶναι, 132a3–4).[11]

Parmenides then uses this description to argue that the form, if we construe it as an individual, seems unable to do the work of explanation; once again, he focuses on the example of the "large." Parmenides says that if someone were to look (ἰδεῖν, 132a7) with the soul (τῇ ψυχῇ, 132a7) over all the many larges, the "large itself" (αὐτὸ τὸ μέγα, 132a6) would appear (φανεῖται, 132a7) with the other larges (τἆλλα τὰ μεγάλα, 132a6). The "large itself," as the explanatory principle, would be that by which (ᾧ, 132a7) all the others appeared as larges. Parmenides argues furthermore that this set of larges—the many larges with which we began and the large itself—require yet another explanatory principle "by which" each is large, and he says that another form (ἄλλο . . . εἶδος, 132a10) of greatness will show up (ἀναφανήσεται, 132a10), having been generated (γεγονός, 132a11) alongside greatness itself (παρ' αὐτό τε τὸ μέγεθος, 132a10–11). This process has no limit, and it threatens an infinite regress. The way Parmenides puts it, each one of his forms (greatness, likeness, justice, etc.) will never be one (ἕν, 132b1–2) but unlimited in multitude (ἄπειρα τὸ πλῆθος, 132b2).[12]

Socrates jumps in to object to the way in which Parmenides seems to have equated the appearing of the form with the appearing of things, and he suggests in reply that there are two kinds of appearing: appearing of the intelligible to the soul and appearing of the sensible to the eyes. By distinguishing between different ways of seeming (δοκεῖν) and appearing (φαίνεσθαι), Socrates is able to hypothesize that each of the forms is a thought (νόημα, 132b4) engendered (ἐγγίγνεσθαι, 132b4–5) in souls (ἐν ψυχαῖς, 132b5). If the form were an ontologically distinct sort of "one," there would be no object field consisting of the form and participants, or the larges and the large itself.

It seems that through the greatness regress Parmenides is calling on us to notice the failure to distinguish between the two distinct types of "one": form and thing ones; and it seems that Socrates makes a partially successful reply to this challenge by introducing an asymmetry between forms and things. But Socrates' reply to Parmenides' objection introduces incommensurability at the expense of the causal efficacy that forms must have. Parmenides points out that being thoughts, they are thoughts of something that is (ὄν, 132c1), that is some one idea (μίαν τινὰ οὖσαν ἰδέαν, 132c4), and that is always the same over all (ἀεὶ ὂν τὸ αὐτὸ ἐπὶ πᾶσιν, 132c6–7). This "one idea" could not be in things either as part or whole unless each thing is "composed of thoughts" (ἐκ νοημάτων, 132c10) and things think (νοεῖν, 132c11), or although being thoughts (νοήματα ὄντα, 132c11) things are thoughtless or they do not think (ἀνόητα, 132c11).[13] Socrates concedes that it would not seem reasonable, or proportionate, to say that things are subject to forms by virtue of thinking them, or that the forms, although thoughts, have their force some way other than by being thought. Thus, forms cannot be in things, and it is ridiculous that forms are thoughts. We might pause, however, to note the there is a turn here at the level of secondary, perhaps unintended, implications toward an account of the incommensurability of forms and things and toward an account of the activity of participation modeled on the activity of thinking. These are not successful moves at this point, but they point to the recognition that some account of these kinds is demanded by the objections.

The dilemma these two objections point to is that the forms, in order to be efficacious, must be incommensurate with things, perhaps in the way thoughts differ in kind from things. The advance that has been made should not be overlooked. It is a positive step forward to acknowledge the problem of the incommensurability of forms and things. It is also important to notice that the discussion of the intelligibility of spatio-temporal ones carries with it discussion of the soul to which things appear and/or are thought. If we draw on the lessons of the previous discussions, we will see that the one "by which" the many larges are large does not itself have a size; indeed, it cannot have size because it is that which constitutes what we call "context," deriving that from the intelligible relations things provide to us in their intelligibility.

The insight to which we are invited by the text is that spatio-temporal presence must be constituted because it is not simply given, and such presence is constituted by participation in forms.[14] Because presence is not an original given, we cannot imagine the form as present without thinking of the form as participating in the forms that make-present, nor can we imagine the thing as present except insofar as it has already participated in the forms out of which its presence is constituted. The circularity that the greatness regress outlines and that the forms-as-thoughts reply is meant to resolve is that we have been presupposing participation in order to imagine the participatory relation. Parmenides' focus on the small, large, equal serves to highlight the problem that something—a form—can only stand in a real relation of proximity or distance to something else commensurate in kind if it is already participating in the forms of large/small/equal. Parmenides' objection works by placing the form in real relation to the things the forms explain and constitute, and the way out of the bind facing Socrates is to think of forms as incommensurate with things as the causes that constitute the very nature of spatio-temporal presences in general.

Review: "One" as Aggregate and Individual

I now want to step back from the flow of the dialogue to comment on the relationship between the aggregate one and the individual one. As I have attempted to show, both aggregate and individual are aspects of any spatio-temporal thing. Just insofar as it is determinately intelligible, a spatio-temporal thing will have an aspect of being one *qua* individual and one *qua* aggregate. What has implicitly changed for us at this point in the analysis of the *Parmenides* is that the relationship between the aggregate and the individual has started to emerge. The specific point I want to argue is that the relative measure which we associated with the aggregate "one" in the section on sharing by part or whole is not complete, i.e., it is not intelligible, without the individual "one" that we have been analyzing in this discussion of the infinite regress.

We need the individual one to make sense of the aggregate one insofar as there is no definite intelligibility in the world of appearances unless there is something to which the appearance can be tied down, or perhaps something by which the tying down can occur. For example, a pen is small relative to the room, and the city is small relative to Greece. There is nothing in the pen, the room, the city, or Greece that would pin down the small, since each is no more small than it is large. Furthermore, the ability to talk about "a" small, or an individual small thing, and to group the individual small thing with other small things explicitly points to the power of the individual one to define (rather than be defined by) its context. That is to say, we can put things together and treat them both as instances of small only because they are intelligible as individuals first and as small secondarily. More specifically, the pen and the city cannot both be small; only one can be small relative to the other, which will be large (or equal). Thus, in both the stability in which we identify a small rather than large or equal, and in the stability by which we group together two smalls, we are relying on the intelligibility of the individual one.

At the same time, we also need the aggregate one to make sense of individuals. Just insofar as any thing in order to be intelligible must in principle be present as small or large, and as taking up a place and being extended in that space and contained by it, there is no spatio-temporal individual that does not carve out a spot for itself. Individuals are present only insofar as they impose limits on a continuum in which they stake out their boundaries. It is out of the continuity with the aggregate surroundings that an individual is able to own boundaries as an individual. No spatio-temporal individual would be intelligible or present were it not carving a space for itself within a larger space. Parmenides is particularly suggestive of this point when he chooses the example of many larges, for they explicitly in their very identity as individuals are implicated in the relational network that extends beyond their individuality.

To sum up this short point, we can only pick out the individual one insofar as we are tacitly aware of the aggregate one, and we can only pick out the aggregate one insofar as we are tacitly aware of the individual one. What this allows us to see is that there is a context in which we relate these two aspects of the one together, and that context must belong to neither one aspect of the individual more than the other. There is a relative intelligibility in which things are measured against each other without independent standard, and this is to be contrasted with a measurability by a fixed (quantitative) standard, so that there is both "taller than that" and "three feet tall," or the height "of" David. On this basis, what is large within its context can be fixed as the greatness of what is numerically (not just relatively) intelligible. Once the individual is prioritized over context, the individual large thing can be brought into proximity with other individual large things, each as numerically one rather than being subject to indefinite relations of larger and smaller.

The intelligibility of any spatio-temporal thing, therefore, is in neither one individual nor in one space. Socrates' suggestion that the object of our knowledge is in thought makes room for this insight. What we want to do in response to the text is to improve on Socrates' suggestion by addressing its shortcomings. I am suggesting that, in a merely provisional way awaiting further analysis, what we should be thinking is the relationship between the indefinite one and the unifying one. We can see the determinate intelligibility of spatio-temporal objects pointing in these two directions.

One step in the direction of such an account can be taken now. It is evident that in order to count many larges or smalls or anything else, there are forms other than large that must be enjoined. It is only once the continuum in which the aggregate "one" is situated is articulated into individual ones that the question of relative measure of the aggregate can be meaningfully posed, and it is only insofar as the triplet of large/small/equal divides the continuum and joins it together as an intelligible tableau that it can be articulated into individuals. The aggregate one and the individual one, therefore, depend on each other. I want to suggest that these two forms participate in each other in order to constitute the eidetic structure of the presence of the spatio-temporal thing. Whether we pick out the aggregate aspect of the spatio-temporal one and subordinate its individual aspect, or we pick out the individual aspect and subordinate (make secondary and accidental) its aggregate aspect, the two aspects depend on each other and belong together.

Thus, if we were to reformulate Socrates' account of the dissimilarity between forms and things, we might have an answer to the regress problem. First, we should notice that there is one register of the spatio-temporal object in which it is aggregate and individual (this "is" joins the two within necessity, as if they were categorial features of the nature of spatio-temporal things), and there is another register, as it were, in which the object is in contingent relations of position, disposition, various qualities, quantities, etc. The objects of knowledge out of which spatio-temporal presence is woven—for instance, greatness, which is constitutive of the aggregate, or number, which is constitutive of the individual—do not occur contingently in any situation but are, similar to Socrates' image of the day, the terms to which anything must submit in order to be present as a spatio-temporal being. The idea of greatness, therefore, does not (and cannot) have any size, nor can it be subject to any locative preposition, such as above and outside, as if it were in the context of spatio-temporal presence.[15]

The soul's grasp of the forms must be prepared to admit a gap between the sources of thinking and the concrete terms in which forms express themselves and from which those forms are known and interrogated.[16] That is, we must be prepared to grasp the distinction between the immanence of forms in things and the prior presence of forms as forms. This theme of the gap between forms as such and forms in things will be extended in the following discussion of the forms as paradigms fixed in nature. For now, we conclude by noting that the relationship between forms and things, in order that forms can be constitutive of the presence of things, is not a real relationship. It seems that Socrates is not in a position to articulate this point explicitly, since there is no reason to believe he would not do so, given the objections Parmenides has raised to the account of participation. The most important point at stake for the dialectician is the notion of a fundamentally constitutive relationship in which the spatio-temporal one is subject to the forms by which spatio-temporal presence is woven. The turn toward paradigms fixed in nature will focus this question in a way that will allow us to continue to wrestle with the idea of the separation and relationship between forms and things.

One in Quality: Likeness and Multiplicity

In this section we will return to the arguments of the dialogue and examine Socrates' final account of participation as the likening of things to forms as "paradigms set in nature." Parmenides will launch an objection that looks on the surface very much like the regress argument above. The differences, however, between this argument and the earlier regress argument will enable us to extend our reading of the way spatio-temporal presence is eidetically structured and fill out the notion of "constitutive participation." Once we examine the metaphysical implications of Parmenides' objection in its specific contrast to the first regress, we will see in particular a way that the ontological solidity and primacy, so to speak, of the spatio-temporal object are eroding as we begin to catch sight of the asymmetry of the relationship between forms and things.

In response to the collapse of the hypothesis that forms are, like thoughts, only in souls, and therefore exempt from the pluralizing regress, Socrates characterizes forms as paradigms, which he introduces somewhat more forcefully as what "appears quite clear" (καταφαίνεται, 132d1) to him: forms are "like paradigms established in nature" (ὥσπερ παραδείγματα ἑστάναι ἐν τῇ φύσει) (132d2). The others (τὰ ἄλλα, 132d2) resemble (ἐοικέναι, 132d3) the forms and are likenesses (ὁμοιώματα, 132d3) of them, and participation is therefore the act of the others being made in the image (εἰκασθῆναι, 132d4) of the forms. This analogy of paradigms as models set in nature has the twofold advantage of not implying that the form is present in things, nor that the form is reducible to the status of a participant. Obviously, however, it is still an analogy, and it still fails to establish incommensurability between forms and things.

Parmenides begins by enjoining the perspective from which something that resembles (ἔοικεν) the form is like (ὅμοιον εἶναι) that which it images (τῷ εἰκασθέντι) to the degree (καθ' ὅσον) that it is made like (ἀφωμοιώθη) the form (132d6–7). Thus, the root of imaging is likeness; as Parmenides puts it, if forms are paradigms that in some sense govern things, forms and things must be "like" each other. There is "great necessity," therefore, that, if one like (ὅμοιον) is reciprocally like the other like, they must both partake in "the same one form" (ἑνὸς τοῦ αὐτοῦ εἴδους, 132d9–e1, Gill's tr.), i.e., the form of likeness.[17] Likes share a quality of likeness: it is by the "form itself" (αὐτὸ τὸ εἶδος) that they are likes.[18] Two cases of the same character, that is, the character of likeness shared by the form and its participants, require a form to explain them. The common character of likeness shared in by the form of likeness and the initial form and its participants would need a supplementary form of likeness to explain them, and so on. Parmenides concludes that the others are not able to be like the form nor the form like any of the others, for if they were, a new form would always show up (ἀναφανήσεται, 132e7) alongside the first, and that form would be like, and another in turn would show up, and this ever-new genesis of form would have no end: "an ever new *eidos* [of likeness] will never cease being generated" (οὐδέποτε παύσεται ἀεὶ καινὸν εἶδος γιγνόμενον, 133a1–2). If there can be no likeness between paradigms and participants, the determinate intelligibility of any individual object of perception cannot be explained by likeness.[19] If it is not "by likeness" that the others partake in the form, "some other" (τι ἄλλο, 133a6) by which (ᾧ, 133a6) the others participate must be sought; Socrates accepts this conclusion, saying "so it seems" (ἔοικεν, 133a7).

At this point Parmenides momentarily rests his case and asks Socrates to notice how great the *aporia* is if one is going to mark off (διορίζηται) forms as beings alone by themselves (εἴδη ὄντα αὐτὰ καθ' αὑτά, 133a9). They break from other objections that might have followed to pass directly to the *aporia*, which Parmenides calls the "greatest": the thorough-going skeptical objection that we cannot have knowledge of the forms, and the gods cannot have knowledge of particulars. Before we continue with our sequential analysis of the arguments, let us pause to consider the implicit metaphysical insights at work in Socrates' new account of participation and Parmenides' new objection.

Metaphysical Asymmetry

Parmenides used his earlier regress argument to show that the form—in that case he used the example of the large itself—was not one but an unlimited multitude. In response to Socrates' "paradigms in nature" account of forms, Parmenides points to what he characterizes as a continuous generation of new forms. I want to suggest that Socrates' new approach suggests a promising metaphysical asymmetry between forms and participants, one that Socrates does not yet master but that will nonetheless ultimately prove compelling.

As images, things are now treated as harboring a kind of incompleteness by which they are able to point beyond themselves toward their paradigm, so the notion of a metaphysically incomplete, or metaphysically secondary, "one" has been introduced. If we hold on to this example of the secondariness and dependence of participants, it will prove fruitful. Similarly, on the side of forms, Parmenides' focus on the generation of new paradigms is suggestive of an important insight regarding the simplicity and uniqueness of forms: insofar as forms are metaphysically incommensurate with the particulars, forms are a metaphysically inexhaustible source that can be indefinitely articulated in new and different images. Each instantiation of the form as an imagined paradigm points beyond itself to the form of which it is the articulation, and thus each paradigm that can be sighted is itself a kind of image dependent on the form. The form speaks of many such paradigmatic instances, and the plethora of paradigms points to a common source "one" that is in principle inexhaustible. Whereas the individual merit of distinct instantiations of "large" might not carry much weight for our insight into the form, it seems that distinct instantiations of, for example, the beautiful would carry significant weight. My point is that the logic of paradigms indefinitely generated suggests a participatory relationship in which (a) each new paradigm cannot fail to manifest the form, but (b) all of the instances combined could not possibly exhaust the form, pointing to an inexhaustibility that belongs to nature of form as such.

On this reading, the account and objection in this regress argument differ from Parmenides' earlier framework for infinite regress by introducing incommensurability into the relationship between forms and things. Parmenides' argument is that likes are reciprocally (symmetrically) like one another, resulting in an ever new generation of forms. Beneath the surface, however, the introduction of the metaphysics of image and likeness acknowledges a fundamental dependence of things on forms and, simultaneously, a limit to the expressibility of forms in things. Thus, there is a deeper and more compelling account of ontological asymmetry that has implicitly started to arise. Earlier, in both the "sharing by part or whole" objection and the "many larges" objection, Parmenides imagined a participatory relation between two fully constituted objects standing in external relation to one another. In the first of those two objections, the object-model was an aggregate "one"; in the second objection, the object-model by which forms and participants were identically grasped was an individual "one." In the account of forms as paradigms, by contrast, Socrates emphasizes the incompleteness and ontological dependency of the participants, entertaining the notion that one member of the relation is dependent and relational in its very being. In Parmenides' objection, the shift from his previous language of an "unlimited plurality" to an "ever new generation" implies a shift from a static participatory relation to a dynamic relationship between form and participant, and a shift to a participatory relationship characterized by its asymmetry.

The Skeptical Objection

Parmenides concludes the discussion of being made like the forms by asking Socrates whether he sees "how great the puzzle" (ὅση ἡ ἀπορία, 133a8) if someone were to mark off the forms as "themselves by themselves" (αὐτὰ καθ' αὑτά). Parmenides begins the next stretch of conversation by emphasizing his view that Socrates does not yet grasp "how great the puzzle is" (ὅση ἐστὶν ἡ ἀπορία, 133b1) if you posit a form whenever marking a distinction between different sorts of things. Parmenides explains that the puzzle is most important owing to the objection that the forms either do not exist or, if they do, they are unknowable. What is at stake, we recall from our earlier review of the terms in which this dialogue operates, is the very foundation of philosophical dialogue. The claim that forms are "themselves by themselves" must respond to the objection that these forms are just hypothetical constructs, in order to facilitate the later deepening of insight into the priority and necessity of form.

Parmenides begins his presentation of the skeptical objection by distancing himself from its content. Parmenides introduces a hypothetical skeptic, and he invites Socrates to imagine what sort of teacher this skeptic would require. Parmenides says:

> If someone were to say that it is not proper for [the forms] to be known (γιγνώσκεσθαι), being the sort of beings (ὄντα τοιαῦτα οἷα) we say the forms need to be, someone would not be able to prove to the one saying these things that he speaks falsely, unless the disputant should happen to be widely experienced (πολλῶν . . . ἔμπειρος) and not without talent (μὴ ἀφυής), and should he be willing to follow many times and from afar the one who points out by toiling through; otherwise the one who [claims] them to be necessarily unknowable would be unpersuaded (ἀπίθανος).
>
> εἴ τις φαίη μηδὲ προσήκειν αὐτὰ γιγνώσκεσθαι ὄντα τοιαῦτα οἷά φαμεν δεῖν εἶναι τὰ εἴδη, τῷ ταῦτα λέγοντι οὐκ ἂν ἔχοι τις ἐνδείξασθαι ὅτι ψεύδεται, εἰ μὴ πολλῶν μὲν τύχοι ἔμπειρος ὢν ὁ ἀμφισβητῶν καὶ μὴ ἀφυής, ἐθέλοι δὲ πάνυ πολλὰ καὶ πόρρωθεν πραγματευομένου τοῦ ἐνδεικνυμένου ἕπεσθαι, ἀλλ᾽ ἀπίθανος εἴη ὁ ἄγνωστα ἀναγκάζων αὐτὰ εἶναι. (133b4–c1)

Parmenides goes on to say that things and forms are separate from one another not by virtue of being ontologically distinct in kind but by being separated by location. The things "in our domain" (ἐν ἡμῖν) and "the things among us" (τὰ παρ᾽ ἡμῖν) are separate from the "being itself by itself for each thing" (αὐτήν τινα καθ᾽ αὑτὴν ἑκάστου οὐσίαν, 133c4). The being of each thing cannot be "in us" (ἐν ἡμῖν, 133c5) as long as it is "itself by itself" (αὐτὴ καθ᾽ αὑτήν, 133c6). In other words, just as two things are "separate" only if they stand outside each other in a real relationship, so too (if the model of thinghood is metaphysically decisive for the conception of forms) forms can only be "separate" from things if the two groups are in different regions. Thus, Socrates is unable to define the incommensurability of forms and things except by simile (e.g., the day), and Parmenides is again taking advantage. Forms are what they are "in relation to each other" (πρὸς ἀλλήλας, 133c9) and have their being in relation to themselves (πρὸς αὑτὰς τὴν οὐσίαν ἔχουσιν, 133c10).

It thus follows that these two regions have nothing to do with one another. Each contains "ones" that are "of themselves" (αὐτῶν, 133e6) and "in relation to themselves" (πρὸς αὑτά, 133e6):

> Neither do those forms have the power they have in relation to the [things] by us, nor do the things by us [have their power] in relation to them; rather, each [has its power] itself in relation to themselves."
>
> μήτε ἐκεῖνα τὰ εἴδη πρὸς τὰ παρ᾽ ἡμῖν τὴν δύναμιν ἔχειν ἣν ἔχει, μήτε τὰ παρ᾽ ἡμῖν πρὸς ἐκεῖνα, ἀλλ᾽ αὐτὰ πρὸς αὑτὰ ἑκάτερα. (134d5–7)

Parmenides uses the example of master and slave to draw out the intuition that we relate to things we can seize hold of. For instance, a human master is master of a human slave. A human master is not and cannot be master of "slave itself," i.e., what it is to be slave. The idea of master has its power in relation to the idea of slave, and the human master has power over the human slave. "Mastery itself" is what it is "of slavery itself" (αὐτὴ δὲ δεσποτεία αὐτῆς δουλείας, 133e3). The things with which we have our dealings, things which we can touch, trade, cultivate, destroy, all have their power in relation to each other and not in relation to forms. Forms are separately "of themselves" and "in relation to themselves" (αὑτῶν καὶ πρὸς αὑτὰ ἐκεῖνα, 133e6).

Parmenides now turns to the crux of the skeptical objection. He says, "knowledge concerning what is would be knowledge of the truth itself concerning what is" (ἐπιστήμη . . . αὐτὴ μὲν ὃ ἔστι ἐπιστήμη τῆς ὃ ἔστιν ἀλήθεια αὐτῆς ἂν ἐκείνης εἴη ἐπιστήμη) (134a3–4). Each type of knowledge, furthermore, would be knowledge of each of the things that are "in themselves." The knowledge that we have, by contrast, would be knowledge of the truth we have (τῆς παρ᾽ ἡμῖν ἂν ἀληθείας, 134a9), and each particular knowledge we have (ἑκάστη ἡ παρ᾽ ἡμῖν ἐπιστήμη, 134a10) is knowledge of particular things "among us" (τῶν παρ᾽ ἡμῖν ὄντων ἑκάστου, 134a10–b1). Because the form of knowledge itself "knows" the forms themselves (αὐτά . . . τὰ εἴδη, 134b3), and because we cannot have the form of knowledge itself (αὐτοῦ τοῦ εἴδους τοῦ τῆς ἐπιστήμης, 134b6–7) by which the kinds themselves (αὐτὰ τὰ γένη, 134b7) are known, we cannot know forms.

Parmenides derives from these remarks the "more fearsome" (δεινότερον, 134c4) consequence that if we do not possess the "more precise" (ἀκριβέστερον, 134c7) kind of knowledge, i.e., knowledge itself, and if only a god has the most precise knowledge (θεὸν . . . ἔχειν τὴν ἀκριβεστάτην ἐπιστήμην, 134c11), then the gods have knowledge of the forms through the form of knowledge itself. But if forms do not have their power in relation to things in our domain, then the gods do not possess knowledge of our affairs, nor do the gods have mastery over us. According to Parmenides, it follows that this many other puzzles seem to follow for anyone who posits that there are ideas and each is defined as the inner nature of things. If Socrates is to live up to the demands of his theoretical commitments, it will be necessary to address the root and cause of the skeptical objection.

Answering the Skeptic

Parmenides' example of master and slave might jump out at the Greek reader as a good way to make the point that the internal, structural relations that govern formal realities are distant from the contingent, external relations that govern spatio-temporal things. Slave is definitionally related to master, but being a slave in Greek society was often simply a matter of bad luck, being in the wrong place at the wrong time, losing a battle, and being forced into slavery. In many cases, master and slave are both free in the sense that they were both citizens at one time, one of whom now serves the other.[20] The master and slave may submit themselves to the structure of an institutionalized relationship, a principle that orders each with respect to the other, but what each member of this relationship is fundamentally exceeds, even challenges, the relationship in which they stand. The skeptic can (and did) object that the relationship between master and slave is purely conventional. The skeptic could argue that all relationality is external and contingent.

It seems, however, that the skeptic would be wrong to conclude that the two members of this structured relation are simply separable from the space of ordered relation. They are not at liberty to approach each other without *some* principle structuring their relationship and constituting its intelligibility. It is only in light of the ordered whole that the parts can gain a sense of themselves as separable from one another, and thus the idea that there can be a realm of forms separable from the realm of things would be false. Thus, the skeptical objection, by forcing us to confront the interpretation of form as regulative and conventional, allows us to consider the specific participatory relationships without which the skeptical objection would not even be intelligible.

I have argued in this chapter that the only response to Parmenides' objection is to see that forms are necessarily prior to and constitutive of things. In support of this view, I have pointed out that one can only separate forms and things in the way the skeptic requires if one believes that each, form and participant, is independently real, which implies that things (one half of the disjunction) are independently real, and therefore explicable and capable of existing without reference to forms. Once we understand that the objection cannot be raised unless we already presuppose the eidetic structure by which individual things are able to be in a region, whether "in our domain" or apart from us, we will have felt the demand that we account for the forms as prior to and constitutive of individual and complex ones.

At the completion of the discussion of the skeptical objection, Parmenides goes on to indicate that it will require hard work and a generous nature to maintain the theory of forms and teach it to a skeptic. In what I have tried to show, the work of owning the hypothesis of forms begins in the refutation of the skeptic, which gains traction with the insight that forms play a constitutive role establishing the intelligibility of the very "ones" on which Socrates bases his account and the skeptic bases her objection. Parmenides tells us that the would-be philosopher must be willing to undergo a strenuous and serious test of truth in order to achieve the kind of facility with the insights we have here outlined necessary for teaching others. If we are going to complete what Socrates in the *Republic* calls the "turning of the soul" from becoming to being, we must work through in detail the exhaustive account of constitutive participation, and we will need to overcome the basic metaphysical attitude to which Parmenides' objections has shown thinking to be subject.

In the following section, I want to look at the way dialectic is characterized in the *Republic*. Parmenides has here characterized the relationship between forms and things as a distinction between two kinds of precision. Gods would have knowledge of the forms, which knowledge Parmenides says is "most precise," and human knowledge is secondary in precision. Between these two degrees of precision lies what Socrates in the *Republic* understands to be the study of mathematics, in which the would-be philosopher must engage in order to adjust to a higher degree of precision than our life "in the cave" allows us to achieve before turning to dialectic.[21] I will argue in what follows that the skeptical objection operates on the basis of mathematical (i.e., pre-dialectical) precision, and that overturning the assumptions on which the skeptical objection is predicated allows us to begin to secure a starting point prior to mathematical thought. In order to progress into philosophy, I will claim, requires that we overcome the object-paradigm that surreptitiously guides Socrates' thinking about the forms and develop a discursively rigorous account of participation.

5. Dialectic in the Republic and Parmenides

At this point in the discussion Socrates can see that his account of the forms might have value for answering Zeno's puzzle, but that it nonetheless faces a number of serious objections. In each of his replies to Parmenides, Socrates has attempted to preserve the status of the form as separate from the things in our domain, i.e., participants, and he finds himself unable to answer the objection that the forms are thereby subject to the very characters they cause; for example, the form of large would be a large thing and subject to the categories of individuality alongside other larges. Freeing himself from the problems to which his account is vulnerable will require that Socrates critique the basic ontological hypothesis of the spatio-temporal one and discover its necessarily prior conditions.

The challenge Socrates faces here bears comparison to the description of the dialectical person in Book 7 of the *Republic*. In Book 7 Socrates says the dialectical person is the one capable of "grasping the *logos* of the being of each [being]" (τὸν λόγον ἑκάστου λαμβάνοντα τῆς οὐσίας, 534b3–4) and submitting that *logos* to the "test of being" (ἐλέγχων . . . κατ' οὐσίαν, 534c1–2). In our case in the *Parmenides*, dialectic will grasp the *logos* of the spatio-temporal one as such in order to specify the determinate intelligibility that belongs to the forms given that they are the causes of the determinacy of things and not simply "objects" of the same kind as the things that participate in them. Socrates will become able to answer Parmenides' challenges by first critiquing the hypothesis of "thinghood" and establishing an ontological difference between participants and forms.

The difficulty of establishing an ontological difference of the sort demanded in the *Parmenides* was announced by the introduction of dialectic in the *Republic*. After describing the Good in Book 6 as that for the sake of which all human beings act and that the soul "divines" (505e1) but is unable to grasp sufficiently, Socrates draws an image of the Good in an analogy with the sun. The person who is said to know in the proper sense of the word grasps particulars not from the perspective of whatever purpose or opinion she happens to have in mind but from the perspective of the *kath' hauto* being of the forms on which particulars depend. According to the analogy with the sunlight, the person who knows is one who sees the *kath' hauto* being of things in the sun's illuminating light. The Good, on this analogy, is like the source from which such being is given, just as the sun is the source that gives the light (i.e., truth) in which the knower truly grasps and the known is truly revealed. As we go on, we learn that this source of truth for the knower and of being for the known cannot become an "object" of knowledge according to the same paradigm as other objects. Socrates characterizes the Good in this way:

> One should claim not only that being known is present because of the Good to those which are known, but also that being and

> essence (τὸ εἶναί τε καὶ τὴν οὐσίαν) are present in them because of it, though the Good is not being, but beyond being inasmuch as it exceeds [being] in reverence and power.
>
> τοῖς γιγνωσκομένοις τοίνυν μὴ μόνον τὸ γιγνώσκεσθαι φάναι ὑπὸ τοῦ ἀγαθοῦ παρεῖναι, ἀλλὰ καὶ τὸ εἶναί τε καὶ τὴν οὐσίαν ὑπ' ἐκείνου αὐτοῖς προσεῖναι, οὐκ οὐσίας ὄντος τοῦ ἀγαθοῦ, ἀλλ' ἔτι ἐπέκεινα τῆς οὐσίας πρεσβείᾳ καὶ δυνάμει ὑπερέχοντος. (*Republic*, 509b6–10)

The Good, as the source of the categories of determinate intelligibility by which things are given to knowing, cannot be made subject to those categories. Given the nature of the Good, Socrates attempts to clarify what he means by offering what has come to be called the "Divided Line." The Divided Line provides initial insight into the difficulties we face specifying the nature of the objects we are investigating in the *Parmenides.*

The key point made in the image of the Divided Line, for our purposes, is to distinguish unreflective inquiry from dialectical inquiry, i.e., reflective from self-critical inquiry. The basic division in the Divided Line is drawn between sensible and intelligible objects, which parallels the distinction in the *Parmenides* between forms and participants. Within each of the two major divisions of the line, Socrates draws a further distinction in which he pairs an independent object with its dependent reflection. In the class of visible things, for example, he divides things, such as animals and artifacts, from their shadows and reflections. In the intelligible section, Socrates divides between the objects of distinct activities of soul:

> In the one [division] of it [i.e., in the intelligible division of the line], the soul is required to inquire from hypotheses, using as images things that were previously [i.e., in the sensible division of the line] imitated, not passing to a beginning but to an end. But in the other [division of the intelligible section of the line]—the unhypothesized beginning—departing from hypotheses and without the images of that [other part], it [i.e., the soul] makes the journey with forms themselves through themselves.
>
> Ἧι τὸ μὲν αὐτοῦ τοῖς τότε μιμηθεῖσιν ὡς εἰκόσιν χρωμένη ψυχὴ ζητεῖν ἀναγκάζεται ἐξ ὑποθέσεων, οὐκ ἐπ' ἀρχὴν πορευομένη ἀλλ' ἐπὶ τελευτήν, τὸ δ' αὖ ἕτερον—τὸ ἐπ' ἀρχὴν ἀνυπόθετον—ἐξ ὑποθέσεως ἰοῦσα καὶ ἄνευ τῶν περὶ ἐκεῖνο εἰκόνων, αὐτοῖς εἴδεσι δι' αὐτῶν τὴν μέθοδον ποιουμένη. (510b4–510b9)

Socrates explains that in geometry and calculation inquiry "hypothesizes" (ὑποθέμενοι, 501c3) things like the odd and even, figures, three types of angle, etc., and takes its foundations as known without exposing those starting points to critique. Investigation of this sort employs assumptions as an unquestioned support and proceeds on that basis. The precision of the knowledge produced is thus only as strong as the blind spot of the starting point that facilitates the inquiry and frames its conclusions. Its conclusions begin from, and are made out of, a kind of ignorance.

The Divided Line is Socrates' way in the context of the *Republic* conversation to show that there are types of knowing and inquiring based on shadows. Unlike shadows, however, these types of knowledge and inquiry do not obviously point beyond themselves to the reality on which they depend. Instead, these objects present themselves as fully constituted and self-sufficient modes of thought, as starting points. Inquiry that is thus blind to its own blindness is, Socrates says, "unable to climb above [its] hypotheses" (οὐ δυναμένην τῶν ὑποθέσεων ἀνωτέρω ἐκβαίνειν, 511a5–6) and grasp them *as hypotheses*.

On the fourth section of the Divided Line, dialectical method wrestles with its assumptions to grasp the starting point directly, without mediation: here "argument itself grasps by the power of dialectic" (ὁ λόγος ἅπτεται τῇ τοῦ διαλέγεσθαι δυνάμει, 511b4) its starting points and treats them as vehicles for further insight, as "stepping stones and impulses" (ἐπιβάσεις τε καὶ ὁρμάς, 511b6). Socrates describes dialectical inquiry as critiquing its hypothetical starting point; inquiry now makes use of nothing belonging to the visible and makes its way in and through forms. As I have been trying to demonstrate, the unreflective hypothesis to be studied in the course of the education of the philosopher in the *Parmenides* is the hypothesis of the spatio-temporal individual, which is subject to the categories of complexity and singularity. This hypothesis has acted as the paradigm by which Socrates has found himself constrained to think of forms. In such a context, Zeno's puzzle serves as a useful occasion for challenging the description under which we understand the manyness of beings, specifically challenging the self-evidence of the givenness of a multiplicity of ones.

Zeno's hypothesis is not dialectical insofar as there is a difference between exposing the incoherence of a certain description of what-is and using that incoherence to transform one's perspective. Zeno succeeds to a degree in securing a critical handle on particulars through his puzzle, and the young Socrates advances things by introducing the forms as a way to rethink the most familiar description of beings. Socrates, however, has not understood the depth of the difference in kind is between forms and participants, and Socrates' account, although insightful, offers him no foothold for making the appropriate progress. The further description of dialectic in Book 7 of the *Republic* prepares us to understand how Parmenides' questioning is a provocation to dialectical exercise. After completing the cave image of "our nature in respect of its education and lack of education" (τὴν ἡμετέραν φύσιν παιδείας τε πέρι καὶ ἀπαιδευσίας, 514a1–2), Socrates goes on to detail five mathematical studies that will place the budding philosopher at the threshold of dialectic. These mathematical studies prepare us for dialectical study and yet fall short of dialectic in a revealing way.

First, the image of the cave reveals many things about the nature of education for a human being, but importantly it shows us that falling short of, even refusing and resisting, dialectical insight is characteristic of dialectical inquiry. The student who is first freed from her bonds is paradigmatic of such a refusal. When she is freed and turns away from the shadows on the cave wall, the new vision that confronts her is blinding and painful, and she wishes to turn back to the shadows and bondage that seem to her more real. Then, having grown acclimated to the new sight over time, the student still has not learned to love education and must be "drawn by force" (ἕλκοι . . . βίᾳ, 515e6) along a difficult path up to the world outside the cave. Outside the cave, the sight of truth is once again too painful to behold, and the student must turn away from the vision; however, note that the turning away is this time experienced as a provisional retreat that preserves the process of acclimatizing the eyes.[22]

The five mathematical studies mitigate the counter-thrust woven into dialectical education by allowing unreflective thinking to proceed unchallenged while at the same time drawing our attention to the basic shape and structure of facilitating assumptions. The first of the five mathematical studies is the study of the one, which we discussed previously at the end of Chapter 1. There we said that the study of the one allowed us to distinguish between the one itself and those aspects of the perceptual one that are commingled in perception. The point in Chapter 1 was to appreciate the categorial specificity of certain forms, i.e., the forms that constitute the very possibility of spatio-temporal presence, and therefore to see the priority of *kath' hauto* being over particular beings. Here we are looking at the hypotheses that, as remnant of cave-thinking, remain in place for the soul undergoing dialectical education. The turning of the soul from becoming to being is a turn from the "is" and "is not" of spatio-temporally determinate ones toward the "is" of *kath' hauto* being. The study of the one allows us to see what must be true of a spatio-temporal one just as the sort of one it is, and this study therefore allows us to engage in categorial thinking without ever questioning the source of the spatio-temporal individuals that are its starting point.

The "springboard" character of this and the other mathematical studies consists in the way that each of them, even while favoring the intelligible aspect of their object over its sensible expression, still rests in an object that is to different degrees individuated. Socrates takes care to show that the individuation of each of these objects of study is not sensible. Socrates says they will study "numbers themselves" (περὶ αὐτῶν τῶν ἀριθμῶν, 525d6) rather than things that are numbered, they will purse plane and solid geometry "for the sake of knowing" (γνώσεως ἕνεκα, 527b1) and will ignore the way geometers speak of making figures and doing things, they will look past the motions of the heavenly bodies studied by astronomers because these motions "fall far short of the true ones" (τῶν δὲ ἀληθινῶν πολὺ ἐνδεῖν, 529d1–2), and they will study the "concordant numbers" (σύμφωνοι ἀριθμοί, 531c3) and their explanatory principles rather than searching out the correct number of "heard concords" (τὰς . . . ἀκουομένας . . . συμφωνίας, 531a1–2) normally mistaken as the proper concern of harmonic theory.

Even as these mathematical studies do abstract from the givenness of spatio-temporal particulars, they still remain beholden to the basic structure of particulars. The "one itself" in the study of the one is a pure one that differs in no way from others, but it still has others and is one of many. The figures of plane and solid geometry are ratios specifically limited to spatiality; similarly, the ratios combining and relating speed and trajectory are limited to spatio-temporal manifolds. Finally, the principles explaining concordant numbers, while they are closest to being the sort of explanatory principle that is not tied directly to particulars, are still ratios rooted in continua of relative degree, such as pitch. Whereas this might fulfill the point of the discussion at the end of Chapter 1 concerning the categorial nature of the forms studied and, thereby, will help us to see that the givenness of spatio-temporal things has an eidetic structure that can and must be explained, we are still thinking in a way that has not learned to detach itself from visualization.

After concluding the description of the five mathematical studies, Socrates says that if the method that goes through these studies sees their "community with one another and their kinship" (ἀλλήλων κοινωνίαν . . . καὶ συγγένειαν, 531d1–2), then they are useful for the turning of the soul, but otherwise these studies are "work without profit" (ἀνόνητα πονεῖσθαι, 531d4). Thus, when Socrates makes the transition from the five studies to dialectic, he makes it explicit that in themselves they are insufficient for their educational purposes. Socrates does not there spell out what it would mean to see them in the way that he says would be of value, and, passing over that explanation, Socrates adds that these studies are a "prelude" (531d7) to the "song itself" (αὐτός ἐστιν ὁ νόμος, 532a1) of dialectic. Turning to dialectic,

Socrates returns to the cave image: just as sight "tries to look at the animals themselves, then the starts themselves, and finally at the sun itself" (πρὸς αὐτὰ ἤδη τὰ ζῷα ἐπιχειρεῖν ἀποβλέπειν καὶ πρὸς αὐτὰ [τὰ] ἄστρα τε καὶ τελευταῖον δὴ πρὸς αὐτὸν τὸν ἥλιον, 532a3–5) outside the cave, so too a student "attempts by *dialegesthai*, through an account without any sensations, to spring toward each thing itself that is" (τῷ διαλέγεσθαι ἐπιχειρῇ ἄνευ πασῶν τῶν αἰσθήσεων διὰ τοῦ λόγου ἐπ' αὐτὸ ὃ ἔστιν ἕκαστον ὁρμᾶν, 532a5–7) and doesn't stop until she grasps by *noēsis* "what is the good itself" (αὐτὸ ὃ ἔστιν ἀγαθόν, 532b1).

The key point for our study of dialectic in the *Parmenides* concerns not what in particular we should define the Good or any other form to be but what sort of "object" forms as such *are*. Socrates' discussion of dialectic in *Republic* 7, after relying on the image of the cave to establish that there are "objects" toward which dialectic strives and which it wants to grasp, then leaves open the possibility that the very notion of "object" by which our anticipation of dialectical insight is here laden will have to be subjected to a sustained and complex critique if we are ever to access what-is. Socrates says that dialectic attempts to grasp "concerning each thing what it is" (αὐτοῦ γε ἑκάστου πέρι ὃ ἔστιν ἕκαστον, 533b2). Socrates contrasts the dialectical grasp with "all the other arts" (ἄλλαι πᾶσαι τέχναι, 533b4), which he describes as directed toward a wide and significant range of human concerns, "toward the opinions and desires of human beings, or toward generation and synthesis, or toward the tending of what is grown or composed" (πρὸς δόξας ἀνθρώπων καὶ ἐπιθυμίας εἰσὶν ἢ πρὸς γενέσεις τε καὶ συνθέσεις, ἢ πρὸς θεραπείαν τῶν φυομένων τε καὶ συντιθεμένων, 533b4–6). Incrementally closer to our goal, mathematical studies nonetheless "dream about what is" (ὀνειρώττουσι μὲν περὶ τὸ ὄν, 533b8–c1) insofar as they rely on hypotheses (of the abstract categories of spatio-temporal determinacy) that are unexplained. Socrates says,

> if the beginning "by which" is something you don't know, and the end and middle are interwoven out of what you don't know, what ever mechanism can there be for 'a general agreement' (τὴν τοιαύτην ὁμολογίαν) to become knowledge (ἐπιστήμη)?
>
> ᾧ γὰρ ἀρχὴ μὲν ὃ μὴ οἶδε, τελευτὴ δὲ καὶ τὰ μεταξὺ ἐξ οὗ μὴ οἶδεν συμπέπλεκται, τίς μηχανὴ τὴν τοιαύτην ὁμολογίαν ποτὲ ἐπιστήμην γενέσθαι; (533c3–5)

This demonstrates the depths to which apparent knowledge penetrates the life of the soul. Even the mathematical studies, therefore, are in the dark about knowledge and weave what they "know" out of non-knowing. Any method that fails to "destroy hypotheses" (τὰς ὑποθέσεις ἀναιροῦσα, 533c8) and return "to the beginning itself" (ἐπ' αὐτὴν τὴν ἀρχὴν, 533c8) cannot be considered "knowledge" (ἐπιστήμη, 533d4). At every level of explanatory completeness and precision in the soul's ascent, only the dialectician will spend her time on earth awake rather than dozing, and only this person will win access to the theoretical education that redeems all the uses to which we put things.[23]

In the *Parmenides*, Parmenides gives Socrates a clear warning that the puzzles of participation will remain unresolved until Socrates begins again from the (dialectical) beginning. Socrates must be right, as we have already noticed, that there is a form for each of the things that are, for otherwise we will have nowhere to turn our thought and one would "destroy dialectic" (τοῦ διαλέγεσθαι δύναμιν παντάπασι διαφθερεῖ, 135c2).[24] Socrates wrongly marks out specific forms, such as "the beautiful, the just, the good, and each one of the forms" (καλόν τέ . . . δίκαιον καὶ ἀγαθὸν καὶ ἓν ἕκαστον τῶν εἰδῶν, 135c9–d1) before "being trained" (γυμνασθῆναι, 135c8). In order that Socrates hit on the truth, and in order that dialectic and thought have something in which to moor themselves, there must be an "idea of each [one] of beings that is always the same" (ἰδέαν τῶν ὄντων ἑκάστου τὴν αὐτὴν ἀεὶ εἶναι, 135c1). I am proposing that this training requires that we determine what we mean when we say that X is something, or that X is one, so that we might preserve the distinct objects of thought and perception from becoming confused by our ways of speaking and habitually thinking about "objects" in general. In Parmenides' view "the impulse that impels you [Socrates] toward accounts is noble and divine" (καλὴ μὲν οὖν καὶ θεία . . . ἡ ὁρμὴ ἣν ὁρμᾷς ἐπὶ τοὺς λόγους, 135d2–3), but Socrates will never be able to receive the truth unless, Parmenides says, he first allows himself to be trained. What is needed is not simply a different definition of a particular form but a purificatory cleansing that removes stubborn, ingrained assumptions about the nature of objects, forms and participants being subject to the same categories. It is not a matter then of the things Socrates knows or opines but his deeply habituated expectation that beings are subject to the paradigm of thinghood that is the goal of his rehabilitory training.

Dialectical training will allow Socrates to correct a deeply ingrained habit. Parmenides has already acknowledged that Socrates should be admired for not letting inquiry wander among the visible nor be about them but about the intelligible character of "those things that someone could most of all grasp by *logos* and consider to be forms" (περὶ ἐκεῖνα ἃ μάλιστά τις ἂν λόγῳ λάβοι καὶ εἴδη ἂν ἡγήσαιτο εἶναι) (135e1–4).[25] But in defiance of the language and upward looking tendency of the *Republic*, Parmenides takes aim at the general form of thought and speech by hypothesizing and examining the consequences "if each is" (εἰ ἔστιν ἕκαστον, 135e9) and "if this same is not" (εἰ μὴ ἔστι τὸ αὐτὸ τοῦτο, 136a1–2), not specifying what the subject of these hypotheses should be. The object of his exercises is the formal system by which thought is ordered and given place. Asked for clarification, Parmenides refers to Zeno's hypothesis of "many" and adds two qualifications:

> For example, he said, if you wish, concerning the hypothesis that Zeno hypothesized, "if many are,"[26] what must be implied both for the many themselves in relation to themselves and in relation to the one, and for the one in relation to itself and in relation to the many.
>
> οἷον, ἔφη, εἰ βούλει, περὶ ταύτης τῆς ὑποθέσεως ἣν Ζήνων ὑπέθετο, εἰ πολλά ἐστι, τί χρὴ συμβαίνειν καὶ αὐτοῖς τοῖς πολλοῖς πρὸς αὑτὰ καὶ πρὸς τὸ ἓν καὶ τῷ ἑνὶ πρός τε αὑτὸ καὶ πρὸς τὰ πολλά. (136a4–7)

Parmenides instructs Socrates to hypothesize something "as being and as not-being and [as] suffering whatever other qualification" (ὡς ὄντος καὶ ὡς οὐκ ὄντος καὶ ὁτιοῦν ἄλλο πάθος πάσχοντος, 136b8–9) and, within each hypothesis, to pursue the implications of that hypothesis in relation to itself and others.[27] Parmenides says that the result of this training will be to "view the truth authoritatively" (κυρίως διόψεσθαι τὸ ἀληθές, 136c5), paralleling the language of the *Republic* account of dialectic as the "finest view" and the "synoptic" insight (504b1-2 and 537c7, respectively).

Socrates is sufficiently baffled by the complexity and nature of the exercise being prescribed that he, with others joining him, asks Parmenides to exemplify his meaning. As we approach the hypotheses, Parmenides' reception and acceptance of the request to offer a demonstration of the exercise call us suddenly back to the themes of embodiment and desire, which were notes struck at the opening of the dialogue. Specifically, it is his desire to hit the mark, the stressfulness of the experience, and the seriousness of character demanded by this exercise that are sounded:

> It is necessary [for me] to obey. But I seem to be suffering [the suffering of] Ibycus's horse. Ibycus compares himself, so old and thus unwilling to be compelled to enter into love's games, to an old horse about to compete by chariot and, on account of past experience, trembling at what he was about to endure. I am struck with fear, thinking back, that at this age I must set sail across such a great sea

> of *logoi*. But I must nonetheless oblige you, especially since, as Zeno said, we are by ourselves.
>
> ἀνάγκη, φάναι, πείθεσθαι. καίτοι δοκῶ μοι τὸ τοῦ Ἰβυκείου ἵππου πεπονθέναι, ᾧ ἐκεῖνος ἀθλητῇ ὄντι καὶ πρεσβυτέρῳ, ὑφ' ἅρματι μέλλοντι ἀγωνιεῖσθαι καὶ δι' ἐμπειρίαν τρέμοντι τὸ μέλλον, ἑαυτὸν ἀπεικάζων ἄκων ἔφη καὶ αὐτὸς οὕτω πρεσβύτης ὢν εἰς τὸν ἔρωτα ἀναγκάζεσθαι ἰέναι: κἀγώ μοι δοκῶ μεμνημένος μάλα φοβεῖσθαι πῶς χρὴ τηλικόνδε ὄντα διανεῦσαι τοιοῦτόν τε καὶ τοσοῦτον πέλαγος λόγων: ὅμως δὲ δεῖ γὰρ χαρίζεσθαι, ἐπειδὴ καί, ὃ Ζήνων λέγει, αὐτοί ἐσμεν. (136e8–137a7)

With these words we are reminded that insight into the forms and the eidetic structure of particulars is something that we must accomplish by concentrating our souls on a new and unfamiliar task. We are both alone in this task, working for our own insight, and we are joined with others, picking up and carrying forward what they have set down for us.

Parmenides agrees to demonstrate his method of exercise and asks whether he may "begin with myself and with my own hypothesis" (ἀπ' ἐμαυτοῦ ἄρξωμαι καὶ τῆς ἐμαυτοῦ ὑποθέσεως, 137b2–3). There is of course a temptation here to assume that the text is referring to something from the historical Parmenides, for Parmenides does cite himself as the source of the hypothesis. But Parmenides glosses what he means, saying that he will be "hypothesizing the one itself, what the consequences must be if one is or if one is not" (περὶ τοῦ ἑνὸς αὐτοῦ ὑποθέμενος, εἴτε ἕν ἐστιν εἴτε μὴ ἕν, τί χρὴ συμβαίνειν, 137b3–4).[28] At this point I take it to be undecided what Parmenides has in mind by choosing to hypothesize "the one itself" (τοῦ ἑνὸς αὐτοῦ, 137b3).[29] All that we do know is that Parmenides sees the exercise as focused on the determinate intelligibility of the hypothesized term, and that he does not want the inquiry to wander between the opposites of what is subject to becoming.[30] It seems that the crescendo of the movement of argument in the dialogue thus far is to allow us to hold open a range of possible meanings in the determinacy of what we say and commit ourselves to when we say "one." Beyond this, we should let the exercises tell us "which one," as it were, we have said.

Conclusion of First Part

Metaphysical inquiry originates in the same place as rhetoric, sophistry, and tyranny. Each suspends the authority of received opinion, established value, and personal momentum to uncover a basis on which something new can be erected. Because rhetoric can, in beginning to speak, create a framework that conceals as much as it reveals, rhetoric can destroy old norms and call new ones into being. It holds a great power by virtue of facilitating forgetfulness in others and permitting them a new attentiveness. The power of words can overturn all opinion, perception, and cultural norms, and therefore sophistry can give rise to a stance in which nothing is true.[31] Because human beings participate in these modes in the destruction and generation of meaning, they can become tyrants, destroyers of worlds. But at the same time this freedom from received opinion allows them to behold the truths that they have concealed from themselves. Rather than allowing what-is to be decided by the received and apparent intelligibility that things have as given, we can overturn the momentum of received wisdom to create a space of receptivity in which what-is may announce itself as perfectly free and unforced. I take human receptivity to the freedom of the unforced to be the subject of dialectical study of forms and the Good.

As we have seen in the objections raised to Socrates by Parmenides, and as we have recalled in our review of the *Republic*, the would-be philosopher's dependence on the unseen and unfelt violence of presupposition does not simply weaken with the initial turn toward philosophy but, ironically, grows stronger as its operation becomes more hidden. Parmenides is aware that philosophical thinking may break down at the threshold of philosophy, and so he asks Socrates to join him excavating the "one" from the constraints of hypothetical thinking, to free determinate intelligibility from the paradigm of the complex individual, and to restore the range of meanings that are invoked when we say "is" and "is one."

PART II

Exercise and Rehabilitation

CHAPTER 3

First Hypothesis (H1)

Parmenides has declared that "the one itself" (τοῦ ἑνὸς αὐτοῦ, 137b3) will act as the subject of the hypotheses.[1] As promised by Parmenides when he originally introduced the exercises in which we are now engaged, our study will examine what follows for what we hypothesize, both in relation to itself and to "each of the others" (πρὸς ἓν ἕκαστον τῶν ἄλλων, 136c1), if it "is" and if it "is not." H1 in particular sets out to study the implications for [a] one if it is, doing so in light of a number of contrasting terms (e.g., being in itself/other, being same, different, like, unlike, equal, unequal, age), terms which I will argue paint a negative portrait of this hypothesized "one."[2]

By the end of this chapter, we can expect to see a parallel develop between the "one" and any form *qua* one prior to complexity and plurality, whether that be the complexity and plurality that characterizes spatio-temporal objects or the complexity that characterizes forms as objects of discursive knowing. In other words, we will see, by the time we reach the end of this introductory hypothesis, that the "one" is (a) partless (internally simple) and (b) unique (the only one of its kind), and we will see these as characteristics consistent with the being of forms. The "one" of H1 is not many, which will lead Aristoteles to conclude toward the end of the hypothesis (141e8) that the one therefore cannot "be," cannot be known, cannot be said, and ultimately (for Aristoteles) cannot be one. Of course, if that were true the hypothesized "one" could not be hypothesized, and the conclusion of the hypothesis would undermine the premise. Thus, the self-refuting reading of H1, the surface reading, invites us to see that we cannot conclude the one "is not" *tout court*, i.e., is nothing at all and therefore must "be" in some sense. On the one hand, the conclusions of H1 will call on us to see that the one must "be" in H5. On the other hand, H1 will call for us to go over things again from the beginning (πάλιν ἐξ ἀρχῆς ἐπανέρχεσθαι, 142b1) and to sort out more completely the complexity and plurality of the one in H2.

Throughout the hypotheses, we will have repeated occasion to see Aristoteles identify "being" with structures consistent with being in space and time while we, attentively and actively engaging the text, will be developing the sense of non-spatio-temporal being. Aristoteles interprets being that is outside of space and time as non-being, so he is perplexed in the face of claims that there is a one outside space and time, and his comments will reflect that in key passages like 141e, 145e, 151a (and preceding), 152a, 159b–c, 161c, 162bff., 163cff., and 166a. If we are careful to sort out the meanings implied by the text but missed by Aristoteles at these important junctures, we will be in a position to rescue the discussion from the apparent contradictions into which Aristoteles falls and beyond which we are summoned to work out in the crucial hypotheses H3, H5, and H7.

Preparatory Discussion of the "One"

The first hypothesis is: "if [a] one is." What is the one (τὸ ἕν)?[3]

Parmenides has sensitized the reader to the ambiguous senses of "one" in his conversation with Socrates, and he has thereby prepared the context of questioning in which the Hypotheses should be read.[4] In the earlier conversation Parmenides probed ambiguities in Socrates' account of participation, specifically in Socrates' shifting understanding of form and participant. At 131a–e, beginning with the question of whether the whole of the form is in each of the participants, Parmenides tested Socrates' understanding of part/whole complexity, challenging specifically the notion that complexity is a universal categorial aspect of what-is. Again at 132a–133a, in what is now referred to as the Third Man Regress, Parmenides tested Socrates' understanding of plurality, specifically again whether plurality is a universal categorial aspect of what-is. These two characters—being one of many and being a whole of parts—characterize participants, and the questions posed by Parmenides examine the extent to which forms and things are for Socrates ontologically distinct kinds of ones or, perhaps more appropriately, whether Socrates acknowledges a genuinely radical ontological distinction in his account of participation. Socrates attempted to answer Parmenides' objections with the similes of day, thoughts, and paradigms, but each of these attempts falls short of conceptual rigor. By proposing to examine the ontological difference in kind between forms and things, Parmenides is offering resources of conceptualization that will develop and mature Socrates' philosophical impulse. We are, in my view, invited to engage the abstraction of the Hypotheses while keeping in mind the puzzles presented by Zeno and Parmenides in the first part of the dialogue. We are invited, that is, to provide the larger context in which the apparent contradictions presented by the Hypotheses might be explained, and the conclusions drawn will have bearing on our account of participation.

I would like furthermore to confirm in this chapter that the Hypotheses are an example of dialectical education. In struggling with the various conflicting senses of the term "one," we find ourselves confronted by the excess of intelligibility that we constantly and inevitably encounter with the world. The intelligibility of any spatio-temporal object, for instance, draws on a wider range of meanings than can be made determinately explicit in any single object. In the hands of Plato, the intelligibility of objects exceeds the limits of any single construal. The Hypotheses of the *Parmenides* allow us to hold ourselves accountable for the way we construe abstract notions such as one.

With that in mind, we should prepare for the possibility that "the one" and "one" do not identify a single referent or single expression but a certain range of distinct senses, e.g., the many ways in which one can be construed. A review of the possible meanings of "the one" includes a stunning array of plausible candidates within the context of philosophical inquiry. The following review of possibilities is preparatory. It is not meant to be exhaustive, nor is it intended to include only those senses of the one established by argument in the *Parmenides* or demanded by specific formulations in the First and Second Hypotheses; that work is yet to come. I am gathering a list of possibilities that we should identify in order to go on to clarify which senses are justified by the text.

The most ubiquitous ones are the spatio-temporal individuals that belong to becoming and are subject to change. They are each one in the sense of being parts comprising one whole, and in the sense of being numerically one relative to other individuals. Socrates earlier made reference to this dual sense of one in his response to Zeno when he said that if you wanted to call him one you would say that he is one of seven people present, and if by contrast you wanted to call him many you would say that he (is one whole that) has many sides, or that he has many parts. Given that such things compose and determine homogeneous materials, i.e., what in other contexts in the dialogues are referred to as continua, "one" might refer to the continuum subject to higher order delimitation, or it may refer to the abstract conceptual *apeiron* (unlimited) that stands beneath that lowest level of composition.

The spatio-temporal sense of "one" in the Hypotheses points immediately to two others. Although it has not been established in the *Parmenides*, in a broader context of Greek thought the flux of becoming occurs within a broader context of the all (τὸ πᾶν), which provides the domain of becoming to which individuals belong. The context of generation and corruption (τὸ περιέχον) is one in a sense distinct from the spatio-temporal individual. The all is the only one of its kind in the sense that it has no other and it has no context: it *is context*.[5] There is an understandable temptation to take "one" to refer to the "all," which seems not very far from Socrates' own example of the oneness of the day. But the *Parmenides* will help us overcome that temptation; more on that later. Alternatively, we might take "one" to refer to an arithmetic unit, the same in every respect as other units of the same kind, following the way the study of the one was approached in *Republic* 7. Individuals can be treated as simply denumerable, i.e., as partless and homogeneous units, and the "one" could refer to the incomposite, indestructible, ungenerated "ones," such as the "apples" and "bicycles," with which many people are familiarized when learning how to add and subtract.

Taken in another sense, "one" means not-many, i.e., one is the opposite of many, so "one" might refer to just what it means to be one in distinction from what it means to be many. Along these lines, "one" might refer to the one that each defining form is, which would be the cause that allows there to be determinate intelligibility in individual beings. "One" might refer to the combination of distinct forms that lays out and defines the defining form as an object of discursive knowing. "One" might also refer to the "one itself," the specific form or cause that is responsible for the oneness of any form or cause.

"One" has a range of potential meanings, including at least: (a) the one itself, the originating source and explanatory principle for any and all instances of unity, whether form or participant, (b) any form or cause taken up in its aspect of being one, (c) the weave of distinct forms in which we lay out any form as an object of discursive knowing, (c) a mathematical unit, (d) a spatio-temporal individual, (e) a continuum in which spatio-temporal individuals stand and take support, (f) the conceptual *apeiron* beneath the lowest level of composition, and (g) the "all" in which participant things are included. It will be my aim in this chapter to explain as we go why we should adopt the view that the "one" refers to any individual just insofar as it is one.[6] Keeping in mind the range of possible interpretations of "one" is a matter of fundamental philosophical importance, and it is something to which we must remain open if we are, with Plato, to conduct ourselves rigorously.

As we find our way, we need not expect that what is referred to as "one" will be identical in each Hypothesis. Socrates has been unable to extract himself with conceptual rigor from the paradigm of the complex individual when answering Parmenides' questions about participation. The specifically contrasting lines of attributes of the "one" in H1 and H2 will I think lead us to make the distinctions that Socrates has struggled with in the first part of the dialogue, such as the distinction between simplicity and complexity and the related distinction between uniqueness and individuality. The various senses of "one" in H1 and H2 will call on us to distinguish meanings that correspond to the distinction between form and participant, and by engaging with and keeping in mind the senses of the one, the dialectical lesson in H1 and H2 will offer insight that will help us to grow accustomed to what in *Republic* 7 is called the light of being and truth.

The One in the First Hypothesis

In H1 we encounter a primary and a secondary aim. The primary aim of the first hypothesis is to elaborate the list of attributes that "[a] one," if it is, cannot have.[7] In each of these many steps, the "one" hypothesized is denied various aspects of complexity, i.e., having parts or being a whole, having a beginning, middle, or end, or having shape, and it is denied aspects of singularity, e.g., sameness and difference, likeness and unlikeness, and equality and inequality. In the end we reach the conclusion that the hypothesized "one," if it is, must not be, must not be known, must not be perceived, and nothing can be said of it. Every intelligible term to which it might be joined ultimately falls short of it, even the initial hypothesis that it is and, thereby, all the consequences that followed from that hypothesis, with the result that the hypothesis is self-undermining. This self-undermining conclusion alerts us to an error along the way and prepares us to seek out a one that "is not" in the specific sense Aristoteles has in mind in H1 but nonetheless still "is" in a different sense and can be and known. The primary aim of H1, then, will be to establish a self-undermining conclusion that puts us on the path toward a newly oriented analysis, pursued most explicitly in H5, in which a "one that is not" must in some sense be and be known.

The secondary aim of H1 is to organize the terms out of which the negative portrait of the one is composed and to shed light on the types of eidetic structures that characterize complex and singular ones. All of the negative consequences drawn in H1 contribute to a positive account of complex singularity, which as a set of characters are consistent with (although not necessarily identical to) spatially and temporally determinate individuals. The secondary aim of H1 will point us in a direction that is more fully developed in H2.

Parmenides' description of the hypotheses proposed to examine the implications of the one hypothesized "as being" and take it up both "in relation to itself" (πρὸς αὑτό) and "in relation to each one of the others" (πρὸς ἓν ἕκαστον τῶν ἄλλων). I take the self/other qualifications to refer to the many paired self/other terms that occur throughout the hypothesis. Given the context in which the precise sense of the "one" is something that we will have to surmise from the consequences that follow from it being hypothesized, we should begin with not a single referent in mind but a range of possible candidates. With the aim of holding that range of referents open, I will employ the indefinite article, if [a] one is, holding tight to the claim that we are hypothesizing an individual but remaining open to the kind to which that individual belongs.

On its own terms and most broadly, being one means being not many. Insofar as an individual is one, it is not many. If we take as our starting point the determinate intelligibility of the "one" in its most inclusive sense, the "one," if nothing else, is not-many. In the sections of this chapter we will go on to study (1) one as complex (structures of complexity include whole of parts, beginning/middle/end, limit and shape of a body, place, and motion), (2) one as one of many (including structures of identity, being the same as and other than another, being like or unlike another), and (3) one as measure (which integrates the relations between distinct ones into relations of part/whole complexity, including greater/lesser/equal, more/fewer in number and age).

Complexity

In this first section our goal is to establish a systematic reading of H1 not only through what seems to be guiding the moves but also through what we are to learn about the aspect of being one. I pay no attention to the role Aristoteles plays in the conversation until we reach the concluding section (Chapter 3, Section C, "Measure"), where Aristoteles exemplifies in a particularly clear way the reduction of being to spatio-temporally determinate being, which in my view the First Hypothesis is designed to diagnose and at least initially repair.

Part/Whole Complexity

After his initial specification of one as not many (εἰ ἕν ἐστιν, ἄλλο τι οὐκ ἂν εἴη πολλὰ τὸ ἕν; 137c4–5), Parmenides turns to the nature of part/whole complexity. If "[a] one" is not many, "then it is necessary that there not be a part of it, nor that it be a whole" (οὔτε ἄρα μέρος αὐτοῦ οὔτε ὅλον αὐτὸ δεῖ εἶναι, 137c5–6). There cannot be a part of it, Parmenides says, nor can it be whole, for in either case it would be many: "thus in both cases, then, that one (τὸ ἕν) would be many but not one" (ἀμφοτέρως ἂν ἄρα οὕτως τὸ ἓν πολλὰ εἴη ἀλλ᾽ οὐχ ἕν, 137c9–d1). Part/whole complexity has two aspects, being whole and having parts. Neither aspect is compatible with the one into which we are inquiring, insofar as the unity of the whole is a unified *plurality*, and the parts remain a plurality when they are unified. Thus, the part/whole complex is only one insofar as its unity implies and includes plurality and is distinct from the aspect of being one, which does not include or entail being many.

On the surface, this is a straightforward denial of complexity, and it adds negative content to our knowledge of the one by specifying that the one in question is not a complex one. This would be consistent with the denial of spatio-temporal determinacy, insofar as spatio-temporal individuals are organized wholes of parts, or aggregates, but it is also consistent with the denial of the mathematical determinacy of certain figures or formulas. In the context of the *Parmenides*, there is some reason to believe that this denial of complexity is a denial of specifically spatio-temporal complexity, given the earlier focus on the relationship between forms and participants. For example, the initial introduction of sharing by parts of whole (131a4) was clearly construed in spatial terms as the distribution of daylight into many places, or the distribution of a sail set over many individuals. The discussion of sharing of the large, equal, small themselves with participants added further clarity to this specification of part/whole complexity as something spatial. But that was the first part of the dialogue. In H1 the analysis is more abstract, and it clearly includes spatiality, it does not clearly include specifically spatio-temporal individuals.

At the same time, there is a consistency in the object of analysis regardless of the relative degree of abstraction in which the stages of analysis proceed. The denial of complexity does not in itself refer to abstract spatiality. However, in just a few steps the denial of part/whole complexity will lead to the denial of shape. If we construe shape spatially, as it seems we are required to, and if the hypothesis is working inferentially in continuous steps, the denial of complexity is implicitly a denial of the complexity of spatiality in the abstract. For now, therefore, let part/whole complexity refer to a specifically spatial whole.

Parmenides furthermore defines this spatial whole in a way that is committed at most to minimally organized parts, i.e., a spatial aggregate as that from which "no part is missing" (μέρος μηδὲν ἀπῇ, 137c7). The whole that he has in mind is not organized but any assemblage that "consists of parts" (ἐκ μερῶν, 137c8). The whole in this instance is a minimal criterion of completeness, a completeness that requires only a unity imposed on parts that are not themselves internally related to one another.[8] Spatial proximity would therefore make each part "a part of the whole" (ὅλου μέρος, 137c6). We can, for example, think of a pie as a one, and we can cut the pie into pieces and think of it as a divided one. However, we can also cut it into pieces and think of the pieces as wholes, each being a one of its own standing in arbitrary relation to the others. The pieces taken as individual ones can be rearranged without making a difference because their unity as a group is arbitrary and falls outside of them; separate ones are indifferent to their relative position and order. Interchangeability of parts presupposes more an aggregate of wholes with no independent, internal, unifying principle. We might object that "whole" implies an internal, unifying principle, but the text suggests that this insight has not yet been achieved. For now, the whole just is a sum of parts.

Notice, however, that as we progress through the initial steps of H1, we are developing and deepening the negative portrait of the one. The "many" that was initially denied to the one is now discussed as a whole, which is a one *of* many; it is a minimal synthesis of initially opposed terms. We first differentiated being one from being many. Now we have a minimally complex combination of a being that is one *and* many. That is to say, part/whole complexity refers to a one that is many and a many that is one. On the basis of the conceptual articulation of our starting point, we can see an intelligible order in the steps taken through the hypothesis. A one that *is not* many has led in the negative portrait to a one that *is* many.

Parmenides now turns away from part/whole complexity to argue that the one has no beginning, middle, or end (ἀρχή, μέσος, τελευτή). Things of this sort would be parts of it (μέρη γὰρ ἂν ἤδη αὐτοῦ τὰ τοιαῦτα εἴη, 137d5), and the one with beginning/middle/end would be as many as its parts. The one cannot be many nor have parts, so it cannot have beginning, middle, or end.

With the introduction of beginning, middle, and end, we notice a further incremental development of the negative portrait of the one. Just as the notion of whole answered the dichotomy between one and many with a one that was (minimally) many, so too the notion of ordered parts transforms the mere aggregate, a multiplicity of unrelated parts, into aspects that are internally related to each other. That is, beginning is determinately related to middle and end, just as middle and end are determinately related to their others. Insofar as each of these parts in the third step of H1 is explicitly tied to its others and cannot be arbitrarily rearranged, beginning, middle, and end again point toward a limiting norm, just as part/whole complexity pointed toward a norm of inclusion, and yet nothing in the text requires or turns on the premise of an ordering norm. All the arguments in the primary movement of the text turn indifferently on the premise that a one, just insofar as it is one, is not many.

If we consider more closely what the structure of beginning, middle, and end introduces to the analysis, we see parts determinately ordered with respect to one another, such that a one [as whole] can be determinately present in many [as parts] rather than outside the many. The inter-dependence and interweaving of parts *qua* beginning, middle, and end demonstrate a reciprocal unity, and thus we discover a new kind of immanence of one in many. Of course, beginning, middle, and end can be aspects of an indifferently ordered aggregate; that is, any aggregate can have parts identified as having a beginning, middle, and end, even if those parts do not themselves take on the order implied by these descriptive terms. That is, just as part/whole complexity could refer to a spatial aggregate that is not internally structured, so too ordered complexity, as it were, can refer to a spatial aggregate that remains indifferent to that (descriptive) order. Thus, we have three distinct levels of analysis: (1) an eidetic structure of determinately ordered parts, i.e., beginning, middle, and end, which do not belong to (2) the "one" hypothesized, which is not many, but which can describe (3) a spatial aggregate that is indifferently ordered. What I think we are meant to see is an increasingly sharp distinction between conditioned individuals and the conditions by which these individuals are constituted.

A Note on Dialectic and the "Secondary Aim" of H1

H1 has offered insight into the one through several negative attributions: the one is not many, not a whole of part, and has nothing that could correspond to beginning, middle, or end. Our method of reading in light of what I am identifying as the secondary aim of H1 has revealed the manifold structure denied to the one. What was initially a stark opposition between one and many led into a unity of one *of* many as part/whole complexity. The unity of one of many in part/whole complexity was further transformed into a one *in* many by the relationship between beginning, middle, and end, which is a many that contains and expresses its unity through an ordered arrangement. The ordered relation of beginning, middle, and end also revealed, negatively, the many as a mere aggregate subject to descriptive structure. Each of these types of complexity unifies a multiplicity of distinct parts. The relationship between a whole that contains indefinitely ordered parts and a whole in which the parts are definitely ordered points to a tighter unity of one and many and, more generally, brings to our attention the unification of one and many and the notion of a unity that can be variously instantiated. Thus, the negative portrait of the one reveals different degrees of normativity governing what are not one. The secondary aim of H1 gathers moments distinguished from the one, so as to point to a type of one that is immanent to the others.[9] Seeking the one that lets stand the distinction between one and many in the organized others exemplifies dialectic. Socrates is there interested in the type of inquiry that can reveal the causal source from which the starting points for being and being-known are revealed, referring to the universal categories of thought and being as hypotheses:

> Understand me to mean by the other division of the intelligible that which *logos* itself grasps by the power of dialectic, making the hypotheses not origins but really hypotheses, such as stepping-stones and impulses, in order to reach as far as the unhypothesized at the origin of all.
>
> Τὸ τοίνυν ἕτερον μάνθανε τμῆμα τοῦ νοητοῦ λέγοντά με τοῦτο οὗ αὐτὸς ὁ λόγος ἅπτεται τῇ τοῦ διαλέγεσθαι δυνάμει, τὰς ὑποθέσεις ποιούμενος οὐκ ἀρχὰς ἀλλὰ τῷ ὄντι ὑποθέσεις, οἷον ἐπιβάσεις τε καὶ ὁρμάς, ἵνα μέχρι τοῦ ἀνυποθέτου ἐπὶ τὴν τοῦ παντὸς ἀρχὴν ἰών (511b4–7)

As we continue working on H1, we will keep in view the secondary aim of the hypothesis with the intention of specifying the various kinds of structured pairs that are set out by Parmenides in the course of his analysis. Our goal is to develop a sense for the noetic source from which these various structures are gathered by grasping these terms as springboards.

Spatiality

Parmenides seems to shift from a discussion of complexity in general to a discussion of the limits that belong to spatial ones in particular. The text requires that we decide whether, when we turn to the discussion of the spatiality of the one, we are clarifying the spatio-temporal framework Parmenides has had in mind from the beginning or introducing a new conceptual framework not implied by abstract part/whole complexity.[10] Either Parmenides' analysis of limit, shape, place, and motion form a new constellation of concepts or they are an elaboration of concepts already invoked by the discussion of the one we have hypothesized. The decision turns on whether we see something fundamentally new being introduced to the inquiry at this point.

At first it seems that we are indeed seeing two fundamentally new ideas introduced. Parmenides argues that if the one has no beginning, middle, or end, and these are each the limit (πέρας) of each, the one must be unlimited (ἄπειρον). "Unlimited" (ἄπειρον) here means that the one is exempt from the plurality of parts implied by beginning and end and is, therefore, shapeless: "it partakes of neither circular nor straight" (οὔτε γὰρ στρογγύλου οὔτε εὐθέος μετέχει, 137d8–e1). Both circular and straight are structured multiplicities. The "circular" is that in which the extremes are equally removed in all directions (πανταχῇ) from the middle, which therefore has two parts, *viz.* center and periphery. The "straight" is that in which the middle is immediately in front of (ἐπίπροσθεν) the two extremes and which therefore has a two-part form of middle and extremes. Parmenides says that the one will be "nowhere" (οὐδαμοῦ) because it will not be able to be in (ἐν . . . εἰμί) either itself or another. If it were in another, he says, it would be contained by another and be touched in many places along that circle, which it could not be if it is partless (ἀμερής) and does not partake of circularity. If the one were in itself it would do and suffer "the same at the same time" (ταὐτὸν ἅμα). Thus, the one is neither in itself nor in another.

As we think through what changes this section of the analysis has introduced, we notice that indexicals suddenly appear in these descriptions of complexity. For example, Parmenides defines "middle" as being "directly in front of" beginning and end; "middle" is also defined as equally distant from limits "in all directions," and there is reference to outside and inside. Implied is the indefinite magnitude of distance, near and far, which is presented in the description of shape and accompanied by the first mention in the hypothesis of participation (μετέχει, 137e1).[11] Parmenides is now being explicit about the indefinite magnitude of spatial ones and the indefinite distances at which they can stand to one another. Although the spatial object of indefinite dimensions may have been implied from the outset, it was not the source for the previous attributes denied the one. It seems to me not that new objects are being introduced but that new types of multiplicity are being excavated within the negative portrait being painted of the one. The new type of multiplicity introduced here is indefinite magnitude.

But we also notice alongside indefinite magnitudes that all such magnitudes are intelligibly structured. For instance, the indefinite distance is articulated into left and right. Indefinite amount is divided into containing and contained. That is, intelligible relations can now be seen in the spatial one as relative position and facing. The indefinite magnitude of the spatial whole and its structured aspects thus belong together. There is no amount that is not structured by shape and position. The spatiality of the whole thus seems implied, at least in the movement of H1, in the type of one and many at issue. I read the one of H1, therefore, as being a spatial individual, and I read the hypothesis itself to be distinguishing the various aspects of this one both from each other and, most centrally, from the aspect of being one against which they are all negatively gathered.

Motion and Rest

The analysis of motion and rest comes on the heels of the discussions of part/whole, beginning-middle-end, and shape. The discussion extends the notion of indefinite magnitude from its purely spatial sense to include a temporal sense, rounding out an initial and basic (albeit abstract) characterization of spatio-temporal individuality. As before, the primary aim of H1 is to clarify the attributes that cannot be possessed by the one hypothesized, but the secondary aim is to elaborate the attributes that belong to a spatio-temporal one. We continue to notice the juxtaposition of the one initially hypothesized and a set of other characters, each of which is manifold in a distinct respect and calls for a unifying principle that is not explicitly provided. With the introduction of motion and change, we are ever more pressingly reminded of a one that underlies and gathers differences, which suggests that what underlies the various conjoined and organized aspects of an individual is neither the stuff out of which it is made nor the sort of thing it is but a one or something of a distinct kind.[12]

After first opposing motion to rest, Parmenides divides motion into "alteration" (ἀλλοιοῦσθαι) and "motion in place," or locomotion (φέρεσθαι). He further divides locomotion into rotational and linear kinds. This final category, linear motion, he analyzes in some detail. In all cases of a locomotion, an indefinite distance and indefinite time of motion is implied. In the specific discussion of motion as alteration, Parmenides infers from its not being many that "the one cannot be altered from itself and still be one" (138c1–2). A spatial aggregate, by contrast, is the kind of thing that can be othered and still be "itself" (ἑαυτό, 138c2 & c8), for this other type of one has the structure appropriate to remaining the same through difference or change. If the one hypothesized in H1 were to change, it would not be itself.

Along with the clarification of the "self" that remains constant in the face of change, there is a discussion of the ordered relation between parts that motion of the whole demands. Parmenides says that rotation requires a center and periphery, which he then construes as parts of a whole. I am paying special attention to the structure of ordered parts implied by these types of motion. Parmenides says,

> And if the one moved spatially, it surely would either spin in a circle in the same [place] or change place from one to another.
>
> Necessarily.

> If it spins in a circle, it must be poised (βεβηκέναι) on (ἐπί) its middle and have other parts of itself that move round (περί) the middle. But for that to which neither middle nor parts are fitting (προσήκειν), by what contrivance will this ever be moved in a circle round its middle?
>
> In no way. (Gill, with modifications)

> καὶ μὴν εἰ φέροιτο τὸ ἕν, ἤτοι ἐν τῷ αὐτῷ ἂν περιφέροιτο κύκλῳ ἢ μεταλλάττοι χώραν ἑτέραν ἐξ ἑτέρας. {—} ἀνάγκη. {—} οὐκοῦν κύκλῳ μὲν περιφερόμενον ἐπὶ μέσου βεβηκέναι ἀνάγκη, καὶ τὰ περὶ τὸ μέσον φερόμενα ἄλλα μέρη ἔχειν ἑαυτοῦ: ᾧ δὲ μήτε μέσου μήτε μερῶν προσήκει, τίς μηχανὴ τοῦτο κύκλῳ ποτ' ἐπὶ τοῦ μέσου ἐνεχθῆναι; {—} οὐδεμία. (138c4–d2)

This argument describes the parts of the whole as if they were separate individuals. In truth the parts compose a single whole only insofar as the whole is "poised" (βεβηκέναι) on its middle, which implies a dynamic dependence of circumference on the middle. Any actual instance of rotational motion demands that parts call for and imply one another (analogous to the way that beginning calls for and fits with middle, end). The axis of rotation needs the spinning circumference so that it may hold itself actively at rest. Conversely, the spinning circumference needs the axis to provide the point of rest in relation to which the activity of the periphery is ordered. Center and periphery imply each other and have their determinacy in relation to one another.[13] Each is actively doing what the other is resisting, and in turn each is suffering the same from the other, which as mentioned above is flagged in the term "poised."[14] The center is doing its best to remain itself, but it is opposed by the motion of the periphery, and their mutual opposition that allows them to participate in a larger unity. Without this mutual interference, there would be no whole in which to participate. Periphery becomes periphery in tension with the center, and center is only the center insofar as it is holding itself in place. Together in tension, the parts establish the normative standard by which each can have its own identity: center relies on periphery, and periphery relies on center. This implies that the being of parts is precisely not that of an aggregate but of a reciprocal harmony. The idea of reciprocal determinacy is missing from Parmenides' account of the whole in terms of separate parts, but it is implied, and we are called on to track and retain this indication.

The discussion of linear motion in similar fashion draws on, but fails to acknowledge or account for, the presence of a principle integrating the spatio-temporal individual under examination. The argument has two parts. In the first, Parmenides demonstrates that it is impossible for the one to move from place to place as a whole because it is impossible for the one to be anywhere (this was shown at 138b). In the second part of the argument, Parmenides shows that it is "more impossible" (ἀδυνατώτερον) for it, part by part, to come to be in something else.[15]

> If something comes to be in something, isn't it necessary that it not yet be in that thing—since it is still coming to be in it—and that it no longer be entirely outside it, if in fact it is already coming to be in it?
>
> Necessarily.
>
> So if anything is to undergo this, only that of which there are parts could so undergo, because some of it would already be in that [thing], while some, at the same time, would be outside. But a thing that doesn't have parts will not by any means be able to be, at the same time, neither wholly inside nor wholly outside something.
>
> True. (Gill, slightly modified)
>
> εἰ ἔν τῴ τι γίγνεται, οὐκ ἀνάγκη μήτε πω ἐν ἐκείνῳ εἶναι ἔτι ἐγγιγνόμενον, μήτ᾽ ἔτι ἔξω ἐκείνου παντάπασιν, εἴπερ ἤδη ἐγγίγνεται; {—} ἀνάγκη. {—} εἰ ἄρα τι ἄλλο πείσεται τοῦτο, ἐκεῖνο ἂν μόνον πάσχοι οὗ μέρη εἴη: τὸ μὲν γὰρ ἄν τι αὐτοῦ ἤδη ἐν ἐκείνῳ, τὸ δὲ ἔξω εἴη ἅμα: τὸ δὲ μὴ ἔχον μέρη οὐχ οἷόν τέ που ἔσται τρόπῳ οὐδενὶ ὅλον ἅμα μήτε ἐντὸς εἶναί τινος μήτε ἔξω. {—} ἀληθῆ. (138d6–e4)

The one cannot move by coming to be in something because it would not only first need to be somewhere, which it cannot be, but it would also need to be split into parts, which is also impossible. Notice, however, that the account of motion includes a division not exactly between parts but between "some [part] of it" (τι αὐτοῦ, 138e2) and some other, as if it were divided into pieces, or continuous magnitudes of indefinite extension. Also, being in motion requires a dynamic determination of the "parts" that are not yet and already inside another. Each of these aspects of the description, therefore, presupposes an indefinitely divisible continuum, and the entire discussion assumes abstract space.[16] The whole does not have specific size or organization, nor does the motion come to rest at a specific point; nothing is calling it to move either here or there.[17] Parmenides is asking us only to consider what would be necessary in the most abstract perspective for something in place to move from place to place. If there were a governing form at work here, it could not govern one individual more than any other. These are abstract descriptions of what is required for something to be in place and time.

The several instances we have examined here in which the argument draws on but fails to acknowledge the principle of unity, or selfhood, of the spatio-temporal individual coalesce in the concluding argument that the one is not at rest. Parmenides premises that something at rest is "in the same." His reference to the "same" here is just another instance in which he points to an ontologically distinct and necessary, but unacknowledged, term without which the description would fail. For instance, in the analysis of rotational motion we saw an example of normativity in the verb "poised" (βεβηκέναι, 138c7) that describes the relationship of the axis to the periphery of motion. As in that previous discussion, the analysis here does not do for us the work of grasping and articulating this ontologically distinct term. Parmenides tacitly, however, points out that the thing in motion and rest must have an integrity of its own. If the spatio-temporal individual were simply what happens to be within certain limits, there would be no individual one, no being in place, and no motion, for there would be no principle of integrity by which to distinguish an individual from its context. Unless there is an internal normative structure such as the opposition of center and periphery in rotational motion, there will be no integrity of the shape, no integrity of the individual in place, or of the individual through time. This integrity, however, implies something other than another shape, place, or motion, by which the indefinite magnitude is unified. The analysis of continuous magnitude, thus, points in the direction of a one that is the "same" in the sense of an abstract self or subject, i.e., the one just insofar as it is one must also be a cause of unity.

To conclude, we see that this section of H1 denies to the "one" the attributes of motion and rest. But more than that, in this section Parmenides allows us to glimpse that a being that has shape, is in place, and in motion and rest is ontologically dependent. The parts of the whole that correspond to center and periphery are at rest and in motion, respectively. These parts cannot be indifferently related but must be set apart and integrated by something other than themselves. Center and circumference are thus analogous to beginning and end in the prior section, and together they point to the need for a normative source by which they are gathered. That source is the principle of sameness that allows the spatio-temporal one to be other than itself, that is, to change and move. It is with this suggestion of an ontologically distinct source of the complex parts that are being contrasted to the one that we now turn to the treatment of "same" and "other."

Same and Other

The first section of H1 has denied to the one the attributes of being many, being a whole or having a part, and having a beginning/middle/end. The second section of H1 has, similarly, denied to the "one" the attributes of limit, shape, location, and motion/rest at the same time as it has studied the structured relationship between the parts of an integrated whole capable of change and locomotion. In both sections, but more explicitly in the second, the secondary aim of the analysis has investigated the abstract spatial determinacy of an individual. The following analysis of sameness and difference continues the call for a normative center around which abstract individual identity is integrated, while it also helps us to articulate the ontological distinctions inherent in our negative portrait of the one. In the previous section on motion and rest it was clear that there must be some principle of identity to gather multiplicity into a unity, whether a multiplicity of individuals gathered into a single field or a multiplicity of parts gathered into a single whole. Parmenides here transforms our sense of the sameness of individual identity.

The consequences in this section are drawn as follows. Parmenides first argues that the one is neither the same as an other or different from itself, and then goes on to argue that the one is neither other than an other nor the same as itself. The basic point is straightforward: sameness and difference imply being many, which the one cannot be. What will interest us in this section are the further indications of ontological difference within and between the objects of the positive and negative analysis. Our attention will be especially drawn to the non-relational and non-individuated character of the one just insofar as it is one.

With regard to the first consequence, that the one is not the same as an other, it is perhaps obvious that nothing is the same as its other, nor is anything other than itself. Neither a thought, loosely speaking, nor a thing, nor a person can be numerically identical with another thought, thing, or person without ceasing to be itself. It may therefore be unsurprising that Parmenides spends relatively little time on these arguments and pursues at greater length the more conceptually transformative insight that the one is neither other than an other nor the same as itself. In spite of being apparently obvious, however, we can learn a great deal from the way Parmenides establishes that the one is the same as itself and other than an other. Parmenides says,

> If [it] were (ὄν) different from itself (ἕτερον . . . ἑαυτοῦ), [it] would surely be other than one (ἑνὸς ἕτερον), and would not be one.
>
> True. (Gill, slightly modified)

> ἕτερον μέν που ἑαυτοῦ ὂν ἑνὸς ἕτερον ἂν εἴη καὶ οὐκ ἂν εἴη ἕν. {—} ἀληθῆ. (139b5–7)

Immediately we are posed with a challenge. Does "other than itself" mean "other than the character of being one" or "other than the individual it is"? In the first case, being "other than itself" would imply being (or being governed by) a distinct aspect, e.g., not "one" but "many." In the second case, being "other than itself" would imply being a numerically distinct individual. I take Parmenides to be talking about an individual just insofar as it is subject to the character of being-one, and as such it seems he could have in mind either the numerically distinct individual or its aspect of being one. Let us read on:

> On the other hand, if it were the same as an other (ταὐτόν γε ἑτέρῳ), it would be that [one] (ἐκεῖνο), and not itself (αὐτό). So in this way, too, it would not be just what it is (ὅπερ ἔστιν)—one (ἕν)—but would be other than one (ἕτερον ἑνός).
>
> Yes, you're quite right. (Gill, slightly modified)

> καὶ μὴν ταὐτόν γε ἑτέρῳ ὂν ἐκεῖνο ἂν εἴη, αὐτὸ δ᾽ οὐκ ἂν εἴη: ὥστε οὐδ᾽ ἂν οὕτως εἴη ὅπερ ἔστιν, ἕν, ἀλλ᾽ ἕτερον ἑνός. {—} οὐ γὰρ οὖν. (139b7–c2)

To be the same as another means to be "that one" (ἐκεῖνο) and not itself (αὐτό) where these terms appear to be construed as opposites. The argument preserves the ambiguity noted above between an aspect of intelligibility and an individual one. However, if we distinguish the aspect of being-one from an individual subject to that character and restrict this discussion to one or the other of these two, we will fail to see that Parmenides is operating on ontologically distinct levels of description simultaneously: the level of the individual subject to the character of being-one as well as the level of the character to which the individual is subject.

When we turn to the counter-intuitive consequences that the one is neither other than another nor the same as itself it becomes more clear that we are distinguishing between an individual one and the characters to which it is subject. In arguing that the one cannot be other than another, Parmenides makes it clear that being one does not imply being different. A one is not, simply by virtue of being one, different from other ones. Parmenides says,

> And it won't be other than another, as long as it is one (ᾗ ἕν); for it is not proper to one (ἑνί προσήκει) to be different from something

(ἑτέρῳ τινὸς), but proper to other-than-another alone (μόνῳ ἑτέρῳ ἑτέρου), and to nothing else.

That's right. (Gill, slightly modified)

ἕτερον δέ γε ἑτέρου οὐκ ἔσται, ἕως ἂν ᾖ ἕν: οὐ γὰρ ἑνὶ προσήκει ἑτέρῳ τινὸς εἶναι, ἀλλὰ μόνῳ ἑτέρῳ ἑτέρου, ἄλλῳ δὲ οὐδενί. {—} ὀρθῶς. (139c3–5)

Leaving aside for the moment questions we might have with the formulation "proper to other-than-another alone" (μόνῳ ἑτέρῳ ἑτέρου, 139c4), what it means to be proper to something is that if X is proper to Y, then something's being Y implies that it is X.[18] Being-one, for example, does not have being-other proper to it in the sense that being-one taken in abstraction from the other characters of an individual does not imply being-other. We, perhaps, can assume that something subject to the character of being-one is also other than other ones, but we cannot assume that it is other by virtue of oneness.

Therefore it won't be other by being one (τῷ . . . ἓν εἶναι). Or do you think it will?

No indeed.

Yet if it isn't different by this [i.e., by being one], it will not be so by itself (ἑαυτῷ); and if it isn't so by itself, it will not itself (αὐτό) be so. And if it is itself in no way other, it will be other than nothing.

That's right. (139c6–d1) (Gill)

τῷ μὲν ἄρα ἓν εἶναι οὐκ ἔσται ἕτερον: ἢ οἴει; {—} οὐ δῆτα. {—} ἀλλὰ μὴν εἰ μὴ τούτῳ, οὐχ ἑαυτῷ ἔσται, εἰ δὲ μὴ αὑτῷ, οὐδὲ αὐτό: αὐτὸ δὲ μηδαμῇ ὂν ἕτερον οὐδενὸς ἔσται ἕτερον. {—} ὀρθῶς.

This argument claims that a one, simply in virtue of being-one or "by itself" (ἑαυτῷ), is not different. It may be clear that spatio-temporal individuals are other than others as soon as they are subject to being one, so to speak, for their manner of being implies the distinction between the same (e.g., spatio-temporal individual) and other (spatio-temporal individuals). However, being-one and being-other are distinct categories to which a one is subject.[19] A one does not have, in virtue of being-one, difference from others.

According to the same *logos*, a one is not the same as itself (οὐδὲ μὴν ταὐτόν γε ἑαυτῷ ἔσται, 139d1). The previous argument showed that a one does not have the relations to others by virtue of being one, and now it will fail to be the same as itself by virtue of being-one. It has being-same and being-other by virtue of participation in sameness and otherness. Parmenides says,

> Nor will [it] be the same as itself.
> Why not?
> The very nature of the one is not, of course, also that of the same.
> Why? (Gill)

> οὐδὲ μὴν ταὐτόν γε ἑαυτῷ ἔσται. {—} πῶς δ᾽ οὔ; {—} οὐχ ἧπερ τοῦ ἑνὸς φύσις, αὐτὴ δήπου καὶ τοῦ ταὐτοῦ. {—} τί δή; (139d1–3)

We can see that a one has a dimension of being "itself" (ἑαυτό), similar to a *per se* dimension but *per se* just as *qua* one. Parmenides calls this selfhood "the very nature of the one" (ἧπερ τοῦ ἑνὸς φύσις, 139d2). I take this to refer to the unity of any individual, which does not rule out the possibility that it have other natures. Under the description as a one, however, it has the specific nature of being-one, and the argument is simply saying that a one is not the same as itself or anything else insofar as it is one. Parmenides goes on to draw out the consequence that if the one were the same as itself, it will not be one with itself (εἰ ἄρα τὸ ἓν ἑαυτῷ ταὐτὸν ἔσται, οὐχ ἓν ἑαυτῷ ἔσται, 139e1–2). To become "same," he says, is always to become "same as . . ." some X or Y; it is for instance to become the "same as the many" (τοῖς πολλοῖς ταὐτόν, 139d4). Because it is possible to become the same as many, and because many is not one, it can be concluded that the nature of the one and the nature of the same are distinct. As distinct, they are two, and if a one were both one and same, it would need to be at least two things, i.e., it would be many. What this shows is that the distinct moments of the determinate intelligibility of a one are subject to certain kinds of determinacy of their own. The being-one, being-many, being-same, being-other, etc., show themselves to be subject to categories of combination and division as objects of discursive knowing, distinguished from one another and added up as many. At the same time, however, Parmenides' emphasis on the uniqueness of being-one and so on has shown us that the terms of the determinate intelligibility of a one are not, by themselves, subject to combination and division. Being-one is not, by itself, same or other.

In the end, the section on the sameness and otherness of a one with respect to itself and its other demonstrates that there is a radical distinction between what participates in the categories of combination and division and the individuals that are subject to those categories. A one of the sort we originally hypothesized participates in the sameness and otherness in terms of which its relations are articulated, such as being distinct from many. At the same time, however, a one has now been shown not to be *properly* subject, *qua* being-one, to categories of relation. A one participates in being-same, being-other, etc., but these terms are prior to categorial relations. In other words, Parmenides has helped clarify a sharp ontological distinction between beings and their being. Because we are now talking about two sides of an ontological difference, we cannot rely on the terms to which things are subject as commensurate and reciprocally determined but, instead, on the terms of incommensurability, for which in this dialogue the category of unlikeness is especially appropriate.

Like and Unlike

The subsequent discussion of likeness and unlikeness is based directly on the premise that the natures of the same and different are distinct from the nature of the one. Parmenides says that to be like is to undergo the same as another. But the nature of the same is separate (χωρίς) from the one. Accordingly, being affected by something "separate from being one" (χωρὶς τοῦ ἓν εἶναι), a one would be more (πλείω) than one. In order for the one to be same in any respect as another or itself, it must undergo the same, and it would therefore be more than one. The argument against the unlikeness of the one is similar. Parmenides says that the one cannot undergo "to be other" (ἕτερόν γε . . . εἶναι), for it would in that case undergo "to be more than one (πλείω . . . εἶναι ἢ ἕν)" (140a7). Thus, prohibition against the one's being like or unlike points to the simplicity of the one. At the same time, this very prohibition points to an implied complexity in any one that undergoes distinct characters.

The ambiguity with which inquiry into the one must wrestle is here plainly marked: just insofar as it is one, a one is not subject to difference. But how could this fail to undermine the relationship between a one and its being one? Without this most basic relationship, we would not be able to say of a one that it is one. It seems we are laying the groundwork for eliminating our ability to hypothesize or speak about a one, which is of course where H1 concludes.[20]

We have now reached the middle of H1. In the following set of arguments, including measure, equal/unequal, and younger/older/same age, we will extend the insight offered in the same/other section. Specifically, we will further elaborate the categories by which spatio-temporal objects are rendered determinate, and we will clarify what must be true in order for these categories to be unified and organized as constitutive of spatio-temporal presence.

Measure

The effort to deny the one any of the attributes of being many, and the complementary effort to cull from these denials the categorial structures consistent with being many,[21] has afforded us insight into the basics of determinate intelligibility. In the section on Complexity (Chapter 3, Section A), the negative attributes denied to the one revealed the many to be characterized by an ordered whole of parts. Subsequently, the section of Same and Other (Chapter 3, Section B) revealed the many to be characterized by structures of relation. The final set of arguments, concerning measure and time, point to the indefinite continuum in which spatio-temporal aggregates are established, as we saw above in the discussion of the motion (both linear and rotational) and spatiality denied to the one. The present analysis of measure moves us incrementally closer to understanding the relation between the categorial structures that characterize the many. This section consists of two main analyses. The first analysis uses the relations of likeness and unlikeness to examine equality. The second analysis consists of a discussion of relative age. In this section our attention shifts to the abstract temporality of individuals.

Having just established that the one is neither like nor unlike, Parmenides makes the transition to the analysis of equality.[22] Parmenides argues that the one, not being like or unlike, cannot consist of measures, either more or fewer. Nor can the one consist of measures that are greater, smaller, or the same size. The introduction of measures that are not only more or fewer in number but also greater or smaller, i.e., measures that do not necessarily share a common unit of comparison, reminds us that measure, although discrete, is set into a continuum. Measure belongs to the continuum in spite of being distinct from it: a body's healthy temperature is a specific ratio within an indefinite range of hot and cold, and the body's tissue and bones are a specific ratio within an indefinite range of hard and soft. Each and every part of an integrated whole is a measured norm standing along a continuum, framed by extremes. The determinacy of those parts then draws on their being-in the continuum and the one beneath composition. As earlier in H1, the negative portrait of the one reveals a detailed account of the others. Here that account sheds light on what are not one, on what are characterized by the least degree of determinacy, in which we start to see hints of the *apeiron* minimally articulated in certain respects as the different types of continuum (e.g., hotter/colder, higher/lower, softer/harder).

Temporality

The ensuing account of age (older/younger/same age) allows us to think further about relationship between measure and its continuum. After showing that being older, younger, the same age as anything would simply imply the ideas of likeness or unlikeness or equality and inequality with respect to time and, therefore, showing that age does not belong to the one, Parmenides says: "So if it is of that sort (τοιοῦτον), that one could not (δύναιτο) even be in time at all, could it?" (141a5–6, modifying Gill).[23] Ratios of older to younger imply that anything subject to them must be in time, and conversely this implies that being in time is *to be* according to a certain ratio. Parmenides says,

> Or isn't it necessary, if something is in time, that it always come to be older than itself?
> Necessarily.
>
> Isn't the older always older than a younger?
> To be sure. (Gill)
>
> ἢ οὐκ ἀνάγκη, ἐάν τι ᾖ ἐν χρόνῳ, ἀεὶ αὐτὸ αὑτοῦ πρεσβύτερον γίγνεσθαι; {—} ἀνάγκη. {—} οὐκοῦν τό γε πρεσβύτερον ἀεὶ νεωτέρου πρεσβύτερον; {—} τί μήν; (141a6–8)

Being in time, because it is a becoming, implies both punctuality (at a moment) and spanning (being between or across moments). A one that is in time is always coming to be older, and, because the older is only what it is in relation to a younger, is always coming to be younger than itself. That is to say that the being of something in time is always incomplete, in process, always relating to itself as an other, differing from itself in the context of an overarching self-relation. What it means to be a spatio-temporal "self" is to be a spread of past and future:

> Therefore it is necessary, as it seems, that as many as are in time and partake of this sort of thing, each of them be the same age itself to itself and, at the same time, comes to be both older and younger than itself (Gill).
>
> ἀνάγκη ἄρα ἐστίν, ὡς ἔοικεν, ὅσα γε ἐν χρόνῳ ἐστὶν καὶ μετέχει τοῦ τοιούτου, ἕκαστον αὐτῶν τὴν αὐτήν τε αὐτὸ αὑτῷ ἡλικίαν ἔχειν καὶ πρεσβύτερόν τε αὑτοῦ ἅμα καὶ νεώτερον γίγνεσθαι. (141c8–d3)

The temporal "one" is always differing from itself by becoming older and younger than itself, and it is always relating to itself throughout these changes as selfsame. Being self-equal in the sense of coming to be "for a time equal to itself" implies difference. When Parmenides says that each is the same age as itself—relating itself to itself for a time equal to itself—and says furthermore that each is becoming ever older and younger at the same time (ἅμα), he is implying that there is a time in which the spatio-temporal one is subject to becoming ever other than—and remaining ever the same as—itself. The spatio-temporal one, ever differing from and relating to itself, is subject to categories of sameness and difference, self and other, and is therefore subject to the timeless categories that structure becoming. Parmenides' ensuing comments invite us to draw this connection more explicitly.

Parmenides asks Aristoteles whether the "one" can partake in anything such as being or becoming older or younger (141d3–4), and Aristoteles responds that it cannot. Parmenides presses him further, then "neither does it partake of time, nor is it in any time" (Οὐδὲ ἄρα χρόνου αὐτῷ μέτεστιν, οὐδ' ἔστιν ἔν τινι χρόνῳ, 141d4–5). The next important step is to establish a parallel between the past, present, and future modes of *einai* and the modes of *gignesthai* (at 141d7–e3). The list of parallel terms is long:

> Isn't it the case that "was" and "has come to be" and "was coming to be" indicate participation in time gone by?
>
> Very much so.
>
> But what of this? Aren't "will be" and "will come to be" and "will be coming to be" in [time] thereafter?
>
> Yes.
>
> Aren't "is" and "comes to be" in [time] now present?
>
> By all means.
>
> τὸ ἦν καὶ τὸ γέγονε καὶ τὸ ἐγίγνετο οὐ χρόνου μέθεξιν δοκεῖ σημαίνειν τοῦ ποτὲ γεγονότος; {—} Καὶ μάλα. {—} Τί δέ; τὸ ἔσται καὶ τὸ γενήσεται καὶ τὸ γενηθήσεται οὐ τοῦ ἔπειτα [τοῦ μέλλοντος]; {—} Ναί. {—} Τὸ δὲ δὴ ἔστι καὶ τὸ γίγνεται οὐ τοῦ νῦν παρόντος; {—} Πάνυ μὲν οὖν. (141d7–e3)

Parmenides concludes that if the one does not partake of time, it cannot partake of any of the forms of "is," and he says that the one does not "partake in being" (οὐσίας μετέχει, 141e9). Notice the form of Aristoteles' answer. Parmenides asks, "Is there a way that something can partake of being otherwise than according to one of these [i.e., past, present, or future]?" ("Εστιν οὖν οὐσίας ὅπως ἄν τι μετάσχοι ἄλλως ἢ κατὰ τούτων τι; 141e7–8). Aristoteles says "It is not possible" (Οὐκ ἔστιν, 141e8).[24] Aristoteles is unknowingly referring to ways of being, conditions of possibility, and not to particular things subject to time. Ways of being have a distinct metaphysical status, and by engaging this ontological level Aristoteles is engaging with a sense of "is" that pertains to what we have been calling "categories": the "is" of the necessary and universal aspects of spatio-temporal individuals. Ironically, he is doing so in the same breath as he is denying any such sense of being. Plato has Aristoteles deny the very distinction between the types of "is" (and "one") that the intelligibility of his words requires. Aristoteles is so deeply unaware of the distinction between the two types of "is" that he draws on the necessary and universal sense of being in order to rule it out, but we are thereby put in a position, potentially with Socrates, to begin to sort out the distinction between the "is" subject to space and time, and the "is" that is atemporal and a-spatial.

Parmenides draws out the implications of Aristoteles' mistaken view that the only kind of being is temporally determinate being, letting the type of atemporal "is" that we have picked out remain unmarked. Parmenides consolidates the view that the "one," if it does not partake in time, "is not," flagging each conclusion following from their previous agreement (note the two instances of ἄρα that pick up the first at 141e9):

> In no way, then (ἄρα), is the one (ἔστι τὸ ἕν).
>
> Evidently not.
>
> Then (ἄρα) in this way it is not such as to be one (ἓν εἶναι), for if it were [one], then it would be being (ὄν) and it would partake in being (οὐσίας μετέχον). But as it seems, the one neither is (οὔτε ἔστιν) nor is one (οὔτε ἕν ἐστιν), if we must put trust in such a *logos*.
>
> So it seems.
>
> Οὐδαμῶς ἄρα ἔστι τὸ ἕν. {—} Οὐ φαίνεται. {—} Οὐδ' ἄρα οὕτως ἔστιν ὥστε ἓν εἶναι· εἴη γὰρ ἂν ἤδη ὂν καὶ οὐσίας μετέχον· ἀλλ' ὡς ἔοικεν, τὸ ἓν οὔτε ἕν ἐστιν οὔτε ἔστιν, εἰ δεῖ τῷ τοιῷδε λόγῳ πιστεύειν. {—} Κινδυνεύει. (141e9–142a1)

The insight offered in this exchange is that there is a distinction drawn between the one that is subject to space and time (and subject to all the unstated categories to which spatio-temporal individuals are heir) and the one that is intelligible in its atemporal and a-spatial determinacy.

Parmenides now concludes H1 by denying to the one that it can be a term of any relation and that it is cognitively accessible. These negative attributes derive, one and all, from the denial of being to the one, which is distinct from the denial of being many, on the basis of which the majority of H1 was conducted. Parmenides says that if the one is not, then it must be deprived of anything belonging "to this is-not" (τούτῳ τῷ μὴ ὄντι) or "of it" (αὐτοῦ, 142a2). It is deprived of all cognitive access, having no name, account, knowledge, perception, or opinion. Parmenides concludes by asking whether such things are possible, and Aristoteles answers that these conclusions seem very wrong.

Lessons and Questions

The inquiry has demonstrated a need to recognize types, or aspects, of being that are distinct from the spatio-temporal individuals we are quickest to recognize. While denying attributes of complexity, relation, and measure to the one, we have gradually built up a negative portrait of the many through an initial study of the structure of spatio-temporal individuals. Grasping the timeless conditions of those individuals, we have also grasped with greater precision the volatility of becoming, and we have started to detect ways in which becoming depends on being. Thus, we have seen ways in which we might start to rethink the distinction between form and participant drawn in the first part of the dialogue and complete the turning of the soul.

Thinking back to the assumptions enabling Parmenides' objections in the first part of the dialogue, we remember that all individuals were taken to belong to a single ontological kind, which led us to think of participation as a real relationship obtaining between one thing and another. The distinction in the senses of being that is indicated throughout H1 but pushed to the point of greatest visibility in the concluding discussion of temporality now prepares us to see the assertion of ontological difference that was called for in response to the skeptic. The very intelligibility of individual things, as complex individuals, demands timeless being that structures and conditions becoming. H1 has shown us a list of attributes to which a one *qua* one is not subject, and it has shown us that these attributes are, in their being, not in space and time. Thus, what H1 allows us to see, from two points of view, is that things in space and time are dependent on a kind of being that is not spatio-temporally determinate. H1 has also revealed division, albeit faint, between the spatio-temporal one and the continuum into which measure and limit are set.

Our first run through the length of the field condensed into the abstract individual does not resolve the challenges laid out in the opening conversation;

indeed, it only gives us an initial sense of the "vast sea" into which we have flung ourselves. But it has alerted us to particular interpretive directions in which we might hear the "one" as we turn to the Second Hypothesis and struggle to make clear what has in a sense already been understood.

CHAPTER 4

The One-That-Is: Second Hypothesis (H2)

Summary of the Chapter

Any instance of intelligibility, no matter how small or brief, contains a plethora of sense. The Second Hypothesis in the *Parmenides* filters this excess of sense and makes its intelligibility accessible to discursive understanding through an elaboration of what Parmenides calls the "one-that-is" (τὸ ἓν ὄν). "One" and "is" live at the center of our encounter with things in the world as place, shape, motion, sameness, mutual affinities, measure, duration, and definitional structures. We can expect in the course of this chapter to elaborate a one that is complex (whole of parts) and individual (one of many) through all the specific aspects that accompany and contextualize complexity and individuality. The Second Hypothesis yields the conceptually transformative breakthrough, in the addendum analysis of the instant (ἐξαίφνης, 155a–157b), that will provide the foundation for the Third, Fifth, and Seventh Hypotheses. The path to that breakthrough lies in first detailing the many-in-one structure of part/whole complexity and the one-of-many structure of individuality.[1]

On the surface, H1 left us with the conclusion that nothing can be said or known or "of" the one. As we progressed through H1, however, I tried to show that there are indications scattered throughout of a one that serves as the normative source for the categorial structure of the many. Far from resulting in saying nothing, the analysis of H1 has prepared a context for reading H2 that points us in the direction of H3, where we are introduced to the concept of limit (*peras*), the one on which limit draws, and the *apeiron* into which it is set. In H2 these later conclusions and insights are once again merely intimated without being substantively developed.

This chapter begins with a prefatory analysis of "one" and "is" that details the foundational role played by one, being, and difference themselves. Following that preface, the first section of the chapter consists of an analysis of the spatiality of the one. The analysis of same and other that issues from the relational structure of spatiality will in turn become a resource for studying the indefinite magnitude, i.e., measure and limit. In the end of the chapter, the categorial structures we uncover will present themselves as the basis for the inter- and intra-individual character of spatio-temporal individuals. H2 will thus be read as a specification of the locative and durative "is" characterizing any spatio-temporal one.

The hypothesis has five main sections. Section 1 (142c–144e) details the individuality and complexity of the spatio-temporal individual, articulating especially the indefinite divisibility and combinability (through iteration) of the one-that-is. The first section is followed by four sections examining the categories to which this individual is subject: Section 2, the spatiality of the one-that-is (145a–146a); Section 3, its qualitative relations (146a–148d); Section 4, its quantitative relations (148d–151e); Section 5, its temporality (151e–155d).

The Abstract Intelligibility of Spatially Determinate Individuals

In both H1 and H2 the hypothesis is "if [a] one is." In the wake of the apparently self-undermining conclusions of H1, however, Parmenides very sensibly asks that we go back to the beginning (πάλιν ἐξ ἀρχῆς, 142b1) to ask whether a recapitulation of the hypothesis will reveal something different (cf. the concluding remarks in Chapter 3, Section 5). The hypothesis is the same, but Parmenides flags a new inflection in sense by changing the order of words, materially emphasizing a gap between its aspects of being and oneness: "[a] one *if* [it] is (ἓν εἰ ἔστιν)" (142b3, b5, c8; emphasis added). Parmenides clarifies his meaning: "But in fact (νῦν δέ), the hypothesis is not 'if [a] one one (εἰ ἓν ἕν) but rather 'if [a] one is' (εἰ ἓν ἐστιν)" (142c2–3; cf. 137c of H1).[2] Unless one were distinct from being, he says, being could not be the being *of* the one, nor could the one partake *in* its being. Therefore "being" and "one" cannot be the same (ταὐτόν, 142b6, b7, b8).[3] With this starting point, Parmenides begins analysis of the one's character as a manifold of aspects.

What this rephrased hypothesis means for the inquiry should not, I think, be separated from the way Aristoteles has steered the conversation at the end of H1. Aristoteles' unreflective insistence that all being is subject to time, specifically that "is" implies being past, present, or future (141e8), is the target of Parmenides' opening articulation of the hypothesis "if one is." My intention in this chapter is to show that Parmenides is calling on Aristoteles and the reader to see in H1 and H2 a deeper continuity between apparently distinct types of timeless and temporal "is" indicated toward the end of H1. The idea of being can, I claim, be understood as what is most basic, and it can be understood as encompassing these apparently distinct ways of construing "is."[4] We saw that in order to limit all being to temporally determinate being, Aristoteles had to unwittingly draw on the intelligibility of atemporal ways of being, and we were called on to see the timeless structure of temporal becoming. The being of the source from which and by which the various aspects of becoming are organized is itself a one. Complementary to that one (i.e., the one of H1) is the complex and individual one that H2 introduces through the re-articulation of the hypothesis "if one is." As Parmenides specifies and expands the "is" of the basic hypothesis, we will start to see the timeless structure of temporally determinate becoming.

The most important point before beginning the examination of H2 is to see that "one exists" is far too restrictive and vague a translation of "one is." What we too loosely call "being" is always shorthand for a specific way of being.[5] In the context of H2, the analysis proceeds from the initial statement of complexity (of "one" and "is") and individuality (of "one," "is," and "difference") to an implied specification in terms of shape, place, motion, etc. But more importantly, in H2, the range of meaning condensed into a "one that is" is filled out and specified, and as we proceed it becomes gradually clear that we are enumerating categories that are at least consistent with spatio-temporal particulars.[6] With this in mind, we begin reading the two short arguments in the preface of H2, in which Parmenides derives "many" from the initial hypothesis of a one-that-is. The first argument runs from 142c7 to 143a2, and the second from 143a4 to 144e5, the two arguments summarized at 144e5–7. At 144e8 to 145a4 Parmenides adds "having limits" to the attributes belonging to the one-that-is, making way for his analysis of spatiality. What we will learn from this opening analysis of complexity and individuality is that the hypothesized one of H2 points to *yet* conceals its ontological dependencies. Our reading begins by attempting to reveal those dependencies.

The first derivation of many from the one-that-is treats the one-that-is as a composite, the second treats it as a unit, and neither grasps combination and division on their own terms. The divisibility and combinability of the one-that-is are understood in terms of the actual multiplicity that is the product or result of indefinite combination and division. Together these first and second derivations of multiplicity use the structure and character of the one-that-is to point to, without being able to explain, the causal sources of complex individuality. By focusing on the products of division and combination rather than their principles, these derivations create the need for later hypotheses (H3 and H7 especially) that will be better able to grasp divisibility and combinability in light of their relationship to the *apeiron*.

One Consisting of Many: The First Argument (142c–143a)

We begin with the hypothesis that "[a] one is." In the first argument as well as the second, Parmenides distinguishes between the aspects of "one" and "being" in the one-that-is, turning to the object of analysis as "something said" (λέγεται, 142d1) and articulating what it "signifies" (σημαίνειν, 142c9). The one-that-is is presented by Parmenides as a whole consisting of a being-part and a one-part. If we keep in mind that the one-that-is will soon be described as a spatial whole (145a ff.), and if we assume that the object of analysis is constant throughout H2, the whole of parts in the first argument should be taken to refer here to a spatial whole of spatial parts. Insofar as the one-that-is is something determinate, it is an aggregate whole indefinitely divisible into similarly constituted parts; it is a whole of many wholes, a one of many ones.

In this first argument there are two sides to the analysis. On the one hand the analysis examines the spatially extended character of abstract magnitudes; on the other hand the analysis examines what follows from what can be said of the one-that-is and what it signifies—that the one-that-is both "is" and is "one":

> Consider whether this hypothesis must not signify that the one is such as to have parts.
>
> How so?
>
> In this way: if the "is" of the one-that-is (τοῦ ἑνὸς ὄντος) is said (λέγεται), as well as the "one" of the being-that-is-one (τοῦ ὄντος ἑνός), but being (ἥ τε οὐσία) and the one [are] not the same [but are] *of* that same (τοῦ αὐτοῦ δὲ ἐκείνου) which we hypothesized, namely, the one-that-is (τὸ ἓν ὄν), then is it not necessary on the one hand for the one-being to be itself a whole,[7] and on the other hand for the one and the being (τὸ εἶναι) to become parts of this?
>
> Necessarily. (Gill, modified)
>
> σκόπει οὖν εἰ οὐκ ἀνάγκη ταύτην τὴν ὑπόθεσιν τοιοῦτον ὂν τὸ ἓν σημαίνειν, οἷον μέρη ἔχειν; {—} πῶς; {—} ὧδε: εἰ τὸ ἔστι τοῦ ἑνὸς ὄντος λέγεται καὶ τὸ ἓν τοῦ ὄντος ἑνός, ἔστι δὲ οὐ τὸ αὐτὸ ἥ τε οὐσία καὶ τὸ ἕν, τοῦ αὐτοῦ δὲ ἐκείνου οὗ ὑπεθέμεθα, τοῦ ἑνὸς ὄντος, ἆρα οὐκ ἀνάγκη τὸ μὲν ὅλον ἓν ὂν εἶναι αὐτό, τούτου δὲ γίγνεσθαι μόρια τό τε ἓν καὶ τὸ εἶναι; {—} ἀνάγκη. (142c8–d5)

Parmenides divides "that same which we hypothesized" (τοῦ αὐτοῦ δὲ ἐκείνου οὗ ὑπεθέμεθα, 142d3) into two aspects, *viz.*, "the one that is" (τοῦ ἑνὸς ὄντος, 142d1) and "that which is one" (τοῦ ὄντος ἑνός, 142d2). The object of analysis is thus treated as both (a) a one that has distinct aspects separable only in *logos*, and (b) a one that is materially divisible into parts that can each be re-described in the same terms.[8] In reference to the necessary character of any "one," whether whole or part, Parmenides says that the being-part cannot "be absent from" (ἀπολείπεσθον, 142e1) the one-part, and reciprocally the one-part cannot be absent from the being-part. When Parmenides then goes on to conclude from this that "whatever is one (ὃ ἂν ἓν ᾖ) both is a whole and has a part" (142d8–9) and is indefinitely divisible, he is subjecting the one-that-is to the paradigm of a spatio-temporal entity, an aggregate whole indefinitely divisible into parts. By contrast, the aspects of being and oneness, unlike separable parts of a spatial whole, cannot "be absent from" each other in the sense that their bond is logically necessary.

The one-that-is thus is conceived (a) as an aggregate whole of parts, specifically implying spatial extension, and (b) a unity of mutually implied aspects. We find ourselves within the context of objects that, abstracting from features unique to each, are construed simply as spatio-temporal wholes with dual aspects of being a *one*-that-is and being a *being*-that-is-one. As spatio-temporal presences, these objects consist of divisible spans, i.e., the spatial wholes are divisible into spatial parts. The result is the one-that-is that can be taken up both as a whole of two aspects and as a spatial aggregate, and it can be divided ad infinitum. Parmenides says:

> Then once again each of the parts [one and the being] will have one and being, and the least part comes in turn to consist of two parts, and according to the same *logos* thus always, whatever proves to be a part, [it] always has these two parts: one always has being (τὸ ὄν), and being [always has] one: with the result that it necessarily is never one because it is always coming to be two (δύ' ἀεὶ γιγνόμενον).[9]
>
> πάλιν ἄρα καὶ τῶν μορίων ἑκάτερον τό τε ἓν ἴσχει καὶ τὸ ὄν, καὶ γίγνεται τὸ ἐλάχιστον ἐκ δυοῖν αὖ μορίοιν τὸ μόριον, καὶ κατὰ τὸν αὐτὸν λόγον οὕτως ἀεί, ὅτιπερ ἂν μόριον γένηται, τούτω τὼ μορίω ἀεὶ ἴσχει: τό τε γὰρ ἓν τὸ ὂν ἀεὶ ἴσχει καὶ τὸ ὂν τὸ ἕν: ὥστε ἀνάγκη δύ' ἀεὶ γιγνόμενον μηδέποτε ἓν εἶναι. (142e3–143a2)

Parmenides draws the inference that, "the one has shown itself to be many" (τὸ ἓν ὂν πολλὰ ἐφάνη, 143a) and concludes: the one-being would be "an unlimited multitude" (ἄπειρον ἂν τὸ πλῆθος).[10]

Stepping back for the moment to consider what has initially and incompletely announced itself thus far in H2, the surplus of meaning condensed into the one-that-is is here reduced to an aggregate whole that is indefinitely divisible. The one-that-is, therefore, is "of such a sort" (τοιοῦτον, 142c10) to have an indefinite plurality of parts. The parts must be kept distinct from the whole if they are to be parts, properly speaking, but there is no basis for making the necessary qualitative distinction between part and whole. Each part is a whole and each whole is a part, without preference, order, or limit. Later in H7 we will study the nature of apparent unity, and there we will take up thematically the kind of indefinite limit that characterizes the one-that-is in these passages. What we have here is just the bare characteristics of complexity. If we want to more adequately understand the nature of any actual thing, we will have to study further the structures of dependency that set the one-that-is into, and allow it to emerge from, an indefinitely divisible continuum and organize it into a definite whole of definite parts. Key to this account will be the discovery of the *apeiron* and the organizing nature, introduced later in H2 but not developed fully until H3 and H7.

Many Ones: The Second Argument (143a–144e5)

The second argument takes as its object the same "one" as the first, but it grasps the aspects of the one-that-is "in thought" (διανοίᾳ), i.e., it takes them up on their own terms as the intelligible characters "one" and "being" that are in, and abstracted from, the one-that-is. By taking the one-that-is as an object, but looking exclusively toward the aspects of being and one "alone by themselves" (μόνον καθ' αὐτό, 143a7), Parmenides turns to the intelligible aspects of the one-that-is insofar as it is and insofar as it is one. In the previous argument Parmenides urged us to see a particular kind of one for which "is" and "one" were always co-implied. In thought, the being and unity characters of the one-that-is are seen standing alone prior to mixing as aspects immanent to the spatio-temporal particular.

Taken on their own, these intelligible principles are prior even to the mixing by which they are known in *legein* and, for example, counted as members of a group or a class, and defined. Parmenides asks Aristoteles to follow along "in this way" (τῇδε): "the one itself" (αὐτὸ τὸ ἕν, 143a6) seized in thought "alone by itself" (μόνον καθ' αὐτό, 143a7) appears to Aristoteles to be one but will prove at 144e5–6 to be many.[11] The argument is that each of these is not other than another, as they must be if they are to be counted, because as forms they are "alone by themselves" and do not have any character other than themselves by which they could be subject to comparison and counting, such as for example the character of "difference" that would allow them to differ with another form.

> Then let us see: Isn't it necessary that its being (οὐσία) is one thing, and it an other, if indeed the one is not being but, as one, partakes of being?[12]
> Necessarily.
> So if being is other and the one is other, it is not "by the one" (τῷ ἕν) that the one is other than being, nor by being being (τῷ οὐσία εἶναι) that being is other (ἄλλο) than the one, but by the different (τῷ ἑτέρῳ) and other (ἄλλῳ) that they are others (ἕτερα) from each other (ἀλλήλων)?
> Of course.
>
> ἴδωμεν δή: ἄλλο τι ἕτερον μὲν ἀνάγκη τὴν οὐσίαν αὐτοῦ εἶναι, ἕτερον δὲ αὐτό, εἴπερ μὴ οὐσία τὸ ἕν, ἀλλ᾽ ὡς ἓν οὐσίας μετέσχεν; {—} ἀνάγκη. {—} οὐκοῦν εἰ ἕτερον μὲν ἡ οὐσία, ἕτερον δὲ τὸ ἕν, οὔτε τῷ ἓν τὸ ἓν τῆς οὐσίας ἕτερον οὔτε τῷ οὐσία εἶναι ἡ οὐσία τοῦ ἑνὸς ἄλλο, ἀλλὰ τῷ ἑτέρῳ τε καὶ ἄλλῳ ἕτερα ἀλλήλων. {—} πάνυ μὲν οὖν. (143b1–6)

Being and oneness do not imply, and cannot account for, their otherness to one another on their own terms because being-other is proper to neither of them. Otherness is a form of its own, and they are subject to otherness by virtue of participation in that form. The one and being are other "by otherness," which is to say that they partake in otherness, and only insofar as they do partake in otherness are the one and being "others" (ἕτερα) in relation to "each other" (ἀλλήλων). Before participation they are not in relation and, therefore, not denumerable.[13]

Each of these terms (i.e., one, being, difference), however, can be subject to *legein*. In themselves, they are not denumerable, since being denumerable requires that they participate in otherness and make themselves available to other ones. But as subject to *legein* and otherness, being, one, and other are counted as three. Parmenides is asking us to see that, although subject to *legein* and countable, the intelligible aspects of the one-that-is have a mode prior to becoming objects of discursive knowing. Parmenides says:

> What then? If we pick out from them, whatever you wish, the being and the different, or the being and the one, or the one and

> the different, do we not pick out in each selection some pair which is correctly called "both"?
>
> τί οὖν; ἐὰν προελώμεθα αὐτῶν εἴτε βούλει τὴν οὐσίαν καὶ τὸ ἕτερον εἴτε τὴν οὐσίαν καὶ τὸ ἓν εἴτε τὸ ἓν καὶ τὸ ἕτερον, ἆρ' οὐκ ἐν ἑκάστῃ τῇ προαιρέσει προαιρούμεθά τινε ὢ ὀρθῶς ἔχει καλεῖσθαι ἀμφοτέρω; (143c1–4)

What the object of analysis is *qua* subject to "picking out" (προαιρεῖσθαι) and "speaking" (λέγειν) it is not on its own. Thus, being, one, and other are three and each is one *qua* subject to *legein*. When Aristoteles asks for clarification of Parmenides' claim that picking out being and one together is to pick out something correctly called "both," Parmenides four times underlines that these are qualities belonging to *things said*. As gathered for a saying, being, one, and other become denumerated ones combined and divided with others. Once Parmenides establishes that together they are "both," and that "both" implies "two," and that two implies that each is "one," he shows that these forms imply both odd and even and all number.[14] Aristoteles agrees on this basis that "if there is one, then there must be number" (εἰ ἄρα ἔστιν ἕν, ἀνάγκη καὶ ἀριθμὸν εἶναι) (144a4). If there is number, then each number is, and there is therefore an "unlimited multitude of beings" (πλῆθος ἄπειρον τῶν ὄντων) (144a6). What they have done is only to clarify the degree to which something subject to *legein* must also be subject to number. This also shows that *legein* is undialectical insofar as it unreflectively treats every "one" in terms proper to its objects, i.e., as subject to the characteristics that belong to them as objects of discursive knowing.

Parmenides uses this account of abstract combination to derive the existence of an unlimited multitude of beings. As he says, if all number partakes in being, then each number partakes in being. We might want to limit the following conclusion, that being is distributed to many things (πολλὰ ὄντα ἡ οὐσία νενέμηται, 144b1), to the claim that being is distributed to many numbers. However, Parmenides rules out limiting the scope of number to the abstract units studied by the mathematician when he specifies that being is missing from "neither the smallest nor the largest" (οὔτε τοῦ σμικροτάτου οὔτε τοῦ μεγίστου, 144b2–3) and then claims that being is chopped up into the greatest and the smallest and "beings of all kinds" (πανταχῶς ὄντα, 144b6, Gill's translation). What is this result trying to tell us?

First, following Jacob Klein, we can see that it is necessary to treat number not first and foremost as an abstract entity but a definite number of definite things.[15] Numbers, as it were, point to things and call for them. Just as "is" implies "is of some particular sort," so too a number implies a number of a certain sort of things.[16] Therefore, the above transition from number to "beings of all kinds" and the "smallest and largest" are natural transitions insofar as the initial invocation of number already implied a certain number of things of definite kinds.[17] Secondly, we trace in this argument a distinction between a denumerated one-of-many structure and a continuum of greater-and-smaller. One-many plurality and part-whole complexity, including relations of abstract spatiality, are aspects of quality and quantity categorially constitutive of the one-that-is.

Parmenides concludes the second argument with a description of the distribution of being into the most unlimited parts and, through the distribution of being, the distribution of the "one itself." Parmenides says "the one itself [is] cut up by being" (κεκερματισμένον ὑπὸ τῆς οὐσίας), and that each "is" must be "some one" (ἕν γέ τι); "insofar as it is, it must be some one thing, it cannot be nothing" (144c4–5).[18] He is simply formalizing the requirement we noticed above; what is must be one. The one is present to (πρόσεστιν) each of the many parts of being and not absent from (ἀπολειπόμενον) any, as he says, neither greater nor smaller than any other (144c6–7).[19] Parmenides concludes that if the one is divisible (μεριστόν, 144d4), "not only is it the case that the one-that-is (τὸ ὂν ἕν) is many [i.e., the first argument], but also the one itself (αὐτὸ τὸ ἕν), completely distributed (διανενεμημένον) by being, is not one, as Aristoteles thought, but is many [i.e., the second argument]" (144e5–7).[20] Parmenides asks: "Then being one, can it be in many places at once as a whole? Consider this carefully."[21] It cannot, and therefore it must be present in many places as "divided into parts" (μεμερισμένον, 144d4), and that therefore "the one itself" is many, distributed by being, just as the one-that-is turned out to be many, in the sense of being divisible, in the first argument. Together the first and second accounts of the one-that-is show that what we are dealing with is characterized by complexity and individuality.

Parmenides offers a third account in which he gathers together the results of the first two accounts in the description of the limit (πέρας) and in the discussion of the one-that-is as something shaped. Each of the many ones-that-are is "limited" (πεπερασμένον) as a whole (144e8). The parts of the one-that-is are contained (περιέχεται) by the whole, he says, and their container is a "limit" (145a1). Parmenides says:[22]

> Furthermore, inasmuch as the parts are parts of a whole, the one would be limited (πεπερασμένον) as a whole. Or aren't parts contained (περιέχεται) by the whole?

Necessarily.
Furthermore, the container (περιέχον) would be a limit (πέρας).
How could it not? (based on Gill)

καὶ μὴν[23] ὅτι γε ὅλου τὰ μόρια μόρια, πεπερασμένον ἂν εἴη κατὰ τὸ ὅλον τὸ ἕν: ἢ οὐ περιέχεται ὑπὸ τοῦ ὅλου τὰ μόρια; ; {—} ἀνάγκη. ; {—} ἀλλὰ μὴν τό γε περιέχον πέρας ἂν εἴη. ; {—} πῶς δ' οὔ; (144e8–145a2)

The divisibility of the one-that-is implies spatial containment of spatially distinct parts, indefinitely divisible. The specific language Parmenides uses for "container" (περιέχον), from which he derives "limit" (πέρας), will serve as the basis from which to begin the spatiality arguments that follow, and the notion of limit will continue as a thematic focus in each of the subsequent sections up through the concluding set of arguments on the temporality of the one. Not until H3 will we find a concentrated study of a whole that, unlike the aggregate, orders and organizes a distribution of contradictory aspects within the distinct parts of the one-that-is. Until then, we are studying the basis upon which an aggregate one can emerge from, and be set into, a continuum.

Conclusion of the Two Derivations (144d3–145a4)

Parmenides now moves to complete the first section of H2, wrapping up and tying together the results. The concluding statement combines a number of apparently incompatible attributions, which quickly becomes the hallmark of H2:

Then the one-that-is is somehow both one and many, both whole and parts, both limited and unlimited in multitude.
It appears so (φαίνεται).

τὸ ἓν ἄρα ὂν ἕν τέ ἐστί που καὶ πολλά, καὶ ὅλον καὶ μόρια, καὶ πεπερασμένον καὶ ἄπειρον πλήθει. {—} φαίνεται. (145a2–4)

Looking over these two arguments in retrospect, we notice the possible range of the different senses of these terms one/many, whole/part, limited/unlimited. The two most important respects uncovered have been the distinction between (a) what appears distinct "in thought," i.e., being, one, and different "themselves," and (b) the spatial continuum in which the one-that-is is set.

The one-that-is presents itself as a middle between its intelligible aspects and the spatial continuum in which it is set.

Our reading of these arguments has taught us to see the one-that-is as a provisional object of analysis—an object that lends itself to being analyzed while simultaneously concealing its conditioning sources. For instance, when we turned to address ourselves to the causes of "being" and being "one" in the second argument, we noted that these causes were prior to difference and therefore not denumerable, and yet they were unceremoniously reduced to their status as objects of *legein* capable of being denumerated and combined indefinitely. Similarly, when studying the aggregate one-that-is in the first argument, the co-implication of "being" and being "one" was taken up as an indefinitely divisible aggregate, but the divisibility of the one-that-is, and the notion of continuum in which divisibility is rooted, was not explained. Thus, the causes that subject what is "by itself" to relation and render it capable of combination and, at the same time, situate the one-that-is in a continuum have not been explicitly elaborated in the analysis. This is not surprising, or should not be, insofar as the analysis is at this point insufficiently dialectical. The one-that-is points both (a) to causes prior to individuation, and (b) to the continuum beneath composition. It is not until H3 that these concealed causes will be revealed as objects of analysis. As we approach H3, I want to outline these as objects of future analysis and emphasize, especially in the case of the continuum, that we are using the one-that-is to provide for us the terms for understanding the ontological difference between being and becoming.

In the remainder of this chapter I will use the limitations of the one-that-is to gain access to its causal sources and the *apeiron* on which it rests. I first focus on the peculiar character of limit as something that is "in" space and time while yet not being subject to space and time, something constitutive of spatio-temporal determinacy without being a spatio-temporal object. I will then examine the arguments for the spatiality of the one-that-is, in which limit both divides the one-that-is from its surrounding context and places the one-that-is into its context. Then from the qualitative distinction between same and other that is teased out of this account of spatiality, I will turn to the arguments in which the relations of same/other and like/unlike show the radically distinct types of one, such as continuum and cause, that are implicit in the structure of the one-that-is. From there we consider contact, measure, and temporality, from which individual ones, both wholes of parts and ones of many, must draw their numerical identity and distinct integrity. In the remainder of H2 we will clarify the distinction between spatio-temporal complexity and individuality and the simplicity and uniqueness on which they depend but to which they can only point.

Our study of the sources toward which the spatio-temporal one points us will not be completed until we have a chance to answer the challenges of H1 and H2 in subsequent chapters. In Chapter 5 we will undertake a four-part analysis of (1) examining the spatio-temporal continuum (H2a, the instant), (2) the primacy of limit vis-à-vis complexity and plurality (H3, constitutive limit), and (3) the veridical structure of eidetic combination and division (H5), and (4) the explicit account of the "is" of spatio-temporal individuals treated not as instances of eidetic structure but as such (H7, the being of appearance). This analysis will enable us to see that the one-that-is—i.e., the one that is the most familiar form taken by our bond with reality—can be seen as secondary to what precedes it and taken as a gift used to transform our trust (*pistis*) in the primacy of individual things into a dialectical study of the sources of being.

Spatial Limit

Parmenides' account of spatiality is a threefold analysis of (1) shape, (2) being-in, and (3) motion/rest. The tacit reliance in the preceding discussion on spatially locative notions of containment and presence is here developed into a more adequate account of the metaphysical structure of part/whole complexity. The whole of parts is a metaphysically enclosed space, with its own self-related integrity and other-related distinctness. And yet, at the same time as it has these formally defining aspects, the whole is a spatial whole of spatial parts continuous with others and divided from itself. The tension between the aspect of the whole as something self-defined and its aspect as being other-defined will serve as a point of special focus in the following analyses.

Spatiality

Parmenides has shown that "the one itself" is chopped up and distributed by being into unlimited parts, and that each part, as part, is "contained" (περιέχον) and therefore "limited" (πεπερασμένον) as a whole (κατὰ τὸ ὅλον, 144e9).[24] As limited, each one-that-is is subject to a twofold character. On the one hand, limit circumscribes the one-that-is and articulates its internal divisions. As a whole, the one-that-is must "have" and not "be absent from" (ἀποστατέω, 145a7) a beginning, middle, and end. Its middle "holds back" (ἀπέχειν) equally from its extremities (ἔσχατα), which give it a shape, either straight, round, or some combination of both (145a7–b2).[25] On the other hand, limit places the one-that-is into the context of relations with respect to other ones. If the one partakes of shape, Parmenides goes on to argue, it follows that it will be both "in itself and in another" (ἐν ἑαυτῷ ἔσται καὶ ἐν ἄλλῳ, 145b6–7). These two senses of limit, external and internal, point to contrasting aspects of external relations to other ones and internal relations of complexity belonging to the one-that-is. As things stand, however, the principle that unifies and coordinates these two aspects of the one-that-is remains concealed.

The one-that-is includes, in its being, the internal divisibility of the place it creates in itself, and it includes the external relations to the other ones in the context of which it is placed. Parmenides points us to the twofold nature of internal complexity and external relations. On the one hand, as Parmenides says, the one is in itself insofar as it is a whole and, as whole, creates a context for its parts. The one is "the whole itself" (αὐτὸ τὸ ὅλον, 145c5), which emphasizes the distinction between the whole *qua* whole and the whole *qua* parts and points to the way the whole is the place for its parts; in this respect, the one-that-is holds itself separate from others. At the same time, "the one is all the parts of itself, and not any more or less than all" (145c1–2).[26] That is, the whole *qua* parts is identical to all of its parts, and the parts are themselves wholes that can be divided, undercutting any organization, indefinitely divisible through the middle between extremities. In its indefinite divisibility the one-that-is *qua* parts is subject to the one-that-is *qua* whole, and the one-that-is *qua* whole implicitly refers to other ones in relation to which it is situated and defined. That is, the account of the way the one-that-is is in itself allows us to see the complexity of the one-that-is in light of its individuality relative to other ones.

The distinction and relationship between the one-that-is *qua* complex and the one-that-is *qua* individual is further captured in Parmenides' subsequent argument for the whole being in another. Within the horizon established by H2, it is a metaphysical necessity to be in some place. To be implies being somewhere; being nowhere implies being nothing.[27] While it is true that the parts are in a space provided by the whole, Parmenides proceeds to argue that the whole is not in the parts, either one, some, or all. The whole, he argues, cannot be in the parts without being in each part. I find the argument here difficult and obscure. Parmenides seems to reject the claim that the whole is in all the parts for the reason that it would have to be in one part, and if it cannot be in two places (i.e., parts) at once, then it is in one and not another, therefore not in all.[28] In a preliminary sense, then, the whole must be in another. Parmenides argues here that the whole cannot be in some of the parts because then the greater would be in the lesser. Insofar as the whole is greater than some of its parts, it is implicitly also lesser than and contained by its surrounding relationship to other ones. Thus, when

Parmenides concludes that the whole must be "in another" (ἐν ἄλλῳ, 145e2), he is pointing to the relationship between complexity of the one-that-is as a whole of parts and the individuality of the one-that-is as one among many.[29]

If we take a step back from the one-that-is, then, we see that it can be taken up from two points of view or in two respects. When Parmenides concludes the analysis of being-in, he introduces for the first time in H2 the idea of respect, i.e., the different directions in which something can be taken up:

> *Insofar* as the one is whole, it is in another, *insofar* as it happens to be all the parts, it is in itself, and thusly it is necessary for it to be in itself and in another.
>
> Necessary. (Gill, modified and emphasis added)
>
> ᾗ μὲν ἄρα τὸ ἓν ὅλον, ἐν ἄλλῳ ἐστίν: ᾗ δὲ τὰ πάντα μέρη ὄντα τυγχάνει, αὐτὸ ἐν ἑαυτῷ: καὶ οὕτω τὸ ἓν ἀνάγκη αὐτό τε ἐν ἑαυτῷ εἶναι καὶ ἐν ἑτέρῳ. {—} ἀνάγκη. (145e3–6)

The two regards in which the conclusion is drawn are set off in the Greek by the ᾗ μέν . . . ᾗ δέ construction. The important point to emphasize is that there are two mutually exclusive but related dimensions in which the one offers itself. I take these complementary and mutually entailing aspects of the one-that-is to be situated conceptually by the duality of the one-that-is as a complex whole of parts and an individual one among many others.

The closedness of the one-that-is, as denumerable, and the openness of the one-that-is, as divisible, can be partially but not adequately captured by the relationship of whole to part and by the relationship of individual to others. The more natural way in which to capture the two aspects of the one-that-is, as I will now attempt to show, is to describe it in terms of motion and rest, i.e., as being one *through* being many, or being open to the motion of change through being held together at rest.

Motion and Rest

In motion and rest Parmenides completes the section on the spatiality of the one-that-is, and his arguments clarify for us the sense in which the one-that-is includes others within its identity. In motion and rest, Parmenides completes the account of spatiality by drawing closer attention to the categories of self and other underlying and structuring the one-that-is.

Parmenides begins by pointing to the constitution of the one as a two-fold structure of containment and limit, calling the relation of being-in-itself and being-in-another aspects of "the one's natural condition" (πεφυκός) (145e7).[30] Being in another, he says, implies that the one is "in motion," for to be "always in another" means always moving out of one place and into another. Conversely, being in itself means being in one place, in itself (ἐν ἑαυτῷ), and not stepping outside of this place (ἐκ τούτου μὴ μεταβαῖνον, 146a1), so it means being always in the same (ἐν τῷ αὐτῷ ἀεὶ ὄν, 146a2–3) and at rest.

The one-that-is that is in-itself is always in-the-same, and therefore it is at rest, corresponding to the way the parts of the one-that-is are contained by the whole, and the whole is a distinct unit separate from other units. The one-that-is in-another is never in the same and therefore in motion. On the one hand, the one-that-is is at rest within itself as enclosed within self-defined limits. On the other hand, the one-that-is is in motion, related to and to a degree subject to other individual ones among which it is. Motion and rest, therefore, describe the being of the one-that-is in its self-relation and other-relation. Both descriptions are of what is "always" (ἀεί), which reminds us of the earlier characterization that being "always has" (ἀεὶ ἴσχει) the one, and the one "always has" (142e3–143a1) being. As divisible, the one-that-is is never one (μηδέποτε ἕν) and always becoming two (δύ' ἀεὶ γιγνόμενον, 143a1). I take the "always" of the coincidence of one and being in any one-that-is to characterize the timeless "is" of categorial determinacy, and the "always" of the indefinite divisibility of the concrete particular that stands in relation to other ones-that-are to characterize the "is" that is subject to temporal determinacy.

In almost Zenonian fashion, Parmenides thinks of motion without potentiality as a series of distinct actualities. This conceptual framing obscures, even occludes the sense in which the one-that-is is categorially (i.e., timelessly) subject to motion and rest, which implies that the one-that-is is subject to the possibility of motion and rest at all times. Whether actually moving or actually resting, the actuality of the one-that-is is characterized by the categorial structure of motion and rest constantly, always. But if we constrain our account to temporally determinate being, we will think of the one-that-is as *either* in motion *or* at rest, i.e., think of these as mutually exclusive states. Categorially speaking, the one-that-is could not be unless it can be in motion and rest at all times, which is to say that the one-that-is is determined by motion and rest. The text pointedly turns away from what I am calling the categorial dimension of motion and rest. If we take note of this and think of it as an incomplete or one-sided account, the account here is forecasting the transformation that will take place in H3–H8 where we learn to think of the "others" as timelessly subject to categorial determination.

Qualitative Relation

Having completed an initial study of the spatiality of individual things in "the previous [things said]" (τὰ πρόσθεν, 146b2), which included an analysis of the spatiality of each whole and the many ones-that-are, we turn now to the relational categories of same and other. The analysis of part/whole complexity and individuality will reveal the idea of sameness and difference to be fundamental, and these ideas will show that the individual is not self-explanatory but rests on a very specific set of prior conditions.

Same and Other

Parmenides frames the discussion with the assertion that the one-that-is must be the same as and other than both itself and the others. We find in this section repeated and systematic mention of "the others" (τὰ ἄλλα), which is directly related to two distinct senses of one.[31] If by "one" we have in mind the one-that-is considered with respect to its number as a single being (second derivation in H2), the term "others" points to other individuals. Conversely, if by "one" we have in mind the one-that-is considered with respect to its wholeness (first derivation in H2), "others" points to what is beneath the threshold of integration.

The section breaks down into four arguments. In the first section, Parmenides takes the "one" to be an individual. He argues that the one must be the same as itself. Here we will note that the one gains its definition from the others—that is, it "is" same as itself because it "is not" other—and its self-sameness is negatively defined. In the second section, the one-that-is shows itself, *qua* whole of parts, to be other than itself. In the third section, the one-that-is shows itself, *qua* individual, to be other than others insofar as it must bear a relation to a numerically distinct other. In the final section, the one is the same as the others in the sense that the one-that-is, *qua* fully integrated whole, is the same as the not-one, i.e., the non-integral; the one-that-is and the not-one are so different that they can occupy the same place without opposition or conflict. I will interpret these arguments to mean that the one-that-is must be other than itself in order to be itself, and that therefore these arguments further underscore the importance of the reciprocal relationship between complexity and individuality.

In the discussion of being-in-the-same and being-in-an-other above, the one-that-is showed itself to be individual (i.e., one among many other individuals) and, at the same time, to be divisible (i.e., a whole of many parts). In the present section, Parmenides opens with the fourfold structure that traces the singular/complex structure of the one-that-is:

> Everything is somehow related to everything in this manner: either it is the same or different; or, if it is neither the same nor different, it would be a part of that toward which it relates, or it would be as whole to part.[32]
>
> πᾶν που πρὸς ἅπαν ὧδε ἔχει, ἢ ταὐτόν ἐστιν ἢ ἕτερον: ἢ ἐὰν μὴ ταὐτὸν ᾖ μηδ᾽ ἕτερον, μέρος ἂν εἴη τούτου πρὸς ὃ οὕτως ἔχει, ἢ ὡς πρὸς μέρος ὅλον ἂν εἴη.[33] (146b2–5)

This description is meant to exhaust the types of relation in which the one can partake. It says, effectively, that what-is is subject to internal divisions as complex (part and whole), and it is subject to external relations as individual (same and other). Something that is, then, is both a complex whole and a one among many individuals, and it can be considered under either aspect. Thus, its sameness or difference is articulated in terms of individuality and complexity. However, in the course of the following four sections, we will see that ontologically distinct kinds can occupy the same identity without interference or contradiction. Thus, this section will further our goal of establishing an ontological difference within our account of the one-that-is and promote our understanding of the categorial characteristics under which the one-that-is stands.

The One Is the Same as Itself. Parmenides demonstrates the sameness of what he here identifies as "the one *itself*" (τὸ ἓν αὐτό, 146b7) as distinct from its parts.[34] He asks: is the one *itself* a part of *itself* (τὸ ἓν αὐτὸ αὑτοῦ μέρος, 146b5–6)? Is it a whole in relation to itself as part of itself (πρὸς μέρος αὑτὸ αὑτοῦ ὅλον, 146b6–7)? Is it different from one (ἕτερόν . . . ἑνός) or different from itself (ἑαυτοῦ γε ἕτερον) (146c1–2)? The answer to each question, with varying degrees of certainty, is "no." If the "one *itself*," i.e., just insofar as it is itself, is not other than itself, not a whole in relation to itself, and not a part in relation to itself, "must it then not be the same as itself?" (146c2–4).[35] Aristoteles says it must. Notice that this consequence that the one is the same as itself rests on an elimination argument. Insofar as the one is not other than itself, it is the same as itself. I take this to imply that the sameness of the one-itself points to others against which it is negatively defined.

The One Is Different from Itself. In the second argument, Parmenides draws on the spatiality of the part/whole relation to show that, because the one is both in itself (as all parts are in the whole) and in another (as the whole of all the parts), the one must be other than itself. Parmenides asks, "What about the following? Must not that which is in an other place than itself, being in the same as itself, be different from itself, if it is to be in a different place?" (146c4–6). The one must be in another (ἑτέρωθι) at the same time as it is in itself (ἐν ἑαυτῷ) (146c7–8).

In the previous discussion, the one-that-is was shown to be the same as itself insofar as it is other than other ones-that-are. In this section, the one-that-is is shown to be different than itself by virtue of being all the parts and the whole of those parts. Taken together, I interpret these first two arguments to show that the one-that-is is the same as itself, i.e., it is itself *qua* individual, insofar as it is other than itself, i.e., it is itself *qua* whole of parts.

The One Is Different than the Others. The same point is made with reference to individuality in the third section. We have seen that individuals are other than other individuals. Each individual as an individual includes reference to other individuals, and those other individuals likewise include and make room for each other. Each one-that-is includes in its being a relation to others, and those others as other ones-that-are mirror relation back to the one-that-is. Parmenides says, "Now, if anything is different from something (εἴ τού τι ἕτερόν ἐστιν), won't it be other than a being-other?" (146d1–2).[36] The first clause invokes a general context of relationality. The second clause attributes to those others not just the qualification "other" but also identities as other ones (ἕτερα). Parmenides says, "Aren't as many as are not-one (μὴ ἕν) quite all others (ἕτερα) from the one, and the one from the (τῶν) not-one?" (146e5–6).[37] Thus, each one is an other, and each other is a one. None could be a one of many unless all were an other to the others.

The One Is the Same as the [Things] Not-One. The fourth argument refers back to the first and points beneath the complex singular individual to the indefinite magnitude of which it is composed and to which it is identical. The types of possible relation were limited within the all (πᾶν) to the relation of complexity (part/whole) and the relation of individuality (one to another). Parmenides here first establishes that the one and the others, or what he here calls "what are not-one" (τὰ μὴ ἕν, 146e6), cannot stand in the relationship of individual to individual, and he goes on to show that they cannot stand in a relation of complexity, i.e., part to whole or whole to part. By analogy to the first argument above, the one and the not-one cannot be other than one another, for the not-ones lack the requisite unity to stand in such a relation. However, in contrast to the first argument, the fourth will help us to see that the one and the not-one still differ, albeit in a way that does not violate the relationships of complexity and individuality.

Parmenides begins on the side of the difference between individuals. The same and the other, he says, are opposites (ἐναντία) (146d6),[38] and opposites will not consent to be "in" each other. Parmenides asks, will the same "ever consent to be in 'the other,' or 'the other' in 'the same'?" (Gill, 146d6–8).[39] Parmenides then points to the one and the not-one, and he says that other will not consent to be in either:

> So if the other will never be in the same, there is none of the things that are (τῶν ὄντων) in which the other is for any time (χρόνον οὐδένα), for if it were in anything for any time whatsoever (ὁντινοῦν), then for that time (ἐκεῖνον ἂν τὸν χρόνον) the other would be in the same (following Chrysakopoulou).
>
> εἰ ἄρα τὸ ἕτερον ἐν τῷ αὐτῷ μηδέποτε ἔσται, οὐδὲν ἔστι τῶν ὄντων ἐν ᾧ ἐστὶν τὸ ἕτερον χρόνον οὐδένα: εἰ γὰρ ὁντινοῦν εἴη ἔν τῳ, ἐκεῖνον ἂν τὸν χρόνον ἐν ταὐτῷ εἴη τὸ ἕτερον. (146d8–e2)

That Parmenides has in mind spatio-temporal individuals is clear from his reference to the things the other is in for "any time whatsoever." Parmenides also has in mind the paired contradictories of sameness and otherness, which is clear from the mutually exclusive relation between same and other, i.e., contradictories that exclude one another. The otherness possible on the basis of complexity or individuality is established between at least partial symmetry between the *relata*. If the one and what are not-one were not at least in some sense each "ones," they would "entirely escape" (πάντῃ . . . ἐκφεύγοι, 147a2) being other.[40]

If they are not other as individuals, they must either be the other as part to whole, which they cannot be if the not-one is "in every way not one" (or simply: in no way one). The one and the not-one cannot stand in part/whole relationship because the not-one does not have the integrity of either a part or a whole. The not-one, that is, does not partake in the one or in number, for if it did it would then not be "not-one" but would be in some way one. The one, by contrast, is "in every way one" (πάντῃ . . . ἕν ἐστι, 147a8), which I am taking to mean "fully integrated." From this Parmenides derives the conclusion that the one cannot be a part of the not-one nor a whole with the not-one as part. If the two do not share the basis for being different, they are incommensurate. Thus, the one and the not-one must be the same in the sense of exceeding the commensurate differences on which the arguments of this section are predicated. They are the same in the sense of lacking any external marks by which they could be distinguished. They simply do not stand in external relation to one another, for this would imply that they were subject to the same structures of identity and difference. The not-one is so different from the one that it cannot stand in relation to it and must be the same, as it were, beneath difference.

I take this section on same and other to teach us a lesson about the unlimited. The complex individual is the basis of our trust (*pistis*) and our most familiar bond to reality, but this individual is not what is most basic. By learning to see through the one-that-is to the background conditions on which it depends, such as the categories of relationality in same and other, we are able to free ourselves from the limitations and restrictions of the cave. One of those background conditions supportive of the one-that-is is the *apeiron* implied by the determinate intelligibility of the complex individual, such as being timelessly subject to the categories of motion and rest, or being timelessly subject to the possibility of division, i.e., being vulnerable to ingress and decomposition. We have been slowly gaining access to the *apeiron* indirectly through our dialectical focus on the part/whole and one/many structures that compose complex individuals because the *apeiron* depends for its intelligibility on those structures. The structure of the one-that-is allows us to conceive the undifferentiated; it is a speculum through which to conduct ontological inquiry. The analysis of the relationship of sameness between the one-that-is and what are not one (τὰ μὴ ἕν, 146e6) gives us a brief glimpse of the way in which the structures of difference and relation will be used to access, through a sort of *via negativa*, the *apeiron* and the other prior conditions that support and give rise to the most familiar and immediate of our bonds to reality.

Like/Unlike

In the discussion of the likeness and unlikeness of the one and the others, the object of analysis is again the character of the one-that-is both as individual and as integrated whole. Parmenides builds on the reciprocal determinacy analyzed in the previous account of same and other, where the one-that-is was shown to share otherness with other individual ones and to be the same as itself. Parmenides has drawn attention to those particular defining characters that the one-that-is, *qua* individual, either shares with others or can be shown with reference to others to possess. In both cases, the selfsameness of the one-that-is includes other ones.

The account of like and unlike builds on sameness and otherness a set of second order attributes, but it does so in a way that is unexpected. Parmenides argues that individual ones are like one another insofar as all are other than one another. The straightforward way to establish likeness between distinct individuals would be to point to their sameness, but Parmenides points to their difference. Why? It seems that the force of this unusual turn in argument is to draw attention to the one's being unlike the others at 148a8–c2, which will revisit the strange account of the sameness that obtains between the incommensurable one and the "not-ones" (τὰ μὴ ἕν, 146e6).

In Parmenides' argument for the likeness of the one and the others, being other than other individuals compels the one-that-is to undergo the same character as them, i.e., being other. Each of the one-of-many is other than the others in such a way that the others are other than it in the same way. Thus, their reciprocal difference was established, and on this basis Parmenides says that the one-that-is is like the others; they are likes, and they are therefore comparable. Each one shares the same character (otherness) as the other ones. Parmenides says,

> Then insofar as it has been so affected as to be different from the others, and they, similarly, [having been so affected as] to be different from it, the one would be affected similarly (ὡσαύτως) as the others, and the others as the one (modifying Chrysakopoulou).
>
> οὐκοῦν ᾗ ἕτερον εἶναι πέπονθεν τῶν ἄλλων καὶ τἆλλα ἐκείνου ὡσαύτως, ταύτῃ ταὐτὸν ἂν πεπονθότα εἶεν τό τε ἓν τοῖς ἄλλοις καὶ τἆλλα τῷ ἑνί. (147c6–8)

Being an other, each is like the others. Otherness serves as the foundation for comparison, and on the basis of their otherness, the ones-that-are can be subject to various shared but more limited respects in which they are all of the same sort. The most inclusive shared respect in which the ones are comparable is the likeness based on their otherness, for any possible individual subject to comparison will also be like in this respect. Parmenides points out that whether we invoke the otherness in things just a single time or many, we call out (προσαγορεύειν) the same thing, and we "always speak of the same" (ταὐτὸν καὶ λέγειν ἀεί, 147d6). Parmenides concludes that what has been affected by the same is alike:

> So in the respect the one is (so) affected as to be other than the others, in this respect itself it would be altogether like them all, because it is altogether other than them all.
>
> So it seems.
>
> ᾗ δὴ τὸ ἓν ἕτερον τῶν ἄλλων πέπονθεν εἶναι, κατ᾽ αὐτὸ τοῦτο ἅπαν ἅπασιν ὅμοιον ἂν εἴη: ἅπαν γὰρ ἁπάντων ἕτερόν ἐστιν. {—} ἔοικεν. (148a4–6)

When Parmenides says the one is "altogether like them all" (ἅπαν ἅπασιν ὅμοιον, 148a5) and "altogether other than them all" (ἅπαν . . . ἁπάντων ἕτερόν, 148a5), "altogether other" refers to the respect in which the one and other ones are numerically distinct. Insofar as one and the others are arithmetically distinct, they are in that respect the same as each and every one of the others.

It is, of course, rather odd that Parmenides uses otherness as the basis for likeness, and as I mentioned above his approach to the likeness argument foregrounds the unlikeness argument and links it back to the previous discussion of the one and what-are-not-one in the same/other section. Parmenides said that the one is "in every way" one (147a8) and the not-one is "in no way" one (147b1), referring to the one as fully integrated and the not-one as in no way integrated. The attributes of being "fully" and "in no way" integrated allowed the one and the not-one to be sufficiently incommensurate as to coincide. Parmenides turns now to the almost mechanical logic that opposing conclusions can be inferred from opposing premises. To wit, if being other implies that the one and the others are like, then we can infer that being same, because it is the opposite of being other, will entail that the one and the others are unlike. Parmenides says, "the same will make it unlike (ἀνομοιώσει), otherwise it [i.e., the same] will not be opposite to the other [i.e., otherness]" (148b5–6).[41]

The inference that the one and the not-one are made unlike by virtue of being the same is formal to the point of being sophistical, but looking to the content of this conclusion, we can see for ourselves that the one that is "in every way one" and the not-one that is "in no way one" are conjoined by their incommensurability. They are in fact "same" in the sense of being in the same one-that-is, and they are "unlike" in the sense of being incommensurate. They cannot exclude one another because they are incapable of entering into structured relation, as set out at the beginning of the section on same and other, between part and whole or one and another. The others, which are named in speech as distinct, are not capable of becoming an object *per se*, even if it is object-like in its distinction from and relation to the one.

To conclude, this section has shown us that the one-that-is cannot be itself without pointing beyond itself to others to which it is commensurate, *viz.* all those others with which it is subject to comparison, and to others with which it is incommensurately related, *viz.* what-are-not-one. In the relations of likeness and comparison, we begin to glimpse a way in which the plethora of intelligibility confronting us in any spatio-temporal individual implies a dichotomy between what is present to us and what constitutes that presence, i.e., what makes presence intelligible without itself becoming present as an object of trust (*pistis*).

Quantitative Relation

It has been my contention that the dialectical study of the one-that-is in H2 allows us to disassemble the type of object in which we primarily place our trust in order to use that object as a vehicle for gaining insight into its prior conditions. I have in the course of this study made the case that the examination of the distinct aspects of complexity and individuality of the one-that-is reveals the principles in which those aspects are gathered and explained. I have suggested that the best way to understand that prior principle of complexity and individuality is to see the complexity of the one as implying the singular individual's relation to other ones, and vice versa. In the present discussion, we will see Parmenides more explicitly join the description of the one *qua* whole of parts to its description as one of many.

In the earlier section on the spatiality of the one-that-is, Parmenides showed that the one-that-is was a spatial whole of spatial parts and, consequently, dependent on certain other categorial aspects, such as shape, being in itself and another, and motion and rest. I argued that the distinction between motion and rest as temporally distinct states of the one-that-is suggested and pointed us in the direction of the timeless "is" of the categories of motion and rest to which all temporally determinate ones are constitutively subject. In the section on the relational categories of same and other, Parmenides used the constitutive relationality of the one-that-is, and its relationship to the "not-one," to show that the incommensurability (unlikeness) of the individual one and the indefinite "not-one" allowed them to be the same, thereby drawing our attention to the *apeiron* of which the one consists.

In the present discussion of quantitative relation, the individuality of the one of many is shown to presuppose and depend on the spatiality of the whole of parts, and likewise the spatiality of the whole of parts is shown to depend on and presuppose the sameness and difference of the one of many, so we are being given a chance to see the prior conditions of the one-that-is gathered together in their structural unity. What we are increasingly given the opportunity to see is that the stepwise dismantling of the one-that-is points to and serves as the basis for describing (through a *via negativa* or negative portrait) the one of H1.

Contact: Coordinating Complexity and Individuality

In the arguments for contact (ἅπτεσθαι), a single feature of the one-that-is, i.e., its capacity for contact, points toward its complexity and individuality. By studying the nexus of complexity and individuality joined in the intelligible structure of contact, these sections on quantitative relation give us further opportunity to dissolve the one-that-is and to see that the ones we take to be basic are dependent on what is not immediately given. There are four conclusions for which Parmenides argues in this section: the one is in contact with itself and with the others (148d6–e7), the one is not in contact with itself (148e5–149a4), and the one is not in contact with the others (149a5–d5).

The first argument uses the complexity of a spatial whole of spatial parts to show that if the one is in itself, it is in contact with itself and "would be prevented from contacting the others" (τῶν μὲν ἄλλων ἀπείργοιτο ἅπτεσθαι, 148e1–2). In the second argument, if the one is in others it is in contact with the others. The one is thus in contact with itself and the others. The first argument points to the way that an individual, i.e., a one of many, has an internal spatiality, i.e., is "in itself," and its internal spatiality implies an external division from others. The second argument does the same. The one is "in the others," so it is in the space that their individuality carves out, separated from itself by their individuality.

In the third and fourth arguments, distinct conclusions are drawn regarding the relationship between the one and the others depending on what sense of others is in play. In the third argument, Parmenides says that the one is one and not two, so it cannot be described as "occupying the seat next to that one" (ταύτην τὴν ἕδραν κατέχον ἣ ἂν μετ' ἐκείνην, 148e6). The point he is making is negative, i.e., the one cannot lie adjacent to itself, insofar as it is one, i.e., individual. But the point we should be noticing is that two individuals touching each other stand in spatial relation to one another. Parmenides says that contact requires that one "lie adjacent to that which it is to contact" (ἐφεξῆς δεῖ κεῖσθαι ἐκείνῳ οὗ μέλλει ἅπτεσθαι, 148e5–6). Contact requires that individuality be the context for complexity. Parmenides emphasizes the sense in which contact draws out the spatiality of distinct individuals: two things in contact must be separate (χωρίς) from each other but adjacent (ἐφεξῆς) (149a5). As an individual, it is impossible that the one would consent, he says, to be in two places (ἐν δυοῖν χώραιν, 149a1).[42] Thus, "the same necessity" (ἡ αὐτὴ . . . ἀνάγκη) that keeps the one from being two keeps the one from being in two places and, thereby, prohibits it from being in contact with itself (149a2–3). In the fourth argument, it is not so much the spatiality of the individual that is being emphasized as the individuality of spatial aggregates. The one cannot contact the not-one because "we said, didn't we, that the others than the one were neither one nor partake in it, if they are others" (149c5–6).[43] If number is not in what-are-not-one, then there cannot be two, and if not two then there is no contact. The one is not in contact with the others insofar as it is individual and they are non-integral, so the two cannot hold themselves in the reciprocal relation necessary for contact.

We can see from these arguments that contact gathers together the aspects of complexity and individuality implied in the one-that-is. The separation necessary for contact between individuals implies that individuality is spatial, such that two numerically distinct ones are implicitly spatial wholes. Conversely, the separation of incommensurability between the one and what-are-not-one, which allows Parmenides to say that there is no contact between the one and the others in the fourth argument, reveals the subjection of spatiality to individuality, i.e., reveals that spatiality is circumscribed and defined in terms of individuals. I am claiming that there can be no spatial relation without individuals, but there can be no individuality without spatiality. When we are discussing the contact between one and other ones, contact implies mutuality and reciprocal difference. Being in contact implies belonging to a shared place, such that being a one implies openness to surroundings in which other ones are in principle present. A correlate to this point is that being one implies being vulnerable at the level of integrity and composition, not simply being comparable to others or gathered together with others at the level of number but also constituted in relation to them and open to them. In this analysis the individual one shows itself to be vulnerable in the sense that it depends on and requires others. Similarly, unless the one were in contact with itself as parts in the whole it would not be in place at all.[44] Thus, the individual's relation to others points to its own internal composition, and its internal composition points to other individuals. Contact shows that the one-that-is is both subject to the context into which it is set and separable from that context as a distinct and fully integrated whole. The limit that joins the one-that-is to its surroundings opens the one to external relation at the same time as it renders the one vulnerable to ingress. The same limit that opens the one to its surroundings as divisible also preserves its individuality.

Continuous Magnitude: Greater/Smaller/Equal

We are now given the opportunity, through fallacies in the arguments that the one is equal to, greater than, and smaller than itself and the others, to determine with greater precision the relationship between the phenomenal character of the one-that-is and its eidetic structure. Key to this section as a whole are two claims: (1) for something, e.g., smallness, to be "in the one" (ἐν τῷ ἑνὶ, 150a1), it must be in the whole or in a part of it (ἤτοι ἐν ὅλῳ ἂν ἢ ἐν μέρει αὐτοῦ ἐνείη, 150a2–3; Aristoteles answers this by saying "necessarily"), and (2) "But of course what is must always be somewhere" (Ἀλλὰ μὴν καὶ εἶναί που δεῖ τό γε ὂν ἀεί, 151a4–5).

Parmenides begins by distinguishing the being-one of the one-that-is from its being greater or less than or equal to others. Just on its own, or with reference to its being-one, a one is no greater than it is smaller. The ones-that-are can enter into relations of relative size, but they cannot explain or account for those relations from their being one. As such, the cause of that relation must be supplied from another source, and Parmenides says the causes of being specifically larger and smaller are the forms greatness and smallness. The size specification into which an individual one-that-is steps must be explained with reference to something other than the individual one. Parmenides says:

> If the one is greater or less than the others, or in turn the others greater than or less than the one, they would in no way be greater or lesser than each other by the one being one and the others being other than the one, that is, by their own being? But if each should have equality in addition to being the sorts of things they are, they would be equals [in relation] to each other: but if the others should have greatness and it smallness, or they [τά] greatness and it smallness, to which ever form greatness attached, that [one] would be greater, and that [one] to which smallness [attached] would be smaller? (modifying Gill)
>
> εἰ μεῖζον εἴη τὸ ἓν ἢ τἆλλα ἢ ἔλαττον, ἢ αὖ τὰ ἄλλα τοῦ ἑνὸς μείζω ἢ ἐλάττω, ἆρα οὐκ ἂν τῷ μὲν ἓν εἶναι τὸ ἓν καὶ τἆλλα (τῷ εἶναι) ἄλλα τοῦ ἑνὸς οὔτε τι μείζω οὔτε τι ἐλάττω ἂν εἴη ἀλλήλων αὐταῖς γε ταύταις ταῖς οὐσίαις; ἀλλ᾽ εἰ μὲν πρὸς τῷ τοιαῦτα εἶναι ἑκάτερα ἰσότητα ἔχοιεν, ἴσα ἂν εἴη πρὸς ἄλληλα: εἰ δὲ τὰ μὲν μέγεθος, τὸ δὲ σμικρότητα, ἢ καὶ μέγεθος μὲν τὸ ἕν, σμικρότητα δὲ τἆλλα, ὁποτέρῳ μὲν τῷ εἴδει μέγεθος προσείη, μεῖζον ἂν εἴη, ᾧ δὲ σμικρότης, ἔλαττον; (149d8–e8)

Because it has magnitude, the one-that-is can exceed or be exceeded by others, but neither of these determinate identities is built into its being-one. Insofar as the ones-that-are have magnitude constitutively, but that magnitude is not qualitatively determined in itself as being greater rather than smaller, the ones-that-are, prior to participation in greatness and smallness, cannot account for the specific qualitative relations in which they stand. If they could account for that relation, they would have to account for it by being what they are, i.e., one, but as Parmenides says, it is not "by being one" (τῷ μὲν ἓν εἶναι, 149e1–2) that the one is greater or smaller than the others.

There must be something that would explain, beyond magnitude, the one's being specifically greater or smaller. Parmenides identifies this cause as the two forms, greater and smaller:

> Then aren't there this pair of forms (εἴδη), greatness and smallness? For surely if there weren't they could not be opposed to each other and engendered in beings (following Gill & Miller)[45].
>
> οὐκοῦν ἐστόν γέ τινε τούτω εἴδη, τό τε μέγεθος καὶ ἡ σμικρότης; οὐ γὰρ ἄν που μὴ ὄντε γε ἐναντίω τε ἀλλήλοιν εἴτην καὶ ἐν τοῖς οὖσιν ἐγγιγνοίσθην. (149e8–150a1)

A one is spatially related to other ones, and it is greater or smaller in virtue of being in relation to these other ones, but it is only as subject to these forms that the one *is large* and *is small.*

Parmenides goes on to argue that these causal sources of being greater or smaller, if they are distinct from being-one, and yet are in the one-that-is, must be subject to the spatiality of being a part or having spatial magnitude of their own. The way he puts it is that the smallness of the one cannot be "engendered in" (ἐγγίγνεται, 150a2) the one, for it would need to be engendered either in the whole of the one or a part, both of which are impossible. If it were in the whole, the small would have to be stretched through (τεταμένη) it, being equal to a stretch of space or containing (περιέχουσα) it (150a4); Parmenides asks:

> Is smallness capable of being equal to something or greater than something, and doing [the works of] greatness and equality, but not its own [works]?
> Impossible.
>
> δυνατὸν οὖν σμικρότητα ἴσην τῳ εἶναι ἢ μείζω τινός, καὶ πράττειν τὰ μεγέθους τε καὶ ἰσότητος, ἀλλὰ μὴ τὰ ἑαυτῆς; {—} Ἀδύνατον. (150a7–b1)

Likewise, if the small were in a part, it would be equal to or larger than the part. Parmenides concludes that the only thing that will be small is "smallness itself" (αὐτῆς σμικρότητος, 150b7). Parmenides' spatialization of the very forms that make for spatial being provokes in us a thought-summoning need to distinguish between spatial being and the non-spatial source of spatial being.

The subsequent argument, namely that there is no greatness in the one-that-is, takes a different approach to make the same point. Parmenides might have shown that greatness could not be in the one-that-is, and indeed he does argue that if greatness were in something, then that something would be greater than the greatness that is in it. But Parmenides also argues that, having just proven that there is no smallness anywhere in anything, there is nothing to exceed (ὑπερέχειν, 150c2), so there is nothing in virtue of which to be larger. This demonstrates again that a one-that-is, whether a one of many or a whole of parts, does not imply determinate relation with others just insofar as it is one, and that therefore the relationship of exceeding and being-exceeded does not belong to the one-that-is *qua* one but to the forms to which the one, by virtue of its relation to other ones, is subject. Nothing has the power to exceed or be exceeded (τὴν δύναμιν τὴν τοῦ ὑπερέχειν καὶ ὑπερέχεσθαι, 150d1–2) except insofar as it partakes in the forms, and the one-that-is has neither greatness nor smallness with respect to the other ones or itself except by participation. Furthermore, greatness and smallness are a dyad in which greatness points internally to smallness, which it exceeds, and smallness points to greatness, by which it is exceeded.

Aristoteles in the end agrees that if the one is neither greater nor less than the others (μήτε μεῖζον μήτε ἔλαττον, 150d5), it neither exceeds nor is exceeded (μήτε ὑπερέχειν μήτε ὑπερέχεσθαι, 150d6), so it follows for him that the one must be equal to them. Parmenides permits this to pass: the one in relation to itself neither exceeds nor is exceeded, because having neither greatness nor smallness, so the one must be equal to itself. Aristoteles is falling prey to the fallacy that not being equal implies being unequal.

What this section allows us to see is that there is a type of relation to spatiality that is non-spatial. Prior to the spatiality of the one-that-is, providing the possibility for its spatiality, there must be being and being-one, whole-part complexity, individuality, same and other, likeness and unlikeness, contact and measure. Only on those bases can there be the phenomenal individual, which has its being determined in all of these ways and is in space and time, and will be able to have spatially extended things in it. Unless we draw a distinction between the prior eidetic structure of the one-that-is and its phenomenal existence, we will not be able to escape the fallacy that the one *qua* one must be equal because it is neither greater nor smaller. We would say first that, taken up as unspecified with respect to relative magnitude, the one is neither greater, nor smaller, nor equal. We have thus addressed the first of our two claims identified above that the only way to be in something is to be spatially extended in a spatially extended part or whole.

The puzzles immediately following in their discussion focus our attention to the second of our two claims from above that what-is must be somewhere, further drawing out the fallacious restriction of being to spatio-temporal being, which we have been tracking for some time. Parmenides asks us to imagine the whole, i.e., the one itself, as a thing that is larger than the parts of the whole. As a whole of parts, Parmenides says, the one is larger than itself, i.e., it is "around itself on the outside" (περὶ ἑαυτὸ . . . ἔξωθεν, 150e6). It is also smaller than itself because it is "in itself" (ἐν ἑαυτῷ, 150e4). The integrity of the one-that-is necessarily implies spatiality; its parts are inside the whole, and the whole surrounds the parts: "containing, it would be greater than itself" (περιέχον μὲν μεῖζον ἂν ἑαυτοῦ εἴη, 150e6–151a1), and "being contained, lesser" (περιεχόμενον δὲ ἔλαττον, 151a1). However, although it is true that the one is a spatial whole of spatial parts, the parts are in the whole, but the whole is not larger than its parts. The whole is all the parts; it does not contain the parts *qua* being a separate complex individual. The sense in which parts are in the whole cannot, it seems, be construed on the model of spatial containment; even the principle by which these parts belong to the whole and are in the whole remains obscure. The fallacy of the whole being a container of parts seems to reproduce the same lesson as the previous set of arguments, i.e., that we should not conceive being in self and other only on the model of spatial containment, i.e., on the model of the lesser being in the greater (ἐν μείζονι ἔσται ἔλαττον ὄν, 151a5–6). But it reproduces these lessons with reference not as much to the layered structure of the one-that-is as to the phenomenal expression of that structure: a whole is its parts; whole and parts are the one-that-is taken up in different respects. There is no whole *qua* container that we can open and empty out the parts, conceiving whole and parts as separate things, like a jar and its marbles.

The final set of arguments, that the one is greater and lesser than the others, provides the complement to the first set, that the one was neither greater nor lesser than the others. These are puzzling arguments, and it is hard to determine whether they are simply fallacious. Parmenides says that the one and the other individuals must be somewhere, if they are something. There is nothing apart from the others and the one, so the one is in the others and the others are in the one. Two things stand out here. The first is that individuals, which are greater and fewer in number, are being treated as indefinite magnitudes, i.e., as greater and smaller in size, and this represents a shift between distinct senses of multitude (πλῆθος), i.e., from number to size. The second is that we are almost obtrusively not positing something like space or context (περιέχον), as Aristotle does in *Physics* 8, when Parmenides says that the one individual is in the others. It seems to me that these two specifics in the text suggest that the eidetic structure of and between ones-that-are is prior to and constitutive of the idea of space as an empty container.

These points ask us to think not primarily in terms of spatial containment but in terms of the continuum of greater and smaller framed at either end by the extremes of one exceeding the other and the other exceeding the one.[46] Indefinite magnitude is the joint instantiation of greatness and smallness. Parmenides presses us to notice that the internal relations of the complex whole and the external relations of one individual to others require explanation that is not imagistic, i.e., is non-spatial. But Parmenides here goes only so far as disrupting the presumption that the one-that-is is basic and providing a context for this insight by showing us the structure of indefinite magnitude. Parmenides now turns to address the intelligibility of measure immanent to spatio-temporal particulars, shifting from quantity as indefinite magnitude to quantity as multitude.

Discrete Magnitude: Measure

Spatiality implies that any spatial one can be compared to any other, and as such any one can serve as the term in relation to which other ones are measured. Just as a smaller individual is the basis upon which the one-that-is can be "larger," so too the individual of a determinate size is the basis upon which another can be determined with respect to size. That basis of indefinite relation, in Parmenides' comments, develops into a definite relation in which magnitude is subject to number and "more than another" becomes "just so many more than the other."[47] Parmenides uses the translation of magnitude into multitude of measure to translate the greater/smaller than and equal to of the last section into more, fewer, and the same number of measures in this section. The obvious omission, particularly given the discussion of measure in H1, is that some indefinite measures cannot be reduced to a common numerical basis. Parmenides is leaving incommensurable magnitudes out of the account in this section.

The two aspects of the one-that-is, i.e., part/whole complexity and one/many plurality, are the two faces of being subject to spatiality. The character of spatiality is such as to be constituted by the forms, in relative measure, of larger and smaller, and also in definite measure, of greater and fewer. We have noted that Parmenides seems to be drawing special attention to the distinction between definite and indefinite magnitude, and he is drawing attention to the distinction between the eidetic and phenomenal being of the one-that-is, but we do not yet have the key that will explain the shifting and sharpening that has taken place.

Temporality

Through the course of H2, the arguments have helped us to see the dependencies of the spatio-temporal individual, e.g., that it be in a place, that it have shape and be capable of motion and rest, that it be the same as itself and other than other ones and not-ones, etc. The determinate character of the one-that-is has implied an eidetic structure by which the spatio-temporal one is articulated, a structure prior to and necessary for its existence. Any spatio-temporal individual rests on an eidetic foundation. Being this or that specific kind of individual will imply further defining structures, but kind-specific defining structures are not the concern of the hypotheses in the *Parmenides.* All individuals in space and time have an articulate structure that is necessarily true of them, and this constitutive eidetic structure will be fully and explicitly developed in H2a and H3 in relation to the notion of immanent form. The other implication of this analysis, namely that there is a general set of preconditions for substance forms, will be investigated in H5.

The temporality section is an analysis of the one-that-is insofar as it partakes of time (χρόνου μετέχει τὸ ἕν, 151e3), which picks up on the discussion initiated toward the end of H1 of temporally determinate being. The one-that-is partakes of being, and, on account of that participation, it "is."[48] Parmenides suggests that "'to be' is proper to it somehow, if one-is (εἴπερ ἓν ἔστιν),"[49] and as proper to the one, Parmenides asks Aristoteles: "is τὸ εἶναι nothing other than participation in being (οὐσία) with time present (μετὰ χρόνου τοῦ παρόντος)?" (151e8).[50] Aristoteles takes this to be true, and the implications are then examined. If being is participation in *ousia* with time present, then "was" is participation in *ousia* with time past, and "will be" is communion with *ousia* (οὐσίας ἐστὶ κοινωνία, 152a2) with time future. The question is not raised whether there is participation in *ousia* without time.

Both the question Parmenides asks and Aristoteles' answer are self-undermining. To define being as being-present points to the tenseless and timeless "is" of the whatness of being. Parmenides asks: "*is* (ἐστιν) being (τὸ εἶναι) nothing other than . . ." and Aristoteles answers "it *is* (ἔστι γάρ)," invoking a timeless *einai* on which Aristoteles relies in order to deny that being can be timeless (151e7–152a2). It is true that *both* the "is" that joins together eidetic structures—such as the "is" to which Aristoteles pointed when he agreed that "there is" a way of being that is not subject to space and time—*and* the temporally inflected "is" partake of *ousia*, but only temporal being partakes of it "with time present." What partakes in being, therefore, can be subject to time, but it is not subject to time because it partakes in being.[51] For if it were the case that all partaking in being is partaking with time present, there would be no temporal structures to discuss, no "what" to identify, and no possibility of agreement about what the one-that-is really is.[52] Thus, insofar as Aristoteles is drawing on a form of *einai* that he pointedly rejects, we readers are left to take responsibility for the conversation and to hold apart the different senses of being that Aristoteles conflates.

The ensuing discussion of temporality has two main parts. In the first they discuss the temporal one's relationship to itself; in the second they discuss its relationship to other ones. My aim in this section is to show that the eidetically structured region of variously interrelated possible attributes, which we have been elaborating step by step, has priority over temporal individuals. The account of the priority of the eidetically structured region over individual things will further clarify the eidetic structure of the one-that-is and will, thereby, point to a type of "is" that cannot be subject to temporality. Furthermore, the complementarity of one-of-many individuality and whole-of-parts complexity will reveal a type of *apeiron* into which individual spatio-temporal beings are set but which does not answer to forms. Thus, at the upper limit of the inquiry, the eidetic structure of any complex individual just as such points to certain universally constitutive forms that structure the one-that-is eidetically, and the lower limit of the inquiry points to a set of continua and an *apeiron* on which any one-that-is must be set. Both upper and lower limit together point to the notion of categorially constitutive participation, according to which the complexity and individuality of any one-that-is are drawn from sources outside the one-that-is. Through a study of limit, which is intimated in H1–2a, we will find ourselves called upon to study the *apeiron* and form in H3.

The Temporality of the One, Relative to Itself

Time passes. Parmenides argues from this that anything subject to time always becomes older than itself (ἀεὶ ἄρα πρεσβύτερον γίγνεται ἑαυτοῦ, εἴπερ προέρχεται κατὰ χρόνον, 152a4–5). But, he says, nothing can become older without becoming older than something younger, and if it is becoming older than itself, it must also be becoming younger than itself. The passing of time is articulated in the difference between two complementary aspects of the one-that-is, i.e., an older and younger aspect; "the older becomes older than a becoming younger."[53] Therefore, to be in time implies the "one" is two.

At the same time, however, the division between the older and younger aspects of what is in time is not between separate ones. It is a difference between aspects that have to be tethered to time somewhere. The one-that-is subject to time is pinned down mid-flight, as it were, with its past and future tethered to the present:

> But is it not older then when, at the now time, it is becoming in between the was and the will be? For I suppose passing from the then to the later it will not overleap the now.
>
> Surely no.
>
> Thus will it not cease becoming older then, when [it] encounters the now and does not become, but then already is, older. For going forward [it] would not then be seized by the now? A thing going forward is in such a condition as to lay hold of (ἐφάπτεσθαι) both the now and the later—releasing the now and reaching for the later, while becoming between both, the later and the now.
>
> True.
>
> If the all [that is] becoming must not bypass the now when it is at this point (κατὰ τοῦτο, 152c7), it always ceases becoming and is then the sort of thing that it happens to be becoming.
>
> It is evident.[54] (Gill, modified)
>
> ἔστι δὲ πρεσβύτερον ἆρ᾽ οὐχ ὅταν κατὰ τὸν νῦν χρόνον ᾖ γιγνόμενον τὸν μεταξὺ τοῦ ἦν τε καὶ ἔσται; οὐ γάρ που πορευόμενόν γε ἐκ τοῦ ποτὲ εἰς τὸ ἔπειτα ὑπερβήσεται τὸ νῦν. {—} οὐ γάρ. {—} ἆρ᾽ οὖν οὐκ ἐπίσχει τότε τοῦ γίγνεσθαι πρεσβύτερον, ἐπειδὰν [152c] τῷ νῦν ἐντύχῃ, καὶ οὐ γίγνεται, ἀλλ᾽ ἔστι τότ᾽ ἤδη πρεσβύτερον; προϊὸν γὰρ οὐκ ἄν ποτε ληφθείη ὑπὸ τοῦ νῦν. τὸ γὰρ προϊὸν οὕτως ἔχει ὡς ἀμφοτέρων ἐφάπτεσθαι, τοῦ τε νῦν καὶ τοῦ ἔπειτα, τοῦ μὲν νῦν ἀφιέμενον, τοῦ δ᾽ ἔπειτα ἐπιλαμβανόμενον, μεταξὺ ἀμφοτέρων γιγνόμενον, τοῦ τε ἔπειτα καὶ τοῦ νῦν. {—} ἀληθῆ. {—} εἰ δέ γε ἀνάγκη μὴ παρελθεῖν τὸ νῦν πᾶν τὸ γιγνόμενον, ἐπειδὰν κατὰ τοῦτο ᾖ, ἐπίσχει ἀεὶ τοῦ γίγνεσθαι καὶ ἔστι τότε τοῦτο ὅτι ἂν τύχῃ γιγνόμενον. {—} φαίνεται. (152b2–d2).

The now is characterized as a separate stopping point between two termini. Not yet having secured itself, already having let go of itself, the one encounters the now like a traveler at the crossroads. In the middle, somewhere between its beginning and end, Parmenides says the one is "seized by the now" (ληφθείη ὑπὸ τοῦ νῦν, 152c2–3), and, wherever it is, "then is the sort of thing that it happens to be becoming" (τότε τοῦτο ὅτι ἂν τύχῃ γιγνόμενον, 152d1–2). Being subject to contingency is a necessary aspect of the structure of the one-that-is as something subject to time.

When we consider the temporal "is" of the one-that-is, we are abstracting from the guided movement of development according to which certain individuals develop toward maturity. We are only considering abstract temporality in which something only ever "is" what it happens to be. There is no fruition, nor any aim, only abstract temporality. Without a governing form to guide its becoming, the is-now is just a midpoint in an abstract span divisible into opposing parts. Before and after, although inseparable, are not meaningfully related to one another, nor do they contain a specific development, shape, or momentum. They are only abstractly related as parts of the same empty temporal unfolding. Neither the process of becoming nor the "is-now" are normatively ordered by a defining form; they are constituted by a categorial form.

But even as an empty becoming, the temporality of the one-that-is has structure and measure, of a sort. Parmenides switches perspectives from the internally self-differentiating now to the externally cumulative span between the beginning and end of the process of becoming. From the outside, the one comes to be for an amount of time equal to itself. Its becoming is its own measure: it is the same age as itself. That is to say, the one participates in a continuous duration that is in principle available to be measured with respect to itself and other ones. Although there is nothing intrinsically ordering and guiding the accumulation of age, it is accumulating into an abstract amount. Just as all incremental change has a before and an after, all continuous change can be taken up in terms of a beginning and end.

This model of temporality is formally structured into two externally and arbitrarily related sides, *viz.* the self-othering advance of the one becoming older than itself (becoming younger) always at some point in time and, second, a distance traversed. There is a structure of time—past and future imply each other—but that structure neither implies nor reflects anything of the specific kinds of thing subject to time. The vector of older and younger, although always pointing toward the future and toward the past at some moment, does not point to a definite future and a definite past from any definite moment. That changes when Parmenides turns to consider the relationship between the one and other ones. That is, the one gains a definite relationship to itself by virtue of being taken up in relation to other ones.

The Temporality of the One, Relative to Others

At first Parmenides addresses the becoming of a one relative to other ones. Parmenides says, "The one comes to be first of all things that have number" (πάντων ἄρα τὸ ἓν πρῶτον γέγονε τῶν ἀριθμὸν ἐχόντων, 153b1–2). After there is the first, there can be a second; the first is therefore older, and the others are necessarily younger. Then Parmenides' arguments invoke the notion of becoming "according to nature" or, more precisely, becoming that is not "contrary to its nature" (παρὰ φύσιν τὴν αὑτοῦ, 153b8), in order to explore the being older, younger, and same-age of a temporally complex one relative to others. Parmenides shifts assumptions from one-of-many plurality to part/whole complexity. If there are parts, he says, there is beginning, middle, and end. The beginning differs from the one that is younger by virtue of not just being accidentally first but being necessarily first, i.e., first by nature. It is on the basis of coming first as a beginning and not simply as a one that there can be a completion to the becoming, i.e., what is last by nature. Parmenides calls this the fully integrated one, for which integrating completion comes last:

> Then doesn't the beginning come first for all things—both for the one itself and for each of the others—and after the beginning, everything else as well, until the end?
>
> Certainly.
>
> Furthermore, we shall say that all these others are parts of the whole and of the one, and that one itself has become one and whole concurrently with the end.
>
> Yes, we shall.
>
> The end, I think, comes to be latest, concurrently with this the one has naturally come to be, so that if the one itself does not become contrary to nature, having come to be simultaneously with the end, it would by nature have become the last of the others.
>
> Evidently. (modifying Chrysakopoulou)
>
> οὐκοῦν πάντων πρῶτον ἀρχὴ γίγνεται, καὶ αὐτοῦ τοῦ ἑνὸς καὶ ἑκάστου τῶν ἄλλων, καὶ μετὰ τὴν ἀρχὴν καὶ τἆλλα πάντα μέχρι τοῦ τέλους; {—} τί μήν; {—} καὶ μὴν μόριά γε φήσομεν ταῦτ᾽ εἶναι πάντα τἆλλα τοῦ ὅλου τε καὶ ἑνός, αὐτὸ δὲ ἐκεῖνο ἅμα τῇ τελευτῇ γεγονέναι ἕν τε καὶ ὅλον. {—} φήσομεν γάρ. {—} τελευτὴ δέ γε οἶμαι ὕστατον γίγνεται, τούτῳ δ᾽ ἅμα τὸ ἓν πέφυκε γίγνεσθαι: ὥστ᾽ εἴπερ ἀνάγκη αὐτὸ τὸ ἓν μὴ παρὰ φύσιν γίγνεσθαι, ἅμα τελευτῇ ἂν γεγονὸς ὕστατον ἂν τῶν ἄλλων πεφυκὸς εἴη γίγνεσθαι. {—} φαίνεται. (153c2–d3)[55]

A whole reaches its point of complete integration when the last in its order of parts is in place; the whole is complete when all the parts that belong to it have come to be. Parmenides goes on from here to conclude that what is last in the order of becoming—i.e., not the last part but the complete whole—is younger than all the others—i.e., the parts that compose that whole. Before the introduction of a "nature" that is becoming, the order of becoming was indefinite, for there was nothing to determine the right moment to stop, nor for that matter was there any proper point from which to begin. There simply was becoming one after another. Here, by contrast, a whole comes to be a complete set of parts. The "one itself," i.e., the complete whole, is younger than the others, i.e., its parts, insofar as the whole implies a complete set of parts. A definite end implies a definite beginning. However, we need not read too much into the idea of a defining nature. The order of parts leads to and prepares for completion, but this can be any order and any completion. The first term will ultimately have prepared for the last, but the order of terms need be no more intelligible than what, at minimum, is required for iteration of the same. For example, as long as we have a series of sounds that can be repeated, we need not have sounds that accord with the specific ratios of a note, harmony, rhythm, or melody.

At the same time, continuing with the image of a repeatable sequence of sounds, the first member of the series has an integrity of its own insofar as it opens up the field in which other series of sounds might have followed. Parmenides characterizes the plurality of moments in which the complete one consists as a plurality that in principle exceeds the whole in which they are ordered. There is a sense in which the previously determined one was indifferent to the other ones that were simply "the more" (τὰ πλείω, 153a7); similarly here the part has a determinacy of its own that is in principle separable from the whole to which it belongs. Parmenides asks,

> But then: must not a beginning, or any other part of the one whatsoever, or of anything else—if indeed it is a part, and not parts—be necessarily one, given that it is a part?
>
> Necessarily.
>
> Then the one would come to be at the same time as the first [part] that comes to be and also at the same time as the second, and fails to attend none of the others that come to be, whatever comes to be added to whatever, until it proceeds to the point of completion and comes to be one whole, leaving off neither middle nor first nor last nor any other in its coming to be.
>
> True. (Modifications on Chrysakopoulou.)

τί δὲ δή; ἀρχὴν ἢ ἄλλο μέρος ὁτιοῦν τοῦ ἑνὸς ἢ ἄλλου ὁτουοῦν, ἐάνπερ μέρος ᾖ ἀλλὰ μὴ μέρη, οὐκ ἀναγκαῖον ἓν εἶναι, μέρος γε ὄν; {—} ἀνάγκη. {—} οὐκοῦν τὸ ἓν ἅμα τε τῷ πρώτῳ γιγνομένῳ γίγνοιτ' ἂν καὶ [153e] ἅμα τῷ δευτέρῳ, καὶ οὐδενὸς ἀπολείπεται τῶν ἄλλων γιγνομένων, ὅτιπερ ἂν προσγίγνηται ὁτῳοῦν, ἕως ἂν πρὸς τὸ ἔσχατον διελθὸν ὅλον ἓν γένηται, οὔτε μέσου οὔτε πρώτου

> οὔτε ἐσχάτου οὔτε ἄλλου οὐδενὸς ἀπολειφθὲν ἐν τῇ γενέσει. {—} ἀληθῆ. (153d5–e5)

The parts of an iterable sequence are ordered toward the whole. Each part awaits the whole, as it were, and holds open the door for the whole coming to be "according to nature." But at the same time the parts have a determinacy of their own. Each is one, and each is attended by the one. The "one itself," i.e., the fully integrated whole, can be one insofar as each part is the one it is. The determinacy of the parts points to the whole to which each gives rise; conversely, the whole renders itself distinct in its parts. It is each part's having a specificity in the context of a culmination that allows the whole to call for and require just these parts. In this sense the one is concurrent with each of the parts and, he says, "has the same age" (τὴν αὐτὴν ἡλικίαν ἴσχει, 153e5) as the others.

Finally, Parmenides turns to address the becoming older and younger, as well as the becoming neither older nor younger, of the one and the other ones. Two ones can have an ordered relationship to each other that remains unchanged by time. They will always remain in the same relationship because any two ones that differ in age by an original amount will become neither older nor younger than each other for any duration in which that difference is measured. At the same time, however, as parts of a total time of existence, the two ones are subject to the context of the whole, such that the longer they stand in relation to each other, the smaller becomes their original difference in age (as long as they are). The younger is always becoming older than it originally was with respect to the older, and, conversely, the older is always becoming younger than it originally was with respect to the younger. The difference between these two examples helps foreground the role that the whole plays in distributing being to its parts.[56] The being of a temporal one is changed by the context it inhabits insofar as the whole demands specificity of its parts, and they stand in a fixed relation to each other giving rise to a context in which their relationship to each other is transformed. The part can, thereby, always become younger (relative to what it was older than) at the same time as it maintains a separate identity as a one, according to which it never is younger. We can see how a single one, i.e., a nature, attends each one of its parts, specifying them, and they in turn in their ordered relationship give rise to a context in light of which their relationship is transformed.

On the basis of these comments establishing the temporal structure of the one-that-is, Parmenides reverses the self-undermining result of H1. The one-that-is can have something that belongs to it and be of it, and therefore there can be knowledge, opinion, and perception of it. What this conclusion fails to recognize is precisely that the determinate intelligibility of the being of the one-that-is cannot be subject to time and space and has not been shown to be so subject. Had Aristoteles been following the elaboration of the ontological difference between being and becoming, he would object to this conclusion, and H2 would be as self-undermining as H1. When, therefore, we start over in H2a, it should come as a surprise to Aristoteles, but it should not come as any surprise to us.

Conclusion of H2

The ideas with which we begin the Hypotheses are difficult because they are the most basic terms of intelligibility and, thereby, the most fundamental. We have engaged in an extended analysis of the various ways in which one and being can be specified and thus rendered accessible to discursive analysis. The two ways in which we have specified these ideas are as (a) any individual just insofar as it is one, and (b) any individual insofar as it is subject to categories of abstract spatiality and temporality. The narrowing down of the one, through specification, into these two objects of analysis has revealed a series of puzzles that arise when different aspects of the one are taken in separation from others. The purpose of H1 and H2 was to separate out the distinct kinds of "is" and "one," so that we may see their mutual interdependence (H2a). Doing so, we begin a study of the way various specific senses of one and being are systematically related. The idea that spatio-temporal becoming implies an eidetic is-structure to support and structure it, and that these sources of intelligibility require the differentiation of becoming to be expressed, will occupy us in the remaining Hypotheses. After we first become more clear about the power of the form to institute limit in the *apeiron* (in H3), we will turn to the "is" of veridical predication (in H5) and clarify for ourselves the being of eidetic determinacy, which will put us in a position to understand the nature of appearance (H7).

CHAPTER 5

Transformed Perspective

In the previous two chapters we have seen that the one of H1, lacking parts and being unique, cannot be specified in any of the ways appropriate to the complex and singular individuals of H2. We have also seen that the one-that-is, in H2, is subject to determinately intelligible aspects that are structurally related. We have also tracked a developing contrast between the determinately intelligible aspects of the one-that-is and the unlimited into which it is set. In the course of this clarification, the foundation has been set for undermining and replacing the familiar assumption that individual spatio-temporal things are the ultimate constituents of reality, preparing us for the insight that the individual is dependent on a set of eidetic conditions that specify being and being one.

Beginning with the addendum to H2, the analysis now focuses on the relationship between the complex and singular individual and its causal conditions. Specifically, in H2a, the previous focus on complementary contraries that compose the intelligibility of the one-that-is shifts to the contradictory contraries that characterize the phenomenal existence of individual things subject to space and time. The instant (ἐξαίφνης), which Parmenides calls a "strange nature," does its work in the context of temporal change. It is an atemporal and a-spatial structure immanent to spatio-temporal individuals. It animates the intelligibility in things by allowing for change.

This chapter has three main sections. (1) The insight that the atemporal instant permeates and moors the one-that-is to its various determinately intelligible aspects will be developed into an account of the relationship between the constitutive limits of the one-that-is and the "not-one" (H3). (2) The clarification of the constitutive limits that integrate the "not-one" into intelligible ones will give way to an analysis of the eidetic structures in which the partless and unique eidetic ones that guide *legein* have a kind of being that allows them to become articulated as the objects of discursive knowing (H5). Finally, (3) the analysis concludes with an account of the appearance of the spatio-temporal one "in the cave" and the perspective to which appearance appears.

H2a—The Instant

The opening of H2a suggests a third attempt at the study of the hypothesis of the one. At first it is not clear exactly which one is now under discussion. The conclusions of H1 and H2 stand in direct contradiction to one another, offering no immediate indication of the route to be taken. H1 ended with the assertion that the one neither is nor is one and, therefore, has nothing that belongs to it, i.e., no name, no account, no knowledge, no perception, assertions that Aristoteles was eager to reject. H2 ends with the opposite assertion that the one is and becomes in the past, present, and future and, therefore, something could belong to it, there would be knowledge, perception, and opinion of it, assertions which Aristoteles is eager to accept. If we are to know how to proceed, we need to assess the referent of the attributions gathered at the outset of H2a.

Parmenides at first invites us to "speak of it a third time," which suggests a study coordinate to the introductions of H1 and H2. But when he looks back to "the sort of [one] we have detailed," he identifies this as something that (a) is "both one and many," (b) is "neither one nor many," and (c) "partake[s] of time."[1] There is no punctuation to suggest that these three characterizations refer to different objects of analysis, so we should hesitate before assuming that we are now discussing both ones of H1 and H2 or that we are discussing some third one formed out of these other two. But what could be both one and many and neither one nor many as it partakes of time? The one of H2, i.e., the one-that-is, is both one and many insofar as it is a whole of parts, i.e., one whole with many definite parts, but the one of H1 was determined to be neither one nor many, so we seem to be looking at attributions gathered from both H1 and H2. However, the one of H2 was also "what is not one" insofar as it is the same as what-are-not-one beneath composition, and, being beneath composition, it was not [a definite] many.[2] Thus, if the one in H2a is only one of the ones we have previously discussed, it would have to be the one-that-is of H2.

The one of H2a, however, is not being analyzed under the same description as the one-that-is. In H2 the one-that-is was discussed in terms of the complementary contraries in which it can be, for example, one *and* many, but in H2a the one is being discussed in terms of the contradictory contraries to which it is subject, for example, at different times. Parmenides describes the relationship between contraries as "partaking in being" and "not partaking in being."[3] He says that the one partakes in being and so is a one-of-many, i.e., a whole of parts. The one, he says, also does not partake of being and "is not" (οὐκ ἔστι, 155e6), i.e., "is not [one]." Between being a one-of-many and being neither-one-nor-many, Parmenides says, there must be coming to be and ceasing to be, i.e., substantial change, which he characterizes as "getting and releasing being" (λαμβάνον τε καὶ ἀφιὲν οὐσίαν, 156a7).[4] As if to emphasize that he has in mind the contrast between being fully integrated (i.e., one-and-many) and being an indefinite plurality (i.e., many), Parmenides describes a transitional period between these two states as processes of "separating and combining" (διακρίνεσθαί τε καὶ συγκρίνεσθαι, 156b5). Being one and not-one are here treated as mutually exclusive periods in time, i.e., mutually exclusive periods in which the one-that-is is integrated and disintegrated. The one-that-is must partake in being, i.e., at the moment the one partakes in being [*viz*., one], it cannot *not* partake in being [*viz*., one]; conversely, when it does not partake in being, it cannot partake in being [*viz*., one], but it must partake in being something else, i.e., many.[5] As Parmenides puts this point, the one that partakes in being one is fully integrated, so it "will not be able" (οἷόν τε ἔσται, 155e7) not to partake in being one, i.e., it will be integrated *until* it ceases to exist, at which point it becomes [indefinitely] many. What is therefore distinctive about H2a is not the object of study, which remains the one-that-is, but the aspect under which that object is studied. That is to say, we are now examining the one-that-is as characterized by contradictories in the context of change, including substantial change, as opposed to studying it as characterized by complementary contraries, as we did in H2.

If the one-that-is is to gain and lose substantial unity, it must seize and let go of being [*viz*., one], which implies transition, either a transition between contradictory states or between a state and its contradictory process. In the transitional instant, such as the moment between being-one and ceasing to be-one, there must be a third thing. There must be an instant in which the one neither "is" nor "is not" one, i.e., is neither of the two contradictory states that are exhaustive of its possibilities for spatio-temporal determinacy. The question is this: given Aristoteles' assumption that all being is spatio-temporally determinate being, what is the one when it neither is one nor many but is in between? What is the one in the instant that it transitions between participation in contradictory characters? It must be in a way that exceeds and comprehends spatio-temporal being and the mutually exclusive and completely exhaustive separate moments into which the contradictory states of substantial change are distributed. Parmenides says that when something in motion comes to rest, or when something at rest begins to move, "I suppose it must be in no time" (δεῖ δήπου αὐτό γε μηδ' ἐν ἑνὶ χρόνῳ εἶναι, 156c1–2). The emphasis for inquiry is the being of what is not in time. Parmenides continues:

> But there is no time in which something is able to be simultaneously neither in motion nor at rest.
>
> Quite right.
>
> Furthermore, it does not change without changing.
>
> Not likely.
>
> So does it *ever* change? For it changes neither being at rest nor in motion, nor being in time.
>
> Quite right.
>
> Χρόνος δέ γε οὐδεὶς ἔστιν, ἐν ᾧ τι οἷόν τε ἅμα μήτε κινεῖσθαι μήτε ἑστάναι. {—} Οὐ γὰρ οὖν. {—} Ἀλλ' οὐδὲ μὴν μεταβάλλει ἄνευ τοῦ μεταβάλλειν. {—} Οὐκ εἰκός. {—} Πότ' οὖν μεταβάλλει; οὔτε γὰρ ἑστὸς ὂν οὔτε κινούμενον μεταβάλλει, οὔτε ἐν χρόνῳ ὄν. {—} Οὐ γὰρ οὖν. (156c6–d1)

Again, the crucial point here is that there is a being that is not in time, and that the "one" must "be" in a way that is not temporally determinate.

With the question of continuity in mind, and given that the one is neither an individual whole of parts nor a disintegrated many at the instant of its transition between the two, what is it that allows the one to be the same through change? What is it that could join contradictory states, or could join a state with a contradictory process? Immediately we can see that there would be a very strong presumption against the sameness of perceptibles if what were "there" were nothing but contradictory characters distributed into distinct times. A mere many, whether decomposed into unrelated integral moments or falling short of integration, cannot be "a" thing at all and, therefore, cannot be at all. The phenomenon of change forces us to see that sameness is the basis on which change and difference are intelligible.[6] Parmenides focuses our attention on the instants of discontinuity at which the one is in transition between the contradictory conditions detailed above.

What we are attempting to think is the causal dependence that determines the one in such a way that it can be subject to temporal change, including genesis and destruction. Attending to the transitional moment thus reveals to us that there is a type of being that exceeds and contains existence within its scope. Becoming one from many or many from one, where these terms describe substantial becoming and destruction, is a shift between two specifications of the being of the one-that-is. The moment of seizing onto being [one individual whole of parts] is a letting go of being [a disintegrated many], where the pivot from one to the other never gets outside or behind being but takes place within the range of being that is laid out for it.

Altogether, Parmenides has laid out the contrary states and processes for being, unity, likeness/unlikeness (ὁμοιοῦσθαί τε καὶ ἀνομοιοῦσθαι, 156b6–7), size (including the process of growth, equalizing, and reduction [αὐξάνεσθαί τε καὶ φθίνειν καὶ ἰσοῦσθαι, 156b8]), and motion/rest). In general summation, Parmenides uses motion and rest (ἵστηται καὶ . . . κινεῖσθαι, 156c1–2) to characterize change (μεταβάλλειν) in the one, *viz.*, change in substance, quality, and quantity is instructively illustrated in terms of motion and rest (κινήσεών τε καὶ στάσεων, 157a2), which are now used to refer to the motion of change and the rest of an at least temporarily stable condition. The instant (ἐξαίφνης), "that strange *phusis*, sits between motion and rest" (αὕτη φύσις ἄτοπός . . . ἐγκάθηται μεταξὺ τῆς κινήσεώς τε καὶ στάσεως, 156d6–7), and it is that from which and to which all change occurs.[7] The question is how we are to think of the relationship between the one-that-is and the instant, for if the spatio-temporal one is situated in the instant, it could never be subject to temporality, but the instant is not in time.

> Then according to the same *logos* [it is] neither one nor many [when] going (εἶμι) from one to many and from many to one, neither divided nor combined. And [it is] neither like nor unlike [when] going from like to unlike and from unlike to like, neither becoming like nor becoming unlike. Also [it is] neither small nor large nor equal [when] going from small to large and from equal to the opposites, it would be neither increasing nor diminishing nor becoming equal.
>
> κατὰ δὴ τὸν αὐτὸν λόγον καὶ ἐξ ἑνὸς ἐπὶ πολλὰ ἰὸν καὶ ἐκ πολλῶν ἐφ' ἓν οὔτε ἕν ἐστιν οὔτε πολλά, οὔτε διακρίνεται οὔτε συγκρίνεται. καὶ ἐξ ὁμοίου ἐπὶ ἀνόμοιον καὶ ἐξ ἀνομοίου ἐπὶ ὅμοιον ἰὸν οὔτε ὅμοιον οὔτε ἀνόμοιον, οὔτε ὁμοιούμενον οὔτε ἀνομοιούμενον: καὶ ἐκ σμικροῦ ἐπὶ μέγα καὶ ἐπὶ ἴσον καὶ εἰς τὰ ἐναντία ἰὸν οὔτε σμικρὸν οὔτε μέγα οὔτε ἴσον, οὔτε αὐξανόμενον οὔτε φθῖνον οὔτε ἰσούμενον εἴη ἄν. (157a4–b3)

The instant reveals the necessity of a causal relationship between the one that is subject to time and, thereby, subject to either one or the other of two contradictories, and a one that is causally prior and not in space and time but in the instant.[8] The spatio-temporal one, which is subject to both being-one and being-many, i.e., integrated and disintegrated, must be neither one nor the other in the transition between them. In order for substantial change between being-one and being-many to occur, and in order for being to be specified as being either one of two contradictories, the one must be neither of these contradictories, which is impossible within the confines of spatio-temporal existence. It is possible only if we extend the existence of spatio-temporal ones to include eidetic being and acknowledge a type of being prior to and foundational for spatio-temporal existence.

It is difficult to characterize the relationship between the founding and the founded term, but it seems prudent to say that what the temporal one is in the instant it is always, throughout its existence. That is to say, the one-that-is is always open to change between its defining contradictories insofar as it is subject to becoming, and change for it is always characterized by these contradictories; they are categorial aspects of its existence. The very flux that characterizes becoming would not be possible unless there were an instant in which and from which the one-that-is could be categorially determined by and open to defining contraries. The various participations of the one-that-is in being-one and being-many, or being-like and being-unlike, etc., call for us to think of something, some specific kind of "one," that would distribute and relate these various contradictories in such a way as to preserve the one-that-is through change. Given that change includes the substantial genesis and destruction of the one-that-is, we are prohibited from thinking of the one-that-is as the ultimate subject of that change. That is, H2a shows that the one of H2 calls for and demands the one of H1, i.e., what we can now identify as the substantial form of the one-that-is. The substantial form specifies the one-that-is as one or as many, in motion or at rest, etc., and the substantial form that determines and relates these different phases of being.

The analysis of the instant shows that for anything subject to time, at each moment (including the moment before substantial genesis and the moment after its substantial destruction), eidetic being is most basic and fundamental. "Exists" and "does not exist" are shorthand for "partakes in being one and many subject to space and time" and "partakes in being neither one nor many subject to space and time," where being-one-and-many refers to substantial unity and being-neither-one-nor-many refers to decomposition. The meaning of the being must be extended beyond the specifically spatio-temporal "is" accepted by Aristoteles and elaborated in H2 to include the type of timeless being negatively elaborated in H1. Furthermore, the discontinuity implicit in the contradictory contraries constitutive of the one-that-is, including substantial genesis and decay, require a type of one that is not subject to time and that can distribute and relate these contradictories. What we will go on to see in H3 is that substantial form is the founding term for the one-that-is, and we will examine how it is permissible to speak of the founding relation. We will also see that the substantial form requires, if it is to be instantiated, that it be instantiated according to certain structured oppositions to which the one of H2 is subject. Thus, it is to the relationship between the ones of H1 and H2 that we turn in H3.

H3–H4—Limit and the Unlimited

According to the plan for the Hypotheses, H3 was scheduled to treat what must result for the others both in relation to the one and in relation to themselves, if [a] one is.[9] It is, of course, left up to us to determine what "one" and "others" mean in this context. As we sort out the referents and arguments of H3, we will begin to see the priority of form over spatio-temporal individuals, and we will want to know how the discovery of this priority transforms the account of the complex individuals in which we place our pre-reflective trust.[10] Key to this hypothesis is the emergence of the concepts of *plēthos* and limit (πέρας) as complements to the instant.

Looking back over the results of past Hypotheses for the sake of situating H3, we recall that H1 has detailed a one that is neither/nor with respect to the very attributes to which the one in H2 is both/and. That is, the one of H1 was said at certain points to be neither one nor many, neither straight nor round, neither in motion nor at rest, neither same nor other, etc., while the one of H2 was said to be both one and many, straight and round, and so on. H2a has alerted us that if the one in H2 is going to be both/and with respect to these attributes, it must in some sense *be* in the instant and not in time. Thus, H2a has alerted us to the possibility that the one of H2 must in some sense be the one of H1, and the purpose of H3, I claim, will be to demonstrate the implications of this truth. Parmenides' goal in this section will be to build on the results of the discussion of temporal continuity in the addendum on the instant to provoke insight into the eidetic structure of the singular and complex others and what we might provisionally call their material trace.

In the analysis of H2a, I suggested that substantial form is prior to temporal existence and that the substantial form assigns contradictory attributes of, for example, being in motion and being at rest to distinct periods of the existence of the one-that-is. Substantial form thus became the source of continuity through change. But Parmenides has not yet detailed the mechanism for the instantiation of this sort of "one" in spatio-temporal particulars. In H3, the mechanism by which the ones of H1 relates to and reconciles the contradictory characters of the one of H2 is described as the imposition of limit on the *plēthos*. Note, however, that unlike the one of H2a, the others of H3 are studied not in terms of their temporal character but in terms of their spatial limits.

The hypothesis opens by contrasting the others to the one, specifically the singularity and complexity of the others to the simplicity of the one. Parmenides says, "If they are others than the one, the others are not that one [that we hypothesized]" (ἐπείπερ ἄλλα τοῦ ἑνός ἐστιν, οὔτε τὸ ἕν ἐστι τἆλλα, 157b8). They are not thereby "deprived in all ways" (στέρεταί γε παντάπασι) but "participate in some way" (μετέχει πῃ) (157c1–2).[11] The others in H3 are one *qua* whole, i.e., composed of many parts (τό γε ὅλον ἓν ἐκ πολλῶν ἀνάγκη εἶναι, 157c6), for if they did not have parts, they would be entirely one (παντελῶς ἂν ἓν εἴη, 157c4).[12] Furthermore, each part is a one *qua* singular, insofar as "the 'each' signifies being one divided (ἀφωρισμένον) from the others and being in accord with itself" (158a1–3).

Parmenides makes it clear that in spite of their similarity to the one-that-is of H2, the others in H3 entail ontological structure by virtue of being ordered parts composing "some one character and some one that we call whole" (μιᾶς τινὸς ἰδέας καὶ ἑνός τινος ὃ καλοῦμεν ὅλον, 157d8–e1). The first decisive argument in H3 shows that the whole of parts is fundamentally distinct from numerical multiplicity, i.e., a many:[13]

> But surely the whole, of which the parts will be parts, must be a one [composed] of many, for each of the parts must be a part, not of many, but of a whole. (Modifying Chrysakopoulou.)
>
> ἀλλὰ μὴν τό γε ὅλον ἓν ἐκ πολλῶν ἀνάγκη εἶναι, οὗ ἔσται μόρια τὰ μόρια: ἕκαστον γὰρ τῶν μορίων οὐ πολλῶν μόριον χρὴ εἶναι, ἀλλὰ ὅλου. (157c5–8)

The parts, therefore, are numerically many, but they are not simply many. If each part were, *per impossibile*, a part of many in which it was a member, Parmenides says, absurd results would follow. Either the part would be part of itself, which is impossible—it is impossible for it to be a part "of itself" (ἑαυτοῦ, 157d1)—or the part would be part of all the others except itself. If the part is not a part of each, Parmenides says, "it will be [a part] of none of the many" (οὐδενὸς τῶν πολλῶν ἔσται, 157d4–5). The argument here is extremely obscure and difficult to interpret even by the high standards set by the *Parmenides*. I favor the view that the many is here simply identical to each and every one of the parts. It would follow that if there were even one of the many to which the part in question did not belong, it would not be part of what is identical to the many.[14] Of course, this logic only works if we do not posit a whole and the many is nothing other than its parts, and the argument is designed to show us that we conceive multiplicity only on the basis of a prior unity.[15] Although this falls short of a fundamental difference in kind between parts and whole, the one whole is ontologically distinct from the ones of which it is composed:

> Then the part is a part neither of the many nor of all, but rather of some one character, of some one which we call a "whole," a complete one having become from all, this is what the part would be a part of.
>
> By all means.
>
> Then if the others have parts, [they] would partake of the whole, namely (καί) of [a] one.
>
> οὐκ ἄρα τῶν πολλῶν οὐδὲ πάντων τὸ μόριον μόριον, ἀλλὰ μιᾶς τινὸς ἰδέας καὶ ἑνός τινος ὃ καλοῦμεν ὅλον, ἐξ ἁπάντων ἓν τέλειον γεγονός, τούτου μόριον ἂν τὸ μόριον εἴη. {—} Παντάπασι μὲν οὖν. {—} εἰ ἄρα τἆλλα μόρια ἔχει, κἂν τοῦ ὅλου τε καὶ ἑνὸς μετέχοι. (157d7–e3)

On the one hand, this description implies a normative source to which the ordered parts are drawn, i.e., "some one character" (μιᾶς τινὸς ἰδέας, 157d8) that organizes and articulates the parts into a whole and is, therefore, the source and condition for its completeness (τέλειον, 157e4).[16] On the other hand, those parts are just "ones" of their own, and to that extent they are the primary reality constitutive of a sum or aggregate. Parmenides thus refers to the part as an "each," which in spite of having its place established by the whole on which it depends, enjoys relatively independent integrity:

> Furthermore there is the same *logos* concerning each part: for it is necessary that this too [i.e., each part] partake of the one. For if each of them is a part, then "each" of course signifies to be one, marked off from the others, being by itself, if indeed [it] will be [an] "each."
>
> καὶ μὴν καὶ περὶ τοῦ μορίου γε ἑκάστου ὁ αὐτὸς λόγος: καὶ γὰρ τοῦτο ἀνάγκη μετέχειν τοῦ ἑνός. εἰ γὰρ ἕκαστον αὐτῶν μόριόν ἐστι, τό γε ἕκαστον εἶναι ἓν δήπου σημαίνει, ἀφωρισμένον μὲν τῶν ἄλλων, καθ' αὑτὸ δὲ ὄν, εἴπερ ἕκαστον ἔσται. (157e5–158a3)

In order that the "others" be able to partake of the one, each part must be "marked off from" (ἀφωρισμένον, 158a2) the others and, in some sense, must have an independently distinctive being (καθ' αὑτὸ δὲ ὄν, 158a2–3). The parts must possess a degree of independence from the whole and from each other, even as they are at the same time drawn toward each other and placed within the whole as subject to a single idea. Insofar as the one whole governs the parts, it demands separate determinacy from each, but insofar as each part is marked off from the others, the whole is just the sum of individually integral parts. The point here is to outline the minimum condition for saying the "others," and what we learn so far is that the others must be complex and singular. What we begin to see through analysis of the arguments is that complexity and singularity, despite their difference, are normative sources that depend on one another reciprocally.

Parmenides now moves to introduce the decisive concepts of "limit" (πέρας, 158d1–2) and "multitudes" (πλήθη, 158c1), which I think will clarify the distinction between normative source and the complex and singular individual. The transition consists of two steps, each of which is intended to establish the ontological specificity of the singular and complex individual between the one in which it partakes and the *plēthos* into which it is set. First, we can distinguish between two types of "limit": the limit received by the "parts" of the whole (158c9–d2), which orders those parts and composes the whole, and the limit received by the "others" (158d6), which integrates the individual and sets it off from other individuals. Both of these limits are imposed upon a prior condition that is, according to its own nature, unlimited in magnitude (πλήθει ἄπειρα, 158b6).

In the imagined moment before participation in the one, neither part nor whole is integrated and definite. It is through participation in the one that the basis for the individual whole is first constituted. Through participation, the others emerge as "more than one," i.e., many ones:

> But since the participants of the one part and the one whole are more (πλείω) than one, must not those participants of the one themselves be, before [participation], unlimited in multitude?[17]
>
> ἐπεὶ δέ γε πλείω ἑνός ἐστι τά τε τοῦ ἑνὸς μορίου καὶ τὰ τοῦ ἑνὸς ὅλου μετέχοντα, οὐκ ἀνάγκη ἤδη πλήθει ἄπειρα εἶναι αὐτά γε ἐκεῖνα τὰ μεταλαμβάνοντα τοῦ ἑνός; (158b5–7)

Before participation, the participants are not even plural. They are disintegrated and not at all one, i.e., the sort of thing that Parmenides first introduced in the argument for the sameness of the one-that-is and the what-are-not-one in H2 (cf. Chapter 4, "The One Is the Same as the [Things] Not-One," above). Participation allows there to emerge an individual whole of parts, i.e., what in H2 was called a one-that-is, which here bears the trace of the unlimited in its identity. The unlimited itself, however, remains a trace that can be accessed only indirectly through a thought experiment:

> Let us observe the following: Then, at the very time when they participate in it, do they participate while not being one and not partaking in that one?
>
> Clearly.
>
> Isn't it the case that [they participate] while being multitudes, in which that one is not present?
>
> Indeed, multitudes.
>
> If we should be willing in thought (τῇ διανοίᾳ) to subtract from these sorts the least we are able, is it not necessary for that [portion] separated, if indeed it does not partake of the one, to be a multitude, too, and not one?
>
> Necessarily.
>
> Ὧδε ἴδωμεν. ἄλλο τι οὐχ ἓν ὄντα οὐδὲ μετέχοντα τοῦ ἑνὸς τότε, ὅτε μεταλαμβάνει αὐτοῦ, μεταλαμβάνει; {—} Δῆλα δή. {—} Οὐκοῦν πλήθη ὄντα, ἐν οἷς τὸ ἓν οὐκ ἔνι; {—} Πλήθη μέντοι. {—} εἰ ἐθέλοιμεν τῇ διανοίᾳ τῶν τοιούτων ἀφελεῖν ὡς οἷοί τέ ἐσμεν ὅτι ὀλίγιστον, οὐκ ἀνάγκη καὶ τὸ ἀφαιρεθὲν ἐκεῖνο, εἴπερ τοῦ ἑνὸς μὴ μετέχοι, πλῆθος εἶναι καὶ οὐχ ἕν; {—} Ἀνάγκη. (158b8–c5)

The multitude has a nature "alone by itself" (αὐτὴν καθ' αὐτὴν, 158c5) that is "other than the form" (ἑτέραν . . . τοῦ εἴδους, 158c6). Prior to their constitution as parts through participation in the one, however, the others are an unlimited multitude. For them, participation consists of the imposition of limit on the unlimited. The two senses of "limit," i.e., part to part within the organized whole and the limit of the individual relative to other whole(s)-of-parts, are captured in these passages:

> Furthermore, when each one part becomes part, it has a limit toward each other and toward the whole, and the whole in relation to the parts.
>
> Certainly.
>
> Accordingly, it follows for the others than the one that from the one and from themselves gaining communion, as it seems, something different (ἕτερόν τι) comes to be in them which provides a

> limit for them in relation to each other; but their own nature, by themselves, provides unlimitedness.[18]
>
> Καὶ μὴν ἐπειδάν γε ἓν ἕκαστον μόριον μόριον γένηται, πέρας ἤδη ἔχει πρὸς ἄλληλα καὶ πρὸς τὸ ὅλον, καὶ τὸ ὅλον πρὸς τὰ μόρια. {—} Κομιδῇ μὲν οὖν. {—} τοῖς ἄλλοις δὴ τοῦ ἑνὸς συμβαίνει ἐκ μὲν τοῦ ἑνὸς καὶ ἐξ ἑαυτῶν κοινωνησάντων, ὡς ἔοικεν, ἕτερόν τι γίγνεσθαι ἐν ἑαυτοῖς, ὃ δὴ πέρας παρέσχε πρὸς ἄλληλα: ἡ δ' ἑαυτῶν φύσις καθ' ἑαυτὰ παρέσχε ἀπειρίαν. (158c7–d6)

"Something else" (ἕτερόν τι) comes to be in multitude, and thereby "a limit is provided" for the things other than the one, which establishes them as individuals in relation to each other.[19] The organized individual, with its standard of completeness, depends on a double imposition of limit as complex whole of parts and as individual among other individuals.

Behind each of these limits the unlimited receives and supports limit as what we might call a material condition. Parmenides makes this point when, concluding H3, he establishes the likeness and unlikeness of the others with respect to themselves and each other: by their own nature, as *plēthē*, the others are unlimited and have an attribute that is the same. Similarly, they all partake of limit and have an attribute the same. But insofar as each is limited and unlimited, their attributes are opposite, which Parmenides says are "as unlike as possible" (ὡς οἷόν τε ἀνομοιότατα, 159a1–2). In respect of both attributes taken together, the others are most opposite and unlike themselves (ἐναντιώτατά τε καὶ ἀνομοιότατα, 159a4), i.e., as a limited one in relation to the *plēthē*, and unlike each other, i.e., as limited ones in relation to the *plēthē* in others. Two ideas, one and the *plēthē*, set the terms: one organizes the part/whole complex through *perata* from above, and *plēthē* are ordered into integral constituents from below. Neither of these terms are in the others. The one is embodied separately by all its various instances, and *plēthē*, which the individual whole(s) emerge from and which they can decompose back into.[20]

The point I would like to make on this basis is that the causal efficacy of the single form is inseparable from the causal facilitation performed or provided by the indeterminacy of the *plēthē*. The whole of parts is, from the ground up, bound by the form's causal priority, but it also owes itself to the power of the *plēthē* to receive limit, such that parts can be separated and brought into relation. Anything that has integrity, i.e., either the whole or its parts, has limits that answer to the form and point to the indefinite multitude in which those limits are set. Those limits are thereby fragile—they can at any moment be decomposed into the *plēthē* on which they rest.

This analysis answers the question of the divisibility presupposed but not explained in the analysis of H1 and H2 (cf. especially the two derivations in Chapter 4, "The Abstract Intelligibility of Spatially Determinate Individuals"). The intelligible structure of the one-that-is was given through the list of complementary contraries in H2, and in H2a we saw that the continuity through time of the one-that-is requires that it "be" in some sense the "one" of H1, not subject to time. H3 has now provided a sense of constitutive limit that renders the whole a complete individual. Thus, the idea of constitutive limit, bearing the trace of the unlimited in the fragility of the limits of the one-that-is, gives us a sense of how an embodied one must be understood and what the limitations of its intelligibility must be.

H4

H4 reinforces our understanding of the necessity of the H3 account by providing a *reductio* argument to show that in the absence of participation, the distinction between the one and the others entails the impossibility of both the one and the others. Parmenides frames H4 as the discussion of whether the things other than the one "are also not so, or only so" (καὶ οὐχ οὕτως ἔχει . . . ἢ οὕτω μόνον, 159b2–3). The structure of the *reductio* will be to show that unless there are complex individuals, which are only possible on the basis of participation, there can be no argument against them.[21]

Parmenides begins by establishing the separation between the one and the others on the basis of a presupposition that what-is must be individual wholes. Specifically, he argues that if there is nothing other than them, there is no third thing "in which" (ἐν ᾧ, 159c2) the one and the others can be; presumably this would mean being distinct parts present together in a whole. The way he puts it is that the one and the others are "all" there is (πάντα, 159c1), and if they are all there is, and they are "other," then they must be separate, which he construes in terms of being distinct individuals. On the one hand, the one is "truly one" (ἀληθῶς ἕν, 159c5), so it is not divisible into a part/whole complex and cannot be in the others as part or whole. The argument, which asserts that the one cannot be in the others, must presuppose that both the one and the others are individuals standing in a relation. The argument is therefore self-refuting and implies the necessity of complex wholes, i.e., the necessity of participation of the others in the one.

Parmenides continues, now from the perspective that the "others" are not many. Here Parmenides makes the claim that the others can be neither one nor many, neither whole nor part, because all of these attributes presuppose being in some respect one, which nothing but the one can be. Apart from emphasizing that the first refutation (i.e., that the others cannot be one) was predicated on the assumption that the separation between the one and the others implied their relation and contradicted its own conclusion, the claim that the others can be neither individual nor whole unless they somehow partake of the one implies that no distinction can stand except on the basis of the structures of concrete determinacy, i.e., being singular and complex. Thus, the refutation draws on the very attributes that it denies, demonstrating negatively the necessity of the H3 premise that there is participation of the others in the one. By positing others that do not partake in number or organization, H4 shows the absurdity of using the structures of intelligibility to deny the possibility of intelligibility.[22]

At the end of H3–H4 we are in a better position to see that the one-that-is-in-space-and-time implies the complementary contraries of H2 and requires the delimitation of the unlimited by which the substantial form assigns attributes to the one-that-is. The determinacy of parts, their organization, the integrity of the whole, owe themselves to the one that governs them. At the same time, the fragility of the limits by which the individual wholes are supported shows that the one toward which they point and which calls them to their determinate limits is fundamentally unlike they are. Incommensurately different, it calls them to measure at the same time as they bear the trace of the unlimited that allows them to be the one of H1 while still being the one of H2.

The analysis that ensues in H5–H6 will clarify this point on a higher ontological level. In H5 we see that individual forms are rendered discursively explicit in spite of their partless simplicity by being bound to other forms (i.e., the forms that belong to them *kath' hauto* as their definition) and bound away from others (both the contradictories of the terms that belong to the form *kath' hauto* and the other terms that simply fall outside this definition). Once again, it will be the relationship of participation that will allow incommensurates to relate to (and be) the same one.

H5–H6—Veridical Predication

In the Fifth Hypothesis, Parmenides is in one respect executing the plan originally laid out in the earlier conversation with Socrates. He earlier promised to hypothesize the one that "is not" and examine the consequences in relation to self and other. In another respect, however, Parmenides is extending insights won in the course of the first four hypotheses. Most important, he is pursuing implications of having discovered in H3 an eidetic one that limits the *plēthē*. These implications will point us to the "is" of a substantial form that binds eidetic ones into an essential structure and that guides the *legein* in which the substantial form is laid bare as the object of discursive knowing. H5 consists of the recognitions that (a) eidetic ones do not have the sort of being that is subject to space and time, but they have a determinate intelligibility that demands explanation (160b–161a),[23] (b) the eidetic one has a constitutive and normative relation to the *plēthē* that we encounter in the fragility of the spatial *perata* of each one-that-is (161a–e), (c) the eidetic one is not only the explanatory principle ordering the intelligibility of spatio-temporal individuals but itself can be subject to *logos* and explicitly articulated as the object of knowledge (161e–162b).[24]

Our first order of business in H5 is to establish an account of the veridical "is." Parmenides refers in H5 to the sort of "is" used properly in a true sentence. The notion of such an "is" was originally implied in H1 when Parmenides and Aristoteles concluded that the one "is not" [in time] (οὐκ ἔστιν, 141e8), and it was developed in the H2 interrogation of the categories by which space and time are articulated. In H2a, eidetic being was implicitly indicated as the condition, in the instant, for the sameness in difference of the one-that-is. In H3 the others were other by virtue of being both many (158b2–3) and wholes-of-parts (157c6–158a3), which allows us to see the one of H3 as the sort of one a form is and connect it with idea (157d8) and *eidos* (158c6). As a form, the one stands in the position of the source that imposes limits on the *plēthē*, differentiating parts and relating them to one another. The veridical "is" has occurred in the analysis whenever we say, for instance, "the one *is* exempt from being." This statement implies recognizing the meaning and truth of saying "one *is* exempt . . . ," which cannot fail to draw on the intelligibility of being and yet cannot be subject to space and time. It is the business of H5 to determine the sense of atemporal being. When we turn to the H5 hypothesis that "the one is not," we are returning to the questions about the knowability and determinacy of the eidetic source of limits in the *plēthē*.

The One-That-Is-Not Partakes of Many Things

Parmenides will assert in this stretch of argument that, although the "one-that-is-not" cannot be, it must be able to partake of many things as something distinct and clearly known. First, according to Parmenides, the hypothesis "if one is not" differs from "if not-one (μὴ ἓν) is not." Parmenides compares this distinction to largeness and smallness, suggesting that if someone were to say that "largeness is not" or "smallness is not" or something of that sort (τι ἄλλο τῶν τοιούτων), "he would make it clear that what he was saying is not were something different" (δηλοῖ ὅτι ἕτερόν τι λέγοι τὸ μὴ ὄν, 160c4). Parmenides thus shifts emphasis from the hypothesis "if one is not" to "what he is saying" (ὃ λέγει, 160c6). The object of his speech, i.e., what the speech is "about" and that by which it is gathered, is something knowable (γνωστόν τι, 160c7) and different from the others (ἕτερον τῶν ἄλλων, 160c7–8).[25]

In the context of Parmenides taking care to point out the determinate intelligibility of the one that is not and, thereby, pointing out its basic commensurability with any and all other objects of speech, we should note that there is still a sharp distinction between one and others carried over from previous hypotheses. Thus, when Parmenides compares the distinction between the one and the others to the large and the small, he is pointing to terms of the same kind. By contrast, the one and others have been established at various points in the previous hypotheses to be incommensurate. What I suggest we notice is that the determinate intelligibility of the one that is not is required if its incommensurability to the others is to become an object of concern in speech.[26]

With these prefatory comments in place, Parmenides offers to start H5 over again on the basis of the insight that "if one is not" there must be knowledge of it, and the others differ from it. When we say 'if one is not' we recognize what we have said, so there is knowledge (ἐπιστήμη) of it, and we recognize that the others are different from it (τὰ ἄλλα ἕτερα αὐτοῦ εἶναι, 160d6–7):

> . . . difference in kind and knowledge belong to it.[27] For one doesn't say the difference in kind of the others when one says that "the one" is different from the others, but [says] the difference in kind of that one.
>
> . . . ἑτεροιότης ἄρα ἐστὶν αὐτῷ πρὸς τῇ ἐπιστήμῃ. οὐ γὰρ τὴν τῶν ἄλλων ἑτεροιότητα λέγει, ὅταν τὸ ἓν ἕτερον τῶν ἄλλων λέγῃ, ἀλλὰ τὴν ἐκείνου. (160d8–e2)

Given that it can be known as an object of *legein*, the eidetic one is an object of knowledge subject to *logos*, and it is subject, in being spoken, to structures required by the cases of grammar. The "one that is not" must also partake of those forms that allow it to be interrogated and known, *viz.*, "that," "of this," "to this," "of these," and it must especially partake of "something" (τινός) (160e2–7).

Notice the care with which Parmenides handles the status of the "one that is not." The others are "different in kind" (ἑτεροῖα, 161a7) relative to the one-that-is-not, and they are "other in kind" (ἀλλοῖα, 161a8) so unlikes (ἀνόμοια, 161b1). But as we recall from the second regress argument, likes are like what is like them (132d5–7), and here too: all unlikes are unlike an unlike. Therefore, it follows that the one-that-is-not would have unlikeness and, Parmenides says, "there would be unlikeness [belonging] to the one" (εἴη δὴ ἄν καὶ τῷ ἑνὶ ἀνομοιότης, 161b2). Here is the important point: it does not follow from the claim that the one-that-is-not has unlikeness that the one is *subject to* unlikeness, nor that the one *is* unlike.[28] Unlikeness is a character of which the one *partakes* such that the others may relate to it as unlike, or so that we may speak of the "one that is not" as standing in some kind of relationship with the others. Similarly, the one *has* likeness in relation to itself in the sense that it can be investigated and understood, but not because the one *is* like. If it did not have likeness in relation to itself, the account (ὁ λόγος, 161b7) would be about something of another kind, and the hypothesis (ἡ ὑπόθεσις, 161b8) would be about something other. Participation in likeness, therefore, allows the "one" to be invoked along a route of inquiry and gradually specified, i.e., to be subject to *logos*. Parmenides says "[That the one must partake of many characters] is necessary, if indeed [the one that is not is to be] the one that is not and not [an] other" (161a1–2).

It is now established that the "one that is not" partakes in those ones that allow it to be an object of knowledge. Parmenides has explained how speech can be about the one-that-is-not, and he has explained how the one-that-is-not can have determinacy. However, he has not shown that the one-that-is-not is the object of knowledge *of* spatio-temporal individuals until he shows that there can be a relationship between the one and the others. In his solution to this problem, notice that Parmenides places the one-that-is-not in relation to spatial others while steering clear of saying that the one is subject to the sorts of quantitative and qualitative relations that characterize the others.

After having established that the "one" has likeness to itself, Parmenides asks Aristoteles about the unlikeness and difference in kind between the one and the others, specifically whether entities that are not equal are unequals.[29] Parmenides pointedly asks Aristoteles whether the denial of equality implies the assertion of inequality. Aristoteles thinks it does. But Aristoteles here fails to notice a distinction that we, as readers, are being called to recognize. Aristoteles does not recognize a difference in kind between beings that are subject to relative magnitude and beings that are not so subject, i.e., a distinction in kind between beings subject to space and time and beings that are atemporal and a-spatial. This distinction, however, has been crucial to reading the hypotheses, and there are a number of important turns of the discussion at which Parmenides has drawn this distinction to our attention. Parmenides here continues the process of backtesting Aristoteles' reductivist assumption that being means what is subject to time and space.

Parmenides says the one partakes (μετέχει, 161c9) of inequality, and the others "are" unequal.[30] Parmenides does not say that the one *is* large, small, and/or equal. Indeed, he is explicitly saying that the one can neither be nor be unlike the others. The one-that-is-not cannot be equal to the others because it would thereby have to "be" and "be like" them. By contrast, the others *are* unequal to the one, i.e., the others are subject to inequality with respect to the one. Thus, the one neither "is" nor "is like" the others, but is subject to being and likeness. The apparent asymmetry between two sides of a relationship of inequality between the one and the others is explained in this way: just as the one *partakes* of likeness with respect to itself as an object of *logos*, so too it partakes of unlikeness with respect to the others. The others both partake of likeness and unlikeness, and in themselves they *are* like and unlike. The one cannot *be* unequal, so it partakes *of* inequality and partakes of large and small in relation to the others. The point of these reflections is to articulate the difference in kind between incommensurate beings, i.e., between those in space and time and those that are timeless and a-spatial.

These initial reflections appear to have answered the question of how the "one that is not" can be knowable *and* related to spatio-temporal others. The being-known and being-distinct of the one refers to the necessary aspects of its intelligibility. On the one hand, the one is accessed by thought and is recognized and is subject to *logos*. The subsequent distinction between "partaking in" and "being subject to" has allowed us to preserve the gap between forms and participants, such that ideas can be causally efficacious with respect to spatio-temporal individuals without being in space and time.

The asymmetry we are thus able to establish between the one and the others offers us the account of normativity implied by H3. The one partakes of greater, smaller, and equal, which enables the others to partake in *and to be*, Parmenides says, unequal to the one.[31] From H3, we remember the *perata* imposed on the *plēthos*. Here, with the addition of the relation of inequality between the others and the one, we are given an opportunity to think not only of the "one" ordering the others but also drawing their organized parts toward normatively determined tipping points of "too much" and "not enough."[32] We thus introduce in H5 the view that the various forms have normative force in spatio-temporal things by virtue of their collaboration with the relevant continua. This would imply that the notion of an unlimited in itself, introduced in H3 as the subject of the *perata* imposed by the one, would be overly abstract, even derivative, and dependent on a normative order. What was previously called unlimited can now manifest to thinking and perceiving only in light of the limit that orders and organizes the continuum into relations of too-much and too-little.[33] The unlimited would be now only manifest as pointing toward, and falling away from, *peras*.

The Bonds of Being and Not Being

We began H5 by investigating the one-that-is-not as something known as different in kind than spatio-temporal others. As mentioned above, the subject of H5, i.e., the one-that-is-not, refers to any subject of hypothesis or speech in general insofar as it is recognized and, therefore, can become the subject of inquiry. A one of the sort Parmenides has been describing in H5, which I believe to be consistent with a form-type one, can be unfolded and known as an object of dialectical inquiry only if it has purchase in being such that it can guide thought and speech through the definite moments of sameness and difference that disclose the one as an object of discursive knowledge and constitute its normative specificity in relation to the others.[34]

Parmenides takes his departure from the claim that when we say the one is-not, we "say true [things] when we say the one is not" (ἀληθῆ λέγοιμεν ἡμεῖς λέγοντες τὸ ἓν μὴ εἶναι, 161e5). Speaking truly, gathering what-is into the light of disclosure, "it is clear that we say things that are (ὄντα αὐτά)" (161e4–162a1).[35] In other words, there is a specific kind of "being" that is invoked when we say that the one "is-not." On that basis, Parmenides feels justified in saying that "it [the one that is not] must partake somehow of being" (οὐσίας γε δεῖ αὐτὸ μετέχειν πῃ, 161e3).

When Parmenides first indicates to Aristoteles that the one-that-is-not must in some sense *be*, Aristoteles' response is "How so?" (πῶς δή;). This of all Aristoteles' comments seems reserved for moments of greatest perplexity, or perhaps moments of least insight. It is the same response Aristoteles gave to the claim that the one is "nowhere" (οὐδαμοῦ) (138a2), and that it is not in time (μηδ' ἐν ἑνὶ χρόνῳ) (156c2). When Aristoteles is confronted with the implication that "being" cannot be reduced to being in space and time, he is clearly at a loss.[36] What Parmenides is asking us to see, in lieu of Aristoteles, is that the one has a specific ontological status as an atemporal and a-spatial "object" on the basis of a participatory relation to being, necessary as the basis for truth. Parmenides therefore elaborates the ontological conditions on which this one, which in a sense "is not," can in another sense *be*:

> As it seems, the one is a not-being. For if it is not to be a not being but in some way gave up its being in relation to not being, it would immediately be a being.
>
> By all means.

> Then it [one that is not] must have a bond of not-being with respect to its being a not-being, if it is going to not-be [in space and time], just as, similarly, what-is must have not-being what-is-not (τὸ μὴ ὄν) in order that it in turn may completely be [in space and time]. For thusly what is would most of all be and what is not would not be: on the one hand by what is partaking of the *ousia* of being a being (τοῦ εἶναι ὄν) and partaking of the non-*ousia* of not being a not-being (τοῦ εἶναι μὴ ὄν), if it is completely to be. On the other hand by what is not [partaking of the] non-*ousia* of not-being a being, and of the *ousia* of being a not-being (τοῦ εἶναι μὴ ὄν), if in turn what is-not will completely not be.

> Ἔστιν ἄρα, ὡς ἔοικε, τὸ ἓν οὐκ ὄν· εἰ γὰρ μὴ ἔσται μὴ ὄν, ἀλλά πῃ τοῦ εἶναι ἀνήσει πρὸς τὸ μὴ εἶναι, εὐθὺς ἔσται ὄν. {—} Παντάπασι μὲν οὖν. {—} δεῖ ἄρα αὐτὸ δεσμὸν ἔχειν τοῦ μὴ εἶναι τὸ εἶναι μὴ ὄν, εἰ μέλλει μὴ εἶναι, ὁμοίως ὥσπερ τὸ ὂν τὸ μὴ ὂν ἔχειν μὴ εἶναι, ἵνα τελέως αὖ εἶναι ᾖ: οὕτως γὰρ ἂν τό τε ὂν μάλιστ᾽ ἂν εἴη καὶ τὸ μὴ ὂν οὐκ ἂν εἴη, μετέχοντα τὸ μὲν ὂν οὐσίας τοῦ εἶναι ὄν, μὴ οὐσίας δὲ τοῦ μὴ εἶναι μὴ ὄν, εἰ μέλλει τελέως εἶναι, τὸ δὲ μὴ ὂν μὴ οὐσίας μὲν τοῦ μὴ εἶναι [μὴ][37] ὄν, οὐσίας δὲ τοῦ εἶναι μὴ ὄν, εἰ καὶ τὸ μὴ ὂν αὖ τελέως μὴ ἔσται. (162a1–b3)

The passages on the bond of being and participation in *ousia* demonstrate what is necessarily entailed given the intelligibility and availability to inquiry of an atemporal and a-spatial one. The bond of "being" (τὸ εἶναι) ties what-is (τὸ ὄν) to its being (ὄν), and it allows a being "to be completely." Similarly, the bond of not-being (τὸ μὴ εἶναι) ties what-is-not to its being a not-being (μὴ ὄν) and allows the one "to not-be completely." In the description of the bonds of being and not-being, the focus is on that to which the subject is tied by the bond. By contrast, participation in *ousia* and non-*ousia* focuses on the subject of that bond: what-is-not partakes of the non-*ousia* of being a not-being and of the non-*ousia* of not being a being (τοῦ εἶναι μὴ ὄν). The difference is the "bond of being" secures a subject to its ontological position as subject to being, and participation treats the subject as prior to, distinct from, and therefore capable of participating in, being. It is my view that nothing in these passages specifies or so much as addresses what the one would "be" prior to its participation in *ousia* or how to talk, no doubt inappropriately and with the requisite twisting of language, about the "being" of the one prior to participation in being. There is no doubt, however, that Parmenides has carved out room for the notion of a one prior to participation in being. The difference between being and not-being is thus secured: the one-that-is-not "is" insofar as it partakes in the *ousia* of being a one that is subject to speech and knowledge, and it "is not" in the sense of being bound to its distinct ontological status as not in space and time.[38] Notice that Parmenides is preserving the distinction between "is" and "partakes in being."

I am puzzled by the evident tension between beings and their being. What Parmenides called the "being in a certain way" of the one-that-is-not does not simply differ from things that are. He says, rather, that the one has a bond of not-being that holds it to not-being [a spatio-temporal being]. If the one were to give up (ἀνίημι) its not-being, it will at once (εὐθύς) be a [spatio-temporal] being (162a2–3). The apparent ontological nearness of atemporal and a-spatial being to spatio-temporal being is intriguing. Both sides of the ontological gap between what-is and not-being are held in place by bonds. But Parmenides' description of the tension between what-is and not-being seems unnecessary, and it therefore calls attention to itself. At the outset of H5, Parmenides drew attention to the intelligibility and determinacy of the one-that-is-not. In that context he specified the one as a distinct subject of *logos*, differing from other subjects of speech and knowledge. Here, by contrast, the one does not simply differ but is held in place by a bond. We have to be cautious assigning meaning to the image of the "bond" in these passages, but I believe that the language of a bond points to the self-undermining nature of intelligibility with which we have been struggling throughout the entire dialogue, especially in Parmenides' objections to participation in the first part of the dialogue. The image of a bond is suggestive of the self-undermining tendency of thought to betray its own insights and take "is" univocally as an object in some sense present. The ensuing discussion of a peculiar non-spatial and non-temporal motion and rest will, I hope, consolidate these points.

Motion and Rest

Parmenides now begins a very strange and provocative discussion that will prove frustrating unless we attend to the limitations in the way Aristoteles responds to questions and take the initiative to restore to the discussion its occluded layer of meaning. Parmenides calls on us to determine the meaning of a very specific, and sparingly detailed, kind of non-spatio-temporal change. I will interpret this change in terms of the way the subject of true discourse is disclosed in true speech (*logos*), and I will use this analysis to extend and confirm insights suggested above in the section on the bond of being and not-being.

Parmenides first, misleadingly we might think, points to the dual aspect of the one-that-is-not as partaking in *ousia* and non-*ousia*, and he asks Aristoteles, "Can something that is disposed in some way (τὸ ἔχον πως) not be disposed in that way without changing (μεταβάλλον) from that *hexis*?" (162b9–10). There is a tempting fallacy in this question. Parmenides has just established that the one, if it is not, partakes in *ousia* and not-*ousia* (162b6–7), and he claims that "everything that is of such a sort, i.e., which is thus and not thus, signifies change" (Πᾶν ἄρα τὸ τοιοῦτον μεταβολὴν σημαίνει, ὃ ἂν οὕτω τε καὶ μὴ οὕτως ἔχῃ, 162b10–c1); Parmenides calls change a motion (μεταβολὴ δὲ κίνησις) (162c1–2). The fallacy here, given the radical unlikeness outlined in the previous section, is to assume that the different states of being and not-being are commensurate and to assume that there is a single subject of change underlying them. Owing to his habits of thinking, Aristoteles is compelled to construe being and not-being in terms of a change of states in the selfsame thing. We, however, are in a position to see that the spatio-temporal being of the one is incommensurate with the being through which it partakes in its eidetic determinacy. What are we to make of this discrepancy?

The answer announces itself as Parmenides strips away the types of motion that characterize spatio-temporal beings. The one is not (in space and time), and it is therefore "nowhere" (μηδαμοῦ). Whatever motion it has, it can move neither by traversal (μεταβαίνειν) nor rotation (στρέφειν) (162c8–d2). Furthermore, the one isn't altered (ἀλλοιοῦται), Parmenides says, for if it were the *logos* would no longer be about (περί, 162d7) the one. Note that the rest attributed to the one here refers back to the likeness that the one has in relation to itself as that "about which" the *logos* speaks. If "the one that is not" is not altered, doesn't rotate, and doesn't move from one place to another, it must be unmoved (ἀκίνητον, 162e1). Parmenides says: "But the unmoved necessarily enjoys repose (ἡσυχίαν ἄγειν), and the thing that enjoys repose is at rest."[39] Thus, Parmenides concludes, the one, since it is not, is in motion of a kind distinct from spatio-temporal change. Parmenides adds to this list of attributes alteration and coming to be (γίγνεται) (163b2–5): if it moves, it is altered, and if it is unmoved, it does not alter. If it alters, it comes to be [in a new state] and ceases to be [in its previous state], and if it is unaltered, it neither comes to be nor ceases to be (163a7–b2).

What has been missing from H5 is an account of the definitional moments by which the one-that-is-not would be revealed to inquiry. We earlier carved out a space for the object of eidetic inquiry as a determinate object of a discourse that differentiates a *definiendum* from other ones that it is not while at the same time relating it to the ones that are in its definition (i.e., what it is veridically). But we have not settled on an account of the movement of inquiry in which the *definiendum* is revealed. For Aristoteles, the discussion of motion and rest looks toward the spatio-temporal thing's distribution of contradictories to different participatory moments, but for us, the discussion of motion and rest points toward the eidetic motion and rest of the truth revealed to inquiry.

If we recall the description of the one's likeness to itself as an object of inquiry (161b4–c2), we saw that the type of motion and rest that would belong to the one would be the sort of alteration and self-sameness that are demanded by *legein* (162d7–8). Inquiry reveals the positive and negative attributes that belong to the one as an object of *legein*, and discursive knowledge consists of a weaving of attributes that classify its object according to what (specifically) it is and what (specifically) it is not. Take for example of the idea of statesmanship: when the Stranger in the *Statesman* characterizes statesmanship as theoretical (γνωστικός) and not practical (πρακτικός) (*Statesman* 259c10–d1), directive (ἐπιτακτικός, 260b3–4) not calculative (λογιστικός, 259e1), self-directive (αὐτεπίτακτος, 260e4–5) and not other-directive (ἐπιτάττειν ἀλλοτριότης) (260c6–261a6), he is delimiting the initially simple and recognizable one (i.e., statesmanship) in accord with positive and negative bonds of being and not-being that will draw the idea into explicitude as an object of knowledge (or, indeed, expose their guiding intuition to critique and revision).[40] By bringing the initially invoked form into relation with attributes that mark it out positively and negatively, the form becomes explicit as a determinate object of knowing. The discursive complex classifies the form as an object of *legein*.

Subject to the *legein* that sorts out the definitional moments of the object of discursive knowledge, the one gives itself to inquiry and is revealed to understanding through the beings (ὄντα) that pick out and mark off the *definiendum*. The precise sense of the motion involved is hard to determine. As we go from end to end of the ideas that belong to the one definitionally, i.e., are said of it veridically, the one is in one sense in motion insofar as its attributes are individually articulated into an ordered relationship of "is" and "is not." The object of knowledge is articulately joined to what it is and divided from what it is not, in that sense moving back and forth between what the one is and is-not. Note, therefore, that true discourse must move through the attributes that positively and negatively characterize the unmoving "what" that the discourse is about (περί, 162d7). Discourse must move from saying what the subject "is" to saying what it "is not" and back to saying what it "is," at the same time as this discourse is guided by a source that remains unchanged. This motion is the motion of truth insofar as the end achieved presents what was already there to be known or, in other words, does not alter the object.[41] Thus, the one is also in motion in the simple sense that the subject of inquiry is disclosed through the gathering of *logos*, and in this sense the motion we have in mind would not focus on the specific beings (*onta*) through which the truth is disclosed but the simple and unique "one" that is the subject of gathering.

As we have already noticed, the form partakes in various characters, such as greatness and smallness, or likeness and unlikeness, and now motion and rest, which allow it to be taken up in a variety of ways distinct from what it is in itself. The form partakes in rest as the source guiding the motion of inquiry and from which the attributes of the form are gathered. As partaking in motion and rest, the form can be an object of inquiry, and there can be knowledge of the form. Prior to motion and rest, the one "is" itself as simple and unique, neither in motion nor rest. As an object of *legein*, however, the form partakes in both motion and rest.

A key point to draw from this, connecting back to earlier hypotheses, is that the one is prior to and, in a sense, exempt from its attributes, including the motion and rest in which those attributes are revealed. And yet, the form can become the object of discursive knowledge only through the forms in which it partakes. The form is therefore twofold. Once we invoke a timeless one by calling it by name, nothing we go on to say will add to the simple and unique "what" that we have invoked (H1). But having said the name only, we do not yet know the object discursively, i.e., in its distinction from and relation to other forms. The form as object of knowledge must therefore be rendered present to discursive understanding through specifying differences. When we speak truly about the one, for instance by saying what statesmanship is definitionally, we thereby make explicit (present to discourse) what was already, in a sense, known (present to intuition). At the completion of that movement, the gathering of terms proper to the idea has revealed the idea guiding that gathering from the beginning. With the discussion of motion and rest in the context of veridical *legein*, Parmenides is asking us to see that the one participates positively and negatively in various other characters.

Parmenides' characterization of the motion and rest of inquiry, however, is puzzling insofar as the "one" is in motion and rest. The form does not move in being known, and the form is not altered when it is articulated, and it is only as *for inquiry* that the idea of, e.g., statesmanship moves and rests. We should expect the one-that-is-not to partake in motion and rest, just as it partook in greatness and smallness above in relation to the others. And yet, in stark contrast to the description of the one's participation in large and small, Parmenides here says that the one *is* in motion and *is* at rest, not that it partakes in them. We are therefore posed with the question of why the one is said to be in motion and rest when Parmenides took such great care previously to avoid saying that the one is great or small.

The answer, which I can only suggest at this point, is that the account of "veridical speech" in H5 of the *Parmenides* points to a structure of weaving that will later, in the *Sophist*, be shifted from the domain of inquiry and *legein* into the complex articulation of forms by other forms. Here in the *Parmenides* the one, as I interpret it, guides and determines veridical speech insofar as it participates in motion and rest, and it remains aloof from itself as an object of knowledge toward which true speech is oriented. In the *Sophist*, therefore, the account of being goes well beyond the confines of the *Parmenides*. Specifically, the Stranger will introduce the notion of eidetic complex, i.e., forms composed of forms, which is here completely avoided. Although this theme is first introduced here, it will not be taken up rigorously until we turn to the *Theaetetus* and *Sophist*, and in ways even more intimate to Platonic metaphysics in the *Statesman* and *Philebus*. In those dialogues we will have occasion to reflect on the distinctive character of truth by first clarifying what we mean by falsity and false speech, which we have not yet had occasion to determine.

H6

H6 provides a complementary *reductio* argument to demonstrate the basic premise of H5 by showing the impossibility of taking this "is not" as the unqualified non-being of the one. If we were to remove all standing from the one-that-is-not, we would thereby remove the possibility of talking about or making sense of the very thing toward which the argument is directed. We are directing the argument at something, so it follows that whatever we name when we say "the-one-that-is-not" cannot be nothing. Parmenides begins H6 by distinguishing what we are addressing from what we are saying about it: "when we say something 'is not' (μὴ ἔστιν), does it indicate anything other than lack of being (οὐσίας ἀπουσίαν) of the very thing we say 'is not'?" (163c1–3). Parmenides then clarifies the sense of the non-being we have in mind, asking whether saying "is not" indicates non-being in some respect, or indicates simply (ἁπλῶς) that "the non-being (τό γε μὴ ὄν) in no way whatsoever partakes in being (οὐδαμῶς οὐδαμῇ ἔστιν οὐδέ πῃ μετέχει οὐσίας) and in no sense 'is' (ἔστιν οὐδέ πῃ)" (163c5–7).

From here it is a short step to show that, if the one of which we speak completely lacks being, nothing can be said of it and, furthermore, it cannot come to light as "is not" or anything else. He underscores this by removing from the one all the cases of grammar that would allow us to make these assertions:

> Concerning what-is-not, will there be "of that," "to that," "something," "this," "of this," "of another," "to another," "then," "later," "now," knowledge, opinion, perception, account, name, or any other beings?
> There will not.
>
> τὸ ἐκείνου ἢ τὸ ἐκείνῳ ἢ τὸ τὶ ἢ τὸ τοῦτο ἢ τὸ τούτου ἢ ἄλλου ἢ ἄλλῳ ἢ ποτὲ ἢ ἔπειτα ἢ νῦν ἢ ἐπιστήμη ἢ δόξα ἢ αἴσθησις ἢ λόγος ἢ ὄνομα ἢ ἄλλο ὁτιοῦν τῶν ὄντων περὶ τὸ μὴ ὂν ἔσται; {—} Οὐκ ἔσται. (164a7–b3)

Thus, Parmenides demonstrates the absurdity of saying anything absolutely "is not," and in H6 he has provided a negative proof that we cannot deny being unqualifiedly to "the one that is not" because doing so implies that sort of being that renders this one intelligible as that about which we are making the denial. Even if Aristoteles does not see the point, we must grant the one being of a certain sort in order to deny it being or anything else for that matter. Therefore, the being of the one-that-is-not is a necessary condition for denying being, now in another sense of spatio-temporal being, to the "one that is not."

H7–H8—Appearance

The subject of H7 is the apparent one. The nature of appearance and seeming have been tacitly at stake in the discussion from early on when Zeno argued for the logical untenability of the hypothesis of many beings, which was undermined by Socrates' account of participation. In the course of the Hypotheses, the nature of apparent being has cropped up in the discussion of spatio-temporal wholes consisting of spatio-temporal parts in H2. For instance, it was shown that the limit that defines the size and shape of the one-that-is is divisible and therefore subject to redefinition. In H7 we learn that this limit, specifically its contingency, is tied to a perceptual context and therefore merely apparent. It is only in light of the analysis in H3 of the one-idea that imposes *perata* on the *plēthē* and the H5 articulation of the one-idea into a manifold of true parts that are truly "of" the one that Parmenides is in a position to give a fuller account of appearance. Having identified the source of the true articulation of spatio-temporal composites, we have implicitly uncovered a basis for acknowledging that spatio-temporal determinacy is given to a plurality of perceptual points of view.

In the language of Parmenides' initial framing, H3 and H7 are the two hypotheses that study the undergoings of the others. H3 keys from the conclusion of H2a that the one is not in time, and H7 builds on the premise that the one is not in time or space, showing that there is no pure one among "the others" and that these others are therefore apparent ones. By showing that reciprocal difference (ἕτερον . . . ἑτέρου, ἄλλο . . . ἄλλου, 164c1–2) cannot apply to the others in relation to the one, H7 presupposes the relationship of incommensurability between distinct ontological levels, echoing the difference in kind (ἑτεροιότης, 160d8–e2) and unlikeness (ἀνομοιότης, 161a6–b2) in H5. Similarly, by showing that the others are different in kind and unlike themselves (ἑτεροῖα καὶ ἀνόμοια ἑαυτοῖς, 165d2), H7 reestablishes the H3 account of unlikeness (ἀνομοιότατα, 159a4) between the one-that-is and both the *plēthē* in itself and the *plēthē* in the others.

Parmenides sets aside the hierarchical relation that obtains between the various levels of description of the "one idea," the *perata* that give physical structure to the parts that compose the whole one-that-is, and the *plēthē* out of which those parts emerge, in order to suspend the thing's normative relationship to the relevant forms and discuss the shifting, divisible, contingent, i.e., impure, unity spatio-temporal individuals have on their own terms.[42] H7 studies the others in relation to themselves, which implies that the others are to be studied here in their extra-normative character. In relation to themselves, the others are taken in terms of their plurality, which is similar to the way they were taken up in H2, but distinct insofar as now the emphasis is on the divisibility of the limiting parts (165a–b) of the one-that-is and the shifting part/whole complexion that the one-that-is presents to different spatial points of view (165c–d). We are studying characteristics that belong to the others "apparently," and yet, although the limits of the others are merely apparent, the others are not thereby nothing.

Parmenides brackets the hierarchically normative immanence of the *eidos* in the *plēthē*, which can now be put aside because its causal priority has been secured, to focus on the relationship of likeness between and among features within the others. The analysis of appearance suspends the normative force by which the others are organized and toward which they are oriented, so that we take them up in their character as a throng, or a spatial mass, as studied in H2. Note that we are not here discussing the *plēthē* that are called up and sorted by *perata* in relation to the defining form. We are discussing the inessential but necessary whole/part structure of the one-that-is as something that occupies space and time. Parmenides says, "the different (τὸ ἕτερον) is different than a different, and the other (τὸ ἄλλο) is other than an other" (164c1–2). As so related, the others differ from one another "as multitudes" (κατὰ πλήθη), and they form "many masses" (πολλοὶ ὄγκοι, 164d7) unlimited in multitude (ἄπειρός ἐστι πλήθει) (164c7–d4):

> So they are other than each other with respect to multitude, for they could not be so with respect to one, if one is not. But, as it seems, each mass (ὄγκος) is unlimited in multitude, and even if someone takes what seems to be smallest, just as a dream in sleep, they [i.e., the seemingly smallest] instantly (ἐξαίφνης) appear (φαίνεται) to be many instead of seeming one, and enormous instead of the smallest, in relation to what are chopped off from it.
> Most correct.
>
> κατὰ πλήθη ἄρα ἕκαστα ἀλλήλων ἄλλα ἐστί: κατὰ ἓν γὰρ οὐκ ἂν οἷά τε εἴη, μὴ ὄντος ἑνός. ἀλλ᾽ ἕκαστος, ὡς [164d] ἔοικεν, ὁ ὄγκος αὐτῶν ἄπειρός ἐστι πλήθει, κἂν τὸ σμικρότατον δοκοῦν εἶναι λάβῃ τις, ὥσπερ ὄναρ ἐν ὕπνῳ φαίνεται ἐξαίφνης ἀντὶ ἑνὸς δόξαντος εἶναι πολλὰ καὶ ἀντὶ σμικροτάτου παμμέγεθες πρὸς τὰ κερματιζόμενα ἐξ αὐτοῦ. {—} ὀρθότατα. (164c7–d4)

The first thing to notice is that once the others are taken up in abstraction from the normative *perata*, they reveal their otherness in relation to one another and the similarity implied by this otherness; their otherness makes them appear similar. The second thing to notice is that the revelation of their unlimited nature takes time. The unlimited multitude reveals its nature not in pointing toward *perata* but rather in the, so to speak, decomposition and recomposition to which the thing lends itself at any moment through a shift in perspective.[43] The limits of the others are fickle insofar as the others do not own the limits that characterize them; as Parmenides says, "So having a limit in relation to another mass (πρὸς ἄλλον ὄγκον πέρας ἔχων), it [the putative one] has neither beginning, limit, nor middle in relation to itself (πρὸς αὑτόν)" (165a5–8). This shifting, in which one limit lends itself to be displaced by another in response to shifting points of view, reveals the composition of the others to be apparent, which we can see in the many references in the texts to appearing (φαινόμενος):

> Because whenever someone grasps something in thought (λάβῃ τῇ διανοίᾳ) as if it were any of these [i.e. beginning, middle, or end], before the beginning another beginning always appears (πρό τε τῆς ἀρχῆς ἄλλη ἀεὶ φαίνεται ἀρχή), and after the end a different end remaining appears, and in the middle others more in the middle than the middle [appear] but smaller, because it is not possible to grasp each of these as one (διὰ τὸ μὴ δύνασθαι ἑνὸς αὐτῶν ἑκάστου λαμβάνεσθαι), since "the one is not." (Chrysakopoulou.)

> Ὅτι ἀεὶ αὐτῶν ὅταν τίς τι λάβῃ τῇ διανοίᾳ ὥς τι τούτων ὄν, πρό τε τῆς ἀρχῆς ἄλλη ἀεὶ φαίνεται ἀρχή, μετά τε τὴν τελευτὴν ἑτέρα ὑπολειπομένη τελευτή, ἔν τε τῷ μέσῳ ἄλλα μεσαίτερα τοῦ μέσου, σμικρότερα δέ, διὰ τὸ μὴ δύνασθαι ἑνὸς αὐτῶν ἑκάστου λαμβάνεσθαι, ἅτε οὐκ ὄντος τοῦ ἑνός. (165a8–b4)

Appearances can decompose, and their decomposition brings to light that all along the others were gathered together into a measure from which they can be detached. The others give the appearance of being many without actually being so; for instance, they have the appearance of continuous and discrete magnitudes, appearing to have number, being even and odd, smaller, larger, and equal, but all are semblances (φαντάσματα) that appear to be without truly being (ὄντα οὐκ ἀληθῶς φαίνεται, 164e2–3). Each mass seems to give, in relation to other masses, the impression of being integrated, but studied on their own these limits reveal themselves to depend on perspective. Insofar as it is relative to another and subject to the attractive forces of reciprocal difference within an overall field of perceptual grasping, mass gives the look of being (relatively) integrated. However, like any look that is based not on an internal measure but on an external relation, this appearance is deceptive and reconfigures on closer inspection.

The being-other of the others implies the perspective from which their unlimited nature is held fast to form an apparent unity, which is to say that the nature of the others implies not only appearance but also seeming. Parmenides says that "such a thing will necessarily appear one to a seeing (ὁρῶντι) from far off and unclearly" (165b7–c3), and again shortly afterward the shadow painting appears one, and all its contents appear like, to someone standing far off (ἀποστάντι). Moving in precisely the opposite direction as the communing of others with the one-idea in H3, the fragility of the masses is here revealed as belonging to a point of view. Every "one" that presents itself implicitly speaks, through its inessential but necessary spatiality, of a range of other points of view that abide and make the others available for reconfiguration, reversal, reconstrual. As fragile and as soliciting a point of view, apparent unities round out the account of the nature of intelligibility.

The others are the occasion for seeing that we are seeing things and taking them to be true so are positioned among them with a perspective on them.[44] Parmenides clarifies the likeness and unlikeness of appearances in a way that reveals the necessity of multiple points of view. The multiplicity of perspectives is built into the nature of appearance. The overarching point in this section is that the spatio-temporal object in its own nature receives and makes room for multiple points of view, and the principle of mass requires that things support points of view. In the end, the priority of the nature of the object over perspectives on the object will, by pointing to the relevant forms that structure the inessential character of those objects, will help shape the account of the priority of form over spatio-temporal particulars to which Platonic education points.

H8

H8 requires us to acknowledge the absurd impossibility of the assertion that "the others" are nothing. Not only does H8 point to the necessity of H7, but insofar as it does so on the basis of invoking key claims of H4 and H6, H8 points to back to H5 and H3 as the necessary basis for H7. Parmenides first establishes the premise that if one is not, others will be neither one nor many. They could not be one because one is not (165e3). They could not be many, for if none of them is one, all would be nothing (εἰ γὰρ μηδὲν αὐτῶν ἐστὶν ἕν, ἅπαντα οὐδέν ἐστιν, 163e5). In a way similar to H4, H8 begins by showing that if there is no one, neither can there be others.

H8 then derives from the premise that there is no one the conclusion that there can be no seeing the others—taking them to be true—or seeming or appearance of the others. Negation of the one results in a lack of qualification and intelligibility across the board, precluding the others from having so much as apparent being. Parmenides says, "then no opinion nor any appearance of what is not pertains to the others, nor is not-being opined in any way at all in relation to the others" (166a4–6).[45] As in H6, the non-existence of the one results in the impossibility of positing the others as the subject of any type of assertion or attribute of being, including asserting of them that they are not. Parmenides sums up: "if one is not, nothing is" (ἓν εἰ μὴ ἔστιν, οὐδέν ἐστιν, 166c1).

The very act of suggesting the premise, considering the argument, and reaching a conclusion demonstrate the falsity of the premise that the one is not (simply speaking). In order to follow the argument in H8, we must be able first to draw on the being of the one, so that when we say "if one is not," we can know what is being posited. Thus, H8 draws on the negative claim made in H6, namely that the "one that is not" must in some sense "be" if it is "not to be" [in space and time]. Apparent being is subordinate to and dependent on eidetic being. Furthermore, H8 draws on the negative claim made in H4 that there must be participation of the others in the one if the others are to show up and be the subject for any attributes, assertions, or perception. The lesson that H8 teaches is that the apparent being of H7 is a necessary condition for conceiving the non-being of the others. In order to show the priority of the object of thought and perception over thinking and perceiving, it is necessary to acknowledge the priority of the "one form" and the participation of the others in form.

The Hypotheses thus conclude with a final *reductio* that ties together the series of H3/4, H5/6, and H7/8. Each of these paired hypotheses demonstrates the self-refuting impossibility for (a) individual part/whole complexes subject to *perata* by the defining form, (b) the defining form that is not in space and time, and (c) the inessential but necessary part/whole structure of the mass extended in space, of the negation of the eidetic principle on which each of these three structures depends. The lesson is that we can turn away from *eidos* only on the basis of *eidos*. That is to say, it is only through the structuring intelligibility provided by form that we can gain access to the extra-normative character of what lacks form and to the perspective that sees and takes up apparent being. The nature of the unity that necessarily, although haltingly, belongs to "mass" reveals the necessity and dependence of the stance for which mass appears to be "one."

Conclusion

We began our study of the *Parmenides* with a consideration of the metaphysical themes raised in the opening scene of the dialogue. The dramatic framing of the dialogue listed a host of examples of place: the unspecified location in which the dialogue is narrated for the reader, the Ionian coast from which the visitors have traveled, the placeless sea across which they journeyed, the Athenian agora in which Cephalus happens to encounter Glaucon and Adeimantus, as well as the home in which Pythodorus long ago hosted Parmenides and Zeno, who had travelled to Athens from Elea. So, too, time was emphasized: the original conversation took place when Socrates was still young, it was later recounted to a young Antiphon by Pythodorus, Antiphon recalled what he memorized and recited it to the Ionian visitors, and these visitors then repeat the conversation to an unidentified audience at an unspecified time. Each one of these specifics of space and time invokes the theme of contingency. Had Pythodorus not arrived when he did to hear the conversation, or Pythodorus not recounted it to Antiphon, or Antiphon not remembered the conversation, or Cephalus not made a safe journey home, the conversation would not be. The dialogue passes along lines of transmission that remind us of the fragile human foundation on which ontological insights rest and of the practices by which these insights are preserved. Also, the written text is characterized by fragility, persisting only insofar as it has been transcribed and handed down to us readers. Thus, at the outset of the discussion we are introduced to both the necessity of spatio-temporal conditions and the contingency of the gift of philosophical insight.

At the same time, the material aspect of the conversation would not be brought to life without understanding and inquiry, without desiring to reach the far shore of "such a great sea of *logoi*" (τοιοῦτόν τε καὶ τοσοῦτον πέλαγος λόγων, 137a5–6). The source of unity, originally present in the image of the Great Panathenaea and its patron goddess Athena, demands hard work for its reception. The importance of the theme of ritual unity for this dialogue is, in my view, that the rituals of the Great Panathenaea and the hypotheses are exercises in accepting that the sources of our being call for recognition and yet exceed our comprehension. In this concluding section, I will show that our study of dialectic has facilitated the turn from becoming to being in such a way as to reveal the ultimate source of intelligibility as the good, calling on us to recognize its primacy and yet exceeding our ability to approach it as an object of discursive understanding.

In the turn toward being, two sides of the educational project were pursued simultaneously. On the one hand, we marked out what it means to be first in the order of being and "manifest" (φαίνεσθαι) as form. On the other hand, we re-situated what it means to be subject to place and time and to be first in the order of becoming. The result has been to upstage what is apparent, in the H7 sense of spatio-temporal particulars, with what truly "is" in sense of forms. For one who has worked through the hypotheses, the familiar sense that the objects of opinion are the primary constituents of reality reveals itself to be predicated on a persistent error that, although necessary to our orientation within the cave, conceals the nature of what is most present in truth and most intelligible.[1] The hypotheses teach us that categorial and defining forms enable the spatio-temporal presence of things, but that forms are self-concealing, and this very self-concealing presence is prior to individual things present in space and time.

The break from our error that reality consists primarily of individual spatio-temporal things occurs in many stages, of which I wish to revisit one in particular. A key initiator in the hypotheses for the turning of the soul from becoming to being was the H2 insight that the one-that-is, simply by virtue of being one, does not stand in spatial relations to other ones (Chapter 4, "Continuous Magnitude: Greater/Smaller/Equal," 149e1–150a9). Parmenides demonstrated that both the spatiality and abstract part/whole structure of the one-that-is are constituted by determinately intelligible aspects, aspects that are prior to the spatial complexity to which they give rise. The things most familiar to us are present only on the condition that forms are what is first and most basic.[2] The exercise provided by Parmenides attempted to spatialize the forms that constitute spatial being, so that, by way of *reductio*, we might see for ourselves the primacy of non-spatial forms. The absurdity of the claim that space could be a container holding the forms that constitute spatiality was an important indicator of the primacy of the forms of spatiality and of being over becoming.

In order to understand how the turn toward being has transformed our understanding of becoming, it is helpful to look back to the things Socrates says about philosophical education in the *Republic*. In *Republic* 7, after detailing the prisoner's escape from the cave, Socrates turns to the mathematical studies that will provide the vehicle for education in the study of the one, imaging for Glaucon the being-large and the being-small of a finger. The "great" and "small" are present in the finger, and without them the finger would not be present to opinion. Socrates wants to show that large and small are mutually exclusive and yet "commingled" (συγκεχυμένα, 524c7) in perception, which he describes as "strange" (ἄτοποι, 524b1), literally "out of place." Socrates is asking us to see that the determinate intelligibility present to perception can neither be explained by perception nor be confined to its objects, awakening intellect (ἐγερτικὰ τῆς νοήσεως, 524d5) and initiating the turn toward being. Socrates is drawing attention to the determinately intelligible aspects of which appearance is composed, so as to set the foundation for dialectical study through the gateway of mathematical study.

In H2 Parmenides challenged the presumed ultimacy of the perceptual object in similar fashion: the one-that-is is not greater or smaller than the others "by being [a] one" (τῷ μὲν ἓν εἶναι, 149e1–2), i.e., not simply by virtue of being a one-that-is. In terms appropriate to the abstraction of the hypotheses, *any individual* just insofar as it is something complex and singular is subject to relations of indefinite spatial magnitude by virtue of the immanent dyadic characters of greater and smaller that are demanded by the defining (substantial) form that instantiates itself as a distinct whole of parts (H3). Parmenides' specific further aim was to show that great and small are a dyad; greater exceeds smaller, and smaller is exceeded by greater, so that together greater and smaller frame a continuum ranging from the exceeding of one over the other to the being exceeded of the other by the one. This continuum is just one of the ways in which *perata* are imposed on the *plēthē* and, moreover, a paradigm way in which form should be thought in relation to what it structures. The *Parmenides* extends Socrates' introductory points made in *Republic* 7 to the point of dialectical fulfillment by showing that form is the immanent structure of spatio-temporal presence, which is properly conceived in terms of limit imposed upon the unlimited.

Dialectical education thus revealed a specific aspect of intelligibility that does not belong to the eidetic ones. The one-that-is is instantiated according to an eidetic structure, e.g., being large, being small, being in motion, being at rest, and so on, understood as constitutive and normative *perata* (limits) set into the *apeiron*. In H7, going back along the "downward path," as it were, the others were accounted for in their appearance and treated independently of the defining and *perata*-bestowing form. These various layers of the individual spatio-temporal thing, i.e., its general spatio-temporal structure, its substantial structure, and its appearance-structure, offer an account of the degree to which such objects are constituted by form. Form founds the general spatio-temporality of the one-that-is in H2, which is subject to normative limits in H3 according to substantial form in H5, but there is no spatio-temporal object without the unlimited, which we accessed indirectly through the appearance-structure of things in H7. Thus, it is not only form that constitutes the proper limits of definite shape and size, of too much and too little, and the defining continua of indefinite magnitude (of this or that specific kind) but also the unlimited.

What dialectical education affords us the opportunity to discover is the necessary errancy that attends spatio-temporal determinacy. Along any continuum constituted by the *perata* of substantial form there are certain definite ratios at which proper measure is established, but beneath these ratios the continuum remains indifferent to proper measure. Independently of the limit-bestowing form, the errancy of the continuum is manifest as indifference to limit. In order to be able to have a proper measure, the determinate limits of the specific individual must be open to drift, either too much or too little, around the proper ratio. The continua constituted by dyadically paired forms, such as large and small, reveal errancy that is indifferent to ordering limit.

Let us review from the top down the layers of intelligibility gathered in dialectical education. The one of H1 is substantial form (i.e., the one-that-is-not of H5) that guides its articulation as an object of discursive knowing as subject to *legein* and inquiry. Substantial form calls for other forms that support and facilitate its instantiation in a spatio-temporally determinate individual (*perata*-bestowing form of H3). For instance, the forms of geometric figures specifically call for only some of those ones directly constitutive of shape and spatiality, and the forms of numbers picks out yet other ones required for number to be instantiated. In the hypotheses, we have examined the set of categorial ones that are demanded by the form if any spatio-temporal individual is to be instantiated, e.g., shape, motion and rest, same and other, likeness and unlikeness, etc. We have also discovered along the way that the substantial form imposes *perata* on the *apeiron*, and that the *apeiron* is in turn made manifest as errancy and indifference to normative limits.

After studying the hypotheses of the *Parmenides*, we may claim to have (a) understood how the one constitutes and then orders the various continua on which substantial form imposes *perata*, (b) elaborated the categorial aspects of the spatio-temporal individual, and (c) understood substantial form as an object of inquiry and knowledge.[3] The dismantling of the spatio-temporal individual, and the correlative discovery of the ones by which it is instantiated in space and time, as well as the sense that spatio-temporal constitution is primarily a matter of participation, allow us to make some concluding remarks about the giftedness of intelligibility. For this, I return to the skeptical objection from the first part of the dialogue and offer a transformed account of knowledge.

The skeptical objection from the first part of the dialogue construed the relationship between knowledge and its object as a relationship between things. The objection achieved its aims by positing a separation between distinct realms of things, one realm of forms and another realm of participants. In each realm, an individual is what it is in relation to itself and others, especially with respect to its opposite. The example used was that "master itself" is what it is in relation to "slave itself," and separately an individual master is what she is in relation to an individual slave. None of the objects of one realm relate to the other, so the forms do not relate to things that we perceive and opine, just as the things with which we have our dealings do not relate to forms. Parmenides then takes "knowledge itself" to be a form that relates only to "truth itself," and he concludes that we have no knowledge of forms or truth itself; reciprocally, a god does not have knowledge of the things that fill our experience.

Several of the errors in the premises of the objection have already been fully addressed in the course of the hypotheses. The objection treats forms and participants as subject to the same categories of abstract individuality, and it therefore fails to appreciate the ontological difference in kind between them. Things have their power in relation to other things, and so too forms have their power in relation to other forms. In the example we have just reviewed, the cause of spatial relations is different in kind than the things subject to spatial relations, and the causes by which spatiality and relative magnitude are instantiated are not themselves subject to spatiality or relative magnitude. Similarly here, form-relations and thing-relations are not isomorphic. This was indicated but not explored when we earlier interpreted Socrates' response to Zeno's puzzle to be predicated on the stipulation that each form is "itself by itself" in the sense of being essentially non-relational and bearing no relation to other forms, specifically opposite forms. This point was partially confirmed and further developed in the H1 description of the one as not being the same as itself or other than another, i.e., a form does not relate to other forms just insofar as each is one. Thus, if the forms are properly understood as each "itself by itself," it will not be true that the form of "master itself" is what it is in relation to the form of "slave itself." The two forms will not have any relation to each other except by participation in other forms, and each form is what it is independently of that relation.

But more importantly for Plato's larger project of ontological inquiry, the hypotheses invite us to wonder what difference there might be between holding the "true predicates" in which a simple form is revealed in speech as an object of discursive knowing (H5) and grasping the simple and unique form by which these predicates are true (H1). Although I think the relationship between H1 and H5 is not explored in the *Parmenides*, we have been given resources for sketching out that relation. As we already know, the grasp of the simple and unique one-that-is-not is articulated through other characters to which the one is subject as an object of discursive knowing. The form *qua* source of knowing (simple and unique one) and the form *qua* object of knowing (complex and singular one) are the same one in distinct modes. The "one-that-is-not" was denied being [in space and time] because it is not spatially and temporally determinate, but it "is" in another sense, i.e., in the sense that it participates in forms that render it distinct as an object of speech and knowledge. The simple and unique form is prior to its participation in other defining characters, and our grasp of that form cannot be extricated from the non-relational simplicity in which the form stands "itself by itself." The form revealed as an object for discursive knowing is an individual properly speaking, i.e., it is the same as itself and other than others. However, the form is on its own terms non-relational, precisely the sort of one we discussed in H1. Insofar as the form is non-relational, it can call for characters in its definition by ruling some characters in and others out; however, it is not itself subject to those characters. This entails a distinction between the form and its *logos*. This is not to say that the form revealed through its definitional moments is not truly revealed. The form is truly revealed in veridical speech, but whereas the form instantiates itself in propositional moments, it is not reducible to those moments.

The ontological distinction between a form "itself by itself" and the form as an object of discursive knowing gives us an ontological basis on which to establish a specifically Platonic account of truth in light of the good. The *logos* of a substantial form can be treated as "true" in the sense of being a template against which correct speech can be measured. But the noetic grasp of the form that guides that *logos* cannot be "true" in this sense. The form guides the inquiry that gathers the *logos*, and in turn the *logos* in which the form is gathered can test the guiding insight and reveal it to be mere opinion. This bi-directional dynamic is something we see at play in the search for the sophist in Plato's *Sophist*: the gathering of *logos* is guided by the noetic insight, but that insight could always turn out to be false or one-sided opinion, spurring openness to renewed insight and inquiry. If we have noetic "certainty" at all, it cannot be the certainty that is rooted in the relations of same and other that determine and define individuals. From the side of the knower, there can only be negative certainty that nothing contradicts our grasp of the form, a sort of qualified certainty to which Socrates often attests. Truth at heart cannot be propositional, even if the predicates that belong to the subject are veridical. Truth at heart must rather be a matter of having a noetic grasp of the form that unifies that set of predicates, and the distinction between the form "itself by itself" and form as participating in the ones through which it is rendered determinate as an object of discursive knowing commits us to an account of truth that acknowledges the primacy of non-propositional insight.

Looking beyond the *Parmenides*, the account of truth that we are given by this account of form and participation is one predicated on self-awareness and inextricably tied to opinion. The form *qua* simple and unique one stands apart from the form *qua* object of knowledge, and therefore our experience of truth cannot be divorced from the possibility that our guiding insight is really otherwise than, even the opposite of, the way we take it to be. For human beings, truth depends on the ability to receive the determinateness of the intelligibility of the form as something capable of being otherwise, and at the same time it depends on the ability to hold noetic insight as incapable of exhaustive reception. Thus, knowledge must be accompanied by wisdom, and heedful speech must restore the natural connection between predicative knowledge and its guiding, non-propositional insight. Just as we discovered in H7 a shifting and untraceable mark through which the *apeiron* showed itself in appearances, here too, in the account of knowledge with which we respond to the skeptical challenge, we discover a shifting and untraceable excess that stems not from the darkness of appearance but from the brightness of being. Although the question of the way the relationship between the form on its own terms (H1) and the form as participating in other forms by which it is an object of discursive knowing (H5) plays out for our account of knowledge is not examined in full detail in the *Parmenides*, we are given sufficient basis on which to say that the ontology of truth offered by the hypotheses shows us that wisdom takes priority over knowledge.

To sum up, then, we have learned a few things. First and most important, we have learned that there is an ordered structure of forms that make present everyday objects. The presence of things in space and time depends on the enabling work of the categorial forms (these were detailed in the list of characters attributed to the one-that-is in H2) and the substantial forms (the one that is participated in by the others in H3 and articulated as true in H5). Beyond these two types of form, the categorial and the substantial, there is the interplay of indefinite magnitude (instantiated, e.g., as the dyadic structure of great and small) and the limits that articulate a continuum by subjecting it to normative limits. We fulfill the educational path here by wondering how the noetic intuition of the simple form (the one of H1) relates to the predicate forms (the *onta* of H5) such that veridical speech can articulate the truth while remaining open to the simplicity and uniqueness of its source. The irreducibility of the simple one to the weaving together of others ones in *legein* suggests an ontological gap between the source and its articulation, and we have initiated a discussion about the excessive relation of the form to its various instantiations. I conclude with the proposal that the love of wisdom demands our receptivity to the giftedness of intelligibility, and that once we learn to see things in light of the giftedness of intelligibility, certain ethical responses to things and people seem not only appropriate but also effortless.

NOTES

Introduction

1. That is not to say that there is a gift-giver. If nothing else, Greek philosophy has a deeply impersonal view of the divine. What counts as divinity for Greek philosophy may be more intimately a part of who each of us is than anything else could be, but as intimately close to us as it may be, divinity itself is completely impersonal.

2. Greek text of the *Euthyphro* is from J. Burnet, *Platonis opera*, vol. 1. Oxford: Clarendon Press, 1900 (repr. 1967): St I.2a–16a. Unless otherwise noted, translations are my own.

3. The link between the educational path described by Socrates in the *Republic* and the dialectical work of the *Parmenides* is a pillar of the interpretation of the *Parmenides* and the later dialogues offered by Mitchell Miller (cf. *Plato's Parmenides: The Conversion of the Soul*, Princeton: Princeton University Press, 1986; reprinted University Park: Pennsylvania State University Press, 1991; cf. also "A More 'Exact Grasp' of the Soul?: Tripartition in the *Republic* and Dialectic in the *Philebus*," in *Truth: Studies of a Robust Presence*, K. Pritzl ed., Washington, D.C.: Catholic University of America Press, 2010).

4. On this point, see also M. Miller, *Plato's Parmenides: The Conversion of the Soul*. Princeton: Princeton University Press, 1986. Reprinted University Park: Pennsylvania State University Press, 1991: 176–183.

5. A key element of the interpretation of the hypotheses in the Parmenides is the sense we assign to the status of the hypotheses as "exercise" (γυμνασθῆναι, 136a2). I take "exercise" to refer to the arduous process of correcting the habits of thinking that belong structurally to human consciousness. Compare Miller's description of the educational situation in which Socrates stands in the dialogue: he "has distinguished, in principle, the forms both from the visible things that partake of them and from one another. But like any thinker who has just begun, he has not worked out the implications of his principle; nor has he freed his thought of the very habits that the principle means to overcome" (Miller, 1986, 42). Constance Meinwald interprets the prescribed repetitions to refer to the variety of different subjects with which the hypotheses should be run, e.g., one, many, like, unlike, etc.: "But if interpretations of the exercise leave nothing of interest to be gained in connection with other potential subjects, they deprive the recommended repetitions of any point" (Meinwald, *Plato's Parmenides* [Oxford University Press, 1991], 23). It seems to me that once we arrive at the so-called middle period dialogues, such as the *Republic* and *Phaedo*, there is remarkably greater attention paid to the momentum and intractability of ingrained habits of thinking, and that the hypotheses can well be repeated with the same subject with the expectation that they will continue to yield new results. Indeed, I take it to be the nature of Platonic writing that it speaks differently to distinct readers or even the same reader at different stages of philosophical education.

6. Cf. Miller (1986), 47. Miller divides two phases of Parmenides' objections to Socrates' account of participation, the first phase addressing the complexity of spatio-temporal individuals in contrast to the simplicity of forms (130e–131e), the second phase addressing

the singularity of such things in contrast to the uniqueness of forms (131e–133a). This division between the essential structure of forms and things is central to Miller's thesis regarding the educational program being offered by the *Parmenides*: "Socrates . . . needs to deepen his grasp of the very difference he declares, the difference of forms as such, in their nature, from the things that partake of them. If forms are really distinct from things, he must learn not to treat them as a sort of subclass of things, subject to the same categories. This, in turn, presupposes a prior understanding of these categories. Unless one grasps what it is, specifically, which forms are not, it will be next to impossible to grasp them for what they are. Thus the task of thinking forms *as forms* presupposes that of thinking things *as things*" (Miller, 1986, 40). I adopt a similar view in my analysis, and I take the goal of the *Parmenides* to be to establish rigorously the ontological distinction between aspects of unity that are necessarily entailed by the determinate intelligibility of things our world. However, like Mary Margaret McCabe and Constance Meinwald, I do not read the hypotheses to be about forms except indirectly. McCabe explicitly sets aside forms in her analysis of the hypotheses to focus on the nature of individuation. McCabe argues (1) that individuals in the sensible world are not self-explanatory (25), (2) that there is a difference between explaining something and simply repeating it, and (3) that the forms, in order to explain, must be uncompromisingly separate (63), with the result that (4) forms must be discarded so that we may understand what it means to be an individual (McCabe, 1994). She writes: "Plato turns his attention away from forms as such and from particulars as such. . . . What Plato badly needs is to consider What is an individual? as a general question, leaving open the issue of which entities qualify" (McCabe, 1994, 99). However, I return to the distinction between form and participants after analysis of the "instant" (ἐξαίφνης) (155e–157b), where I think that the dialogue re-founds the ontological starting point and starts to offer a new account of participation on that basis.

7. G. E. L. Owen and Gilbert Ryle see the hypotheses as a *reductio* resulting in an unacceptable pure negativity (G. E. L. Owen, "Plato on Not-Being" in *Plato I: Metaphysics and Epistemology*, ed. Gregory Vlastos [New York: Doubleday, 1970]; Gilbert Ryle, "Plato's 'Parmenides,'" *Mind* 48, no. 190 [1939]:129–151). I take a very different approach that has its roots in the neo-Platonic reading of the *Parmenides*, according to which the apparent contradictions point beyond certain limits of thinking and being to a one that has being in some sense that we must work to understand. The distinction between different approaches to the hypotheses is clearly articulated by Miller (1986, 236n.4) and Constance Meinwald (1991, "Introduction," esp. 19–26).

8. I share this reading with Miller, for whom this point is crucial in developing the thesis that there are distinct subjects of H1 and H2 (Miller, 1986, 90–91).

Chapter 1

1. Text of the *Parmenides* is from J. Burnet, *Platonis opera*, vol. 2. (Oxford: Clarendon Press, 1901, repr. 1967), St III.126a–166c.

2. See Nancy Evans, *Civic Rites: Democracy and Religion in Ancient Athens* (University of California Press, 2010).

3. See Jenifer Neils, *Goddess and Polis. The Panathenaic Festival in Ancient Athens* (Hood Museum of Art and Princeton University Press, 1992).

4. As Mark Munn points out, the formula καλός τε κἀγαθός had associations with Athenian empire as a means by which the elite of Athens could distinguish themselves from the less affluent citizens who constituted the polis through its civic institutions in

the Assembly and law courts (Mark Munn, *The School of History: Athens in the Age of Socrates* [University of California Press, 2000], 10).

5. The issue of concatenations of power will return later in the opening conversation when Parmenides brings up the example of the relationship between master and slave (133c2–134c2).

6. Furthermore, the critique launched in the *Parmenides* will draw on, even as it overturns, the impact of the study of mathematics as described in the *Republic*. The third level of the divided line and the study of mathematics will help us to clarify the intelligible foundations of the stance of mastery, so that dialectic can expose the dependencies and incommensurable foundations of the metaphysics on which it stands.

7. This is, of course, a controversial point and one that I make in this context only for the sake of understanding Plato. It is commonly argued to the contrary that Parmenides denies the reality of our lived world and argues instead for a strict monism. It is my view, to the contrary, that the historical Parmenides is arguing for the distinct character of the "is" that lets all intelligible opposition and therefore determinacy stand forth. That is, prior to combination and division of determinate intelligibility, the "is" shows itself as what lets difference be, which is why the Parmenidean "is" has nothing other than itself to which it stands in contrast or which it "is not" and why it cannot be explained in according to any of the modes of intelligibility that it founds (e.g., neither more here nor there, neither earlier nor later). For a thorough account of the Platonic reception of the historical Parmenides, see John Palmer, *Plato's Reception of Parmenides* (Oxford University Press, 1999). For an interpretation of the Parmenidean "is" that lines up with my own, see Miller, "Ambiguity and Transport: Reflections on the Proem to Parmenides' Poem," *Oxford Studies in Ancient Philosophy* 30 (2006):1–47, and Mourelatos, *The Route of Parmenides* (Princeton: Princeton University Press, 1970). Later on, we will have the opportunity to consider the way that the account of "is" in Greek philosophy generally figures in to what I am here only suggestively indicating (see C. Kahn, "A Return to 'Be' and the Concept of Being," in *Essays on Being* [Oxford University Press, 2009], and L. Brown, "Being in the *Sophist*: A Syntactical Inquiry," in G. Fine, ed., *Plato 1* [Oxford University Press, 1999].)

8. Mary Margaret McCabe locates the structural co-implication of opposites in what she calls the "contextualizing feature of relations," i.e., having one relation in one respect implies having the opposite in another: "each particular is enmeshed in a variety of relations to other particulars" (McCabe, 1994, 43). With reference to the *Phaedo*, McCabe relates the character of self-sameness in forms to the modality of being "always" what they are, and she distinguishes this from the cognitively unreliable and shifting character of particulars, which are "never" the same as themselves (McCabe, 1994, 44). McCabe's emphasis on phenomenality and explanatory adequacy helpfully singles out the nature of appearance as such, or spatio-temporal presence as such, which will be instrumental in understanding the basic lesson offered by the *Parmenides*. Once we distinguish between the eidetic structure that explains spatio-temporal things and their relational character, we will be in a position to explain the relationship of the eidetic "ones" to the spatio-temporal "others." We will have occasion below to consider the various ways in which Socrates fails in the early parts of the *Parmenides* to maintain the rigorous distinction between ontological levels that his account of participation requires.

9. There is a way to explain their failure from the perspective of the virtues. They, like the Democratic Man in *Republic* 8, interpret justice as numerical equality, leading them to

privilege no one over any other, and committing themselves to stream continuously from one to the next.

10. Greek text of the *Republic* is from J. Burnet, *Platonis opera*, vol. 4 (Oxford: Clarendon Press, 1902, repr. 1968): St II.327a–621d.

11. There are many other instances in the dialogues at which the relationship between the one and the many arises, and in some of those instances it appears that the problem goes right to the core of an important philosophical issue. In the *Meno* Socrates asks Meno about virtue—what is it (τί ἐστιν)? And when Meno gives him various types of virtue, Socrates asks Meno to stop making many from one (πολλὰ ποιῶν ἐκ τοῦ ἑνός), as the jokers say when someone breaks a plate. Socrates tells Meno to leave virtue "whole and sound" (ὅλην καὶ ὑγιῆ) and tell him what it is (*Meno* 74a–b).

12. Miller stresses the relationship between Platonic ontology and Aristotle's account of categories (Miller, 1986, throughout Chapter IV, but esp. 119n.62, 121n.64).

13. The move to take "like" and "unlike" not as referring to a particular respect in which a thing is subject to relation among other things is not unusual in the Platonic context. In other dialogues, eristic also demands of an account that its terms and claims be taken up simply on their own without their elided content (see the argument in the *Euthydemus* that if the dog is a father, and you have a father, then the dog is your father; see also the argument in *Republic* 5 that what instantiates the formula *x* "is" and "is not" is anything that both is F and is not F). This approach to intelligibility can be purely destructive and therefore irresponsible in the hands of those who are not beholden to the forms. However, this is also the approach by which the sophistries of thinking are overturned. We will revisit this point below when we consider the way rhetoric and sophistry pave the way, through their use of contradiction and opposition, for scientific philosophy. The basic point I will make below is that by setting received opinions in opposition, we are able to expose the sources (that is, the forms) guiding our formulations of those sources. In the case of the formulations of those things we hold in honor, such as justice, there is a normative order toward which our various formulations strive. In contrast to that normativity, scientific philosophy reveals the constitutive basis for determinacy, and in that case there is no striving at all without a constitutive basis upon which striving is possible.

14. I leave to one side the intellectual-historical context of the pluralist attacks on the historical Parmenides. In my view, Zeno and Parmenides are primarily interested in what *logos* can and cannot sustain as evidence, with Parmenides focusing on the primacy of the nature of intelligibility itself and Zeno focusing, in concert with Parmenides, on the apparent incoherence of our way of talking about beings.

15. It is for this reason that forms are characterized as what "is" most of all, or most truly. For instance, justice is what is just, and beauty is what is beautiful. This has become known as the "self-predication" of forms. I take self-predication to refer to the simple source from which all formulations and specific instances of, e.g., justice have their intelligible determinacy. That source is not determinate in the same way as its instances, and self-predication should be taken, in my view, to be nothing more than the invocation of the source from which determinate instances draw their being just.

16. As Allen notes, Socrates' account of participation seems a poorly measured response to Zeno's paradox; he says, "the Theory of the Forms seems curiously beside the point. Critics unite in regarding [Zeno's paradox] as an empty sophism, . . . But they do not explain why, if this is true, Socrates should trundle in the Theory of the Forms, irrelevantly, as a solution. They do not explain why he should use heavy artillery to shoot at fleas—

and miss" (R. E. Allen, "The Interpretation of Plato's *Parmenides*: Zeno's Paradox and the Theory of the Forms," *Journal of the History of Philosophy*, vol. 2, 1964, 145–46). Allen's point is well taken. The critics of Zeno's paradox intend to solve the puzzle with reference to the distinct relations in which something is like and unlike. But even if the same thing is not like and unlike in the same respect, it is still necessary that the same thing possesses the opposing characters somehow, for it is the condition of their being present. Socrates explains the presence of like and unlike in beings by participation in distinct forms, each of which is "itself by itself" and, as indicated above, apart from other forms. Participation is thus necessary even to explain the case of relational predicates. Furthermore, Allen draws our attention to the important distinction between those forms responsible for intelligibility as such and forms responsible for the character of this or that thing. The forms of likeness and unlikeness belong to the former category insofar as they extend beyond the sensible realm into the intelligible: every form (including likeness) will be unlike the others, and conversely every form (including unlikeness) will be like the others (Allen, 1964, 150–152). Socrates assumes that the forms themselves, because they do not combine and divide, are not subject to forms, but it then becomes impossible for him to explain how forms can become objects of knowledge at all if they do not bear at least some of the characteristics proper to objects in general.

17. Socrates lists parts that are indifferently related to each other as the necessary aspects of spatial presence (front/back, left/right), without regard for functional priority, e.g., initiating movement with the right side, facing forward, standing upright. These are the aspects the individual has in relation to other individuals, and not the complex internal organization of the individual body.

18. Socrates' use of "the likes themselves" as equivalent to "likeness itself" reveals a lack of precision in his distinction between forms and things. The work of sorting out the difference between, e.g., the idea of the "many" and the presence of many things will continue throughout the dialogue, and we will address other implications of Socrates' imprecision in this passage below. Miller has made this point clearly: The "mixing of the intensive substantive, αὐτὸ τὸ . . . ("the . . . itself"), with the plural adjective seems to reflect a residual confusion in Socrates' thinking. He both distinguishes the form from its instances and yet still treats it as if, like the instances, it were subject to plurality" (Miller, 1986, 39). McCabe dismisses the concern: "How much hangs on the plural here (cf. the anxieties that commentators display about the plural 'the equals themselves' at *Phaedo* 74c)? Nothing, in my view; Socrates clearly intends to contrast the particulars which are both like and unlike and the Form of Likeness; the use of a plural expression for the Form may be mere carelessness after the plural for the particulars, and not meant to imply (at least before the Third Man arguments) that the Form of Likeness is itself many" (McCabe, 1996, 9n.7). It seems that Socrates' carelessness regarding the characteristics to which forms are subject is, however, precisely what is most seriously wrong with Socrates' current understanding of forms. Socrates cannot grasp his own theory with sufficient rigor; Parmenides' objections will point this out, until he learns to disentangle the ontological status of a "something" (τί) from spatio-temporal particulars.

19. This second formulation comes closest to positing, in the form of a question, the part/whole complexity of forms toward which H5 will point when, for instance, Parmenides says that the "one that is not" must be subject to bonds of being and not-being. However, Socrates does not use part/whole complexity to refer to forms or eidetic ones anywhere in the *Parmenides*.

20. I will show later (in the analysis of *exaiphnes*) that this is a serious omission on Socrates' part, and that addressing this omission will result in a radical inversion of the subject/predicate relationship as it is, even here, being imagined in the pre-philosophical perspective.

21. It is common to translate the hypothesis here as "if the all is one," and doing so responds sensibly to the immediate context in which Socrates has just attributed to Parmenides the claim that "the all is one" (ἓν φῂς εἶναι τὸ πᾶν, 128a8–b1). But of course the subject "the all" is not made explicit by Zeno, and it would not contradict the claim that the "all is one" to say "there is one." In my translation I am attuned to the questions that will become more pressing later concerning the translation of the hypotheses themselves and Parmenides' introduction of them (see Chapter 2, Section 5, n.72).

22. As Allen points out, "[Zeno] apologizes for the polemical tone of his book but nowhere implies that he questions the validity of its arguments" (Allen, 1964, 147 n.). Kenneth Sayre notes that Zeno nowhere dismisses the main intent of his treatise, and he would not have brought it with him to Athens unless it contained something of philosophical value (Kenneth Sayre, *Parmenides' Lesson: Translation and Explication of Plato's Parmenides* [University of Notre Dame Press, 1996, 64]). Miller reads Zeno as attempting to be the inheritor of Parmenidean wisdom and being displaced by Socrates (*Plato's Parmenides: The Conversion of the Soul* [Princeton: Princeton University Press, 1986; reprinted University Park: Pennsylvania State University Press, 1991: 29–30]). I think Miller's reading applies too strict a criterion of success to Zeno's arguments. It seems that Zeno's arguments are successful enough in this context at soliciting an important set of strengths and weaknesses from Socrates, which would be a valid reason for Zeno to continue to read and discuss his book after so much time has elapsed and his relationship toward its contents has changed. I do however believe that there is a pervasive concern in the Platonic dialogues for philosophical inheritance and preservation of insight, and that the transformative reception of the past is key to the style of Platonic philosophy.

23. Zeno, on this reading, is taken to be pointing out limitations in the way we speak and think more than as champion of any particular thesis (let alone a champion of whatever he may take Parmenides' thesis to be). Phil Hopkins makes this point in "Zeno's boêtheia tôi logôi: Thought Problems about Problems for Thought," *Epoché*, 11:1 (2006). As he says, "Zeno's paradoxes are paradoxes about the way we think and represent the world to ourselves." Zeno's puzzle concludes only that "the many are not," arguing on the evidence that a certain hypothesis of the many would suffer impossible self-contradictions. As Rose Cherubin points out about the historical Zeno, Zeno did not go on to draw a positive conclusion from the negative arguments, in spite of what was attributed to Zeno by the philosophical tradition that followed him (Rose Cherubin, "Inquiry and What Is: Eleatics and Monisms," *Epoché* 8.1, 2003; cf. also Trish Glazebrook, "Zeno against Mathematical Physics," *Journal of the History of Ideas* 62, no. 2 (2001): 193–210). Although it is important to notice that Zeno is not explicit about his intentions, Socrates seems right to say "not many" and "one" is "saying nearly the same thing" (σχεδόν τι λέγοντας ταὐτά, 128b5). I take Zeno to be subjecting our unreflective ways of describing beings to critique through refutative *reductios*, and that chief among our mistaken views is the way we understand what it means to be one. On a certain description of being present as a one, Zeno's puzzles show us that there cannot be motion and that beings cannot be many. I think Zeno's contribution to the *Parmenides* is significant at the level of method, and that the hypotheses in the dialogue (not only the negative ones) are a brilliant reception and philosophical fulfillment of Zenonian method.

24. Gregory Vlastos makes this point ("Plato's Testimony Concerning Zeno of Elea," *The Journal of Hellenic Studies*, vol. 95 [1975]: 136–162), pointing to Socrates' charge that Zeno is trying to deceive everyone into thinking that he has his own philosophical contribution to make apart from Parmenides' claim that the "all is one." As Vlastos reads it, Zeno does not "say anything to imply that he had avowed positively his alliance with Parmenides anywhere in the book: had this been the case Socrates' charge could hardly have been made in the first place" (Vlastos, 1975, 138n. 11). Vlastos goes on to challenge Cornford and Fränkel, who make the charges that Zeno did not take his own work seriously (Cornford) and that Zeno is trying to deceive his reader (Fränkel). Later in the same essay Vlastos says Plato tells us that Parmenides and Zeno are saying nearly the same, but on the basis of this prior observation that Zeno never positively avows his allegiance with Parmenides it seems significant that it is *Socrates* who sees the parallel between Zeno and Parmenides, which may tell us more about what Socrates stands to learn than it does about what Plato takes to be the case (Vlastos, 1975, 149n. 52). Solmsen agrees that the text of the dialogue seems to claim that Parmenides and Zeno are saying the same thing, but he qualifies this with reference to the claim in the dialogue that Parmenides' hypothesis is the "one," which he says is only one predicate of being found in the poem and not necessarily the most important predicate. He concludes that if Plato has distorted Parmenides, he could just as easily have distorted Zeno's intentions, and we should not place our trust in the claim that Parmenides and Zeno are saying the same thing (Friedrich Solmsen, "The Tradition about Zeno of Elea Reexamined," *Phronesis*, vol. 16 [1971], 120–121).

25. It is rhetoric's freedom from external standards that grants its power for beginnings. The power of rhetoric is lost once it is subject to the rigors of craft, for under that paradigm rhetoric would be something measured by an impersonal standard. If rhetoric were measured by the "just things" (τὰ δίκαια, see *Gorgias* 460b7), it would no longer be free to operate solely on the way truth appears to the non-knower.

26. Key to our study will be to see that Socrates unwittingly treats forms ambiguously as prior *and yet subject to* the categories that determine things. Clarifying the distinction between forms and things will allow us to see the extent to which the determinate intelligibility of things, universally and necessarily, owes itself to the forms. As Socrates says in the *Philebus*, characterizing the distinction between forms and ultimate participants, "human beings nowadays—those who are wise—make one and many haphazardly and any which way, faster and shorter than they ought to, and immediately after the one they make things unlimited, but the middle things escape them. It is by the middle things that the separation has been made between our talking with one another dialectically and eristically" (Plato, *Philebus*, tr. S. Benardete [University of Chicago Press, 1993, 10 (16e4–17a5)]), I am proposing the thesis that the "middle" to which the *Parmenides* especially draws our attention is categorial determinacy, which mediates between forms and participants of all sorts. By distinguishing properly between forms and things, and by articulating the eidetic structure of things, we will be in a position to break free from the hypothesis of things by which the philosophical attitude is smothered.

27. Miller holds that the entirety of Parmenides' comments early in the dialogue are unified by the educational needs of the young and immature Socrates (Miller, 1986, 43). The smiling admiration of Socrates' first attempted response to Zeno need not be an exception to this interpretive principle—Parmenides and Zeno are smiling because now they see the young philosopher's brilliance as clearly as they see the educational path the young Socrates must follow.

28. This first group of forms in particular (*viz.* one, many, likeness) has direct bearing on the remainder of the dialogue as a preliminary indication of the sort of abstract terms that we will engage exhaustively in the hypotheses.

29. As Miller provocatively suggests, this list also parallels the investigation of the *Republic*: "justice is the form sought in *Republic* II-IV; beauty (τὸ καλόν) is Socrates' exemplary focus in introducing the conception of the forms in *Republic* V (see 474d ff., 475e, 476bff.); and the good is revealed as the highest form in *Republic* VI (505a ff., especially 506a and the following simile of the sun)" (Miller, 1986, 44n. 12).

30. I interpret the "abyss of nonsense" to refer to the recognition that all materiality and phenomenality is normatively structured, even "worthless" things such as hair, mud, and filth. The insight to which this points us is that all indexicality, or "thisness," is rooted in a causal basis of form. I take the lesson here to be a pre-cursor to Aristotle's claim that matter is not a "this," and that actuality precedes potentiality. Miller identifies the "abyss of nonsense" as the point to which Socrates must be led back repeatedly before he can move forward and develop his account of participation, with which I agree. However, Miller takes the abyss to refer to the problem of interpreting the being of forms, at least in the case of the "things that we see," in such a way that they possess the same characteristics that they are (Miller, 1986: 46–47), e.g., as justice "is" just, so too hairiness would be hairy or muddiness muddy. As different as these approaches are, each adopts the view that Socrates must differentiate between what is subject to normative and constitutive eidetic structures and those prior, causally efficacious, structures themselves.

31. John Russon points out that the fact that two sticks are subject to comparison as equal and unequal implies there is a single dyad of comparison *and* a multiplicity of other qualities, or respects, in which they can be compared. Comparison also implies a standard of measuring longer and shorter, or better and worse, that is, a reality that both share and neither exhausts. Lastly, comparison implies that the differing of the two sticks is something constitutive of what they are, not simply an external imposition on them. Thus, the recognition of equality, Russon concludes, requires (a) the ability to recognize being, sameness, and difference, as well as the "as" or "*qua*" of respect, (b) the ability to recognize that these are inseparable from one another, and (c) the ability to recognize all of these aspects as invoked from within each member of any comparison (John Russon, "We Sense that They Strive," in *Retracing the Platonic Text*, John Russon and John Sallis, eds. [Northwestern University Press, 2000: 72–73]). What I want to emphasize in Russon's analysis is the discovery of the inseparability of the co-implicated aspects that belong to any spatio-temporal object just insofar as it is subject to space and time.

32. Russon describes the metaphysical situation of the individual thing as "a double harmonious tension" (Russon, "We Sense that They Strive," in *Retracing the Platonic Text*, ed. Russon and Sallis [Evanston, Ill.: Northwestern University Press, 2000, 79]). He explains: "It is at odds with others from which it cannot separate its identity. It is at odds with a value which it itself projects. To be a determinateness is thus to be a striving—a striving to be this and not that, and this striving to be not that is thus a pursuit of itself, which means it projects a good in terms of which it is to be measured—what Aristotle would call its *telos*" (Russon, 2000, 79). The important point to carry away from this discussion of the *Phaedo* is that the very nature of being an individual subject to space and time is to be the site from which what Socrates calls "mind" orchestrates the way things occupy space and time.

33. Note that in the *Phaedo*, the issue of being "present in" can refer not to the structure of the spatio-temporal individual but to the way the participant has the form present in it

as a real property. At 102b1–2, Phaedo says that the people in the cell that day agreed "each of the forms are something" (εἶναί τι ἕκαστον τῶν εἰδῶν) and that the others that participate (μεταλαμβάνοντα) in them get their names from the forms, and Phaedo then quotes Socrates: when you say that Simmias is greater than Socrates but smaller than Phaedo, aren't you saying that "both the large and the small are in Simmias?" (εἶναι ἐν τῷ Σιμμίᾳ ἀμφότερα, καὶ μέγεθος καὶ σμικρότητα; 102b4–5). On the subject of the forms' being "in" participants, see Gail Fine, "Immanence," *Oxford Studies in Ancient Philosophy* 4, 1986, and Verity Harte, *Plato on Parts and Wholes: The Metaphysics of Structure*, Oxford University Press, 2002: 65–66, 70; see also McCabe's discussion of "natural inherence" (McCabe, 1994, 29–37). We will return to the argument that the form "large" is present in things in the discussion of Parmenides' "sharing by parts or wholes" objection below (Chapter 2, Section 1).

34. Note that in spite of referring to the "one itself," Socrates cannot be talking about the form of unity. The one Socrates has in mind is essentially related to other ones, so it must be a one that is denumerable, i.e., one *qua* number, i.e. a "something."

35. *Republic*, ed. Giovanni Ferrari, tr. Tom Griffith (Cambridge University Press, 2000).

36. πειρᾶται λογισμόν τε καὶ νόησιν ψυχὴ παρακαλοῦσα ἐπισκοπεῖν εἴτε ἓν εἴτε δύο ἐστὶν ἕκαστα τῶν εἰσαγγελλομένων, 524b4–5.

37. There is some difficulty determining to what "the one itself" (αὐτὸ τὸ ἕν) here refers. After singling out the ones that are the objects of thought and calculation, Socrates says that the soul will think these (e.g., large or small) as separate (κεχωρισμένα, 524b10–c1) and as each one. The act of singling out the characters large and small will provide the basis for the distinction between the sensible and the intelligible (νοητόν & ὁρατόν, 524c11–13). This step appears to lead McCabe to take "the one itself" to be a form: "Before we ask 'What is large?' then, we must sort out 'the large,' which, in its manifestations, appears both one and many. The large is itself subject to the compresence of opposites, namely, one and many; so the primary question the soul must ask is not 'What is large?' but 'What is one?' before any dialectic can get off the ground. For our question cannot begin to be settled until the item about which we ask the questions is itself a determinate one something, itself by itself" (McCabe, 1994, 65). Her analysis is linked to her overall thesis that being an individual (being one) is basic to being anything and is prior to the form/participant distinction. While I agree with her characterization of forms, i.e., that they are "austere individuals" and cannot be subject to the compresence of opposites, it seems that the "one itself" cannot here refer to form. Socrates prefaces the final leg of his discussion by stating again that a one seen "itself by itself" (αὐτὸ καθ' αὑτό, 524d10) will not summon intellect; specifically he refers to the finger "itself by itself." It seems that this language, which we normally associate with forms, is here being used to describe distinct aspects of sensible particulars. I think the reason for this is that we are singling out formal aspects of a compound. When we say "the one itself," we are referring to "that very one" that we perceive and judge, and we are talking about it primarily as the "something" in which contradictories can co-habit. Meinwald makes a similar point with regard to the use of "nature" and "itself by itself" referring to *plēthos* in H3 (at 158c5–6 , 158d5–6 , 158e2): "such phrases as 'in itself' and 'taken by itself' may be used, in a context where some compound or complex is being discussed, to isolate a subject for discussion that is one of the elements to be combined, but will now be considered in abstraction from the combination" (Meinwald, 1991, 137). Just as the *plēthos* is an aspect of the "others" distinguished in thought and discussed "itself by itself," so too the "one" in the *Republic* 7 discussion is an aspect of the finger taken in abstraction from the other aspects with which it is combined in, for example, the finger.

38. Socrates' focus on the important one–many relationship strikes especially deep chords in the *Philebus* (15a–b), where he acknowledges the potentially childish (παιδαριώδη) purposes to which the puzzles involved in a rigorous, discursive understanding of the relationship can be put. He says that whenever someone divides the parts and members (μέλη τε καὶ ἅμα μέρη) of anything, he can playfully refute himself, declaring that he has done the impossible and compelled the one to be many and unlimited (τό πολλά . . . καὶ ἄπειρα) and the many to be only one (ἓν μόνον). These puzzles concerning things that are generated and destroyed, the things with which we are commonly familiar, are of no interest to Socrates, and are easily solved by pointing out the different respects in which things appear. However, when someone posits the good as one (τὸ ἀγαθὸν ἕν), man as one (ἕνα ἄνθρωπον), ox as one (βοῦν ἕνα), or, as we have just discussed in the context of the *Republic*, beauty as one (τὸ καλὸν ἕν), "great zeal with division of these henads and the like gives rise to dispute" (περὶ τούτων τῶν ἑνάδων καὶ τῶν τοιούτων ἡ πολλὴ σπουδὴ μετὰ διαιρέσεως ἀμφισβήτησις γίγνεται, 15a4–7, consulting Frede). Socrates tells Protarchus that the issues are: (1) whether we should assume that such "ones" "truly are" (ἀληθῶς οὔσας, 15b2), (2) how each, being always the same, can remain steadfastly this one, and (3) given the plethora of things that come to be as these ones (i.e., as ox, as beautiful, etc.), whether the "one" is dispersed (διεσπασμένην, 15b5–6) into many or wholly separate from itself (ὅλην αὐτὴν αὑτῆς χωρίς, 15b6–7). These last two puzzles, i.e., being dispersed and being separate from itself, refer to the complexity and individuality of participants. Socrates says that the questions about these "ones" cause the greatest perplexity if they are not agreed on properly, but if they are well resolved, they provide "good passage" (εὐπορία, 15c2). The questions are fundamental: First, do such ones truly exist? If they do, then how (πῶς) are they supposed to be? Can they be permanently (βεβαιότατα) this one, selfsame thing? And, given the unlimited number of things that come into being and are destroyed, must it be dispersed, or separate from itself, or at the same time in one and many? These questions, Socrates says, cause the utmost perplexity if they are poorly agreed upon, but if they are well agreed upon they provide smooth passage (εὐπορία). These questions will come up in the detailed study of the Hypotheses. The issue will be threefold: (1) whether these ones truly are, (2) being one and selfsame, in what sense they have permanence, (3) whether and how they can be in many. Greek text of the *Philebus* is from J. Burnet, *Platonis opera*, vol. 2. Oxford: Clarendon Press, 1901 (repr. 1967): St II.11a–67b.

39. Cf. Miller, "Figure, Ratio, Form: Plato's Five Mathematical Studies," in "Recognition, Remembrance and Reality: New Essays on Plato's Epistemology and Metaphysics," ed. Mark McPherran, special issue, *Apeiron* 32, 4 (Dec. 1999), 73–88. Miller argues for the philosophical importance of the mathematical studies in *Republic* 7 as a way to move from the imagistic thinking characteristic of the cave and into the sunlight of discursive accounts of intelligibility and being. The mathematical objects that are identified in *Republic* 7 are studied as intermediaries between sensibles and forms, able to capture the universality of the form at the same time as touching on the spatiality of the sensible. By approaching the one-that-is in H2 as a mathematically abstract description of concrete particulars, we might be able to see this one as just such an intermediary, perhaps most importantly as a paradigm with specific limitations pointing us in the direction of the more complete account of the "others" in H3.

40. Later, after the objections have all been raised, Parmenides returns to the problem that Socrates marks out the good, the just, and the beautiful too early. Parmenides will recommend the Hypotheses as gymnastic training (γυμνασθῆναι, 136a2), which others

consider idle talk (ἀδολεσχία, 135d5), and which produce what in the *Republic* Socrates calls the "synoptic" understanding of the dialectician (cf. *Republic* 537c7). I am interpreting this to mean that Socrates must habituate himself away from the authority of received wisdom and perceived norms in order to be, as Socrates puts it in the *Republic*, "eager to test [his insights] in accord with being" (κατ' οὐσίαν προθυμούμενος ἐλέγχειν) (*Republic*, 534c2–3). Cf. n. 5 to the introduction to this book.

Chapter 2

1. As Allen reminds us, Parmenides ultimately accepts and endorses the account of participation, so criticisms of the account must be motivated not by the desire to assert a contrary account but by the desire to help Socrates develop a stronger insight into the account of participation. Parmenides makes objections in order to reveal assumptions and enable the account to mature, not simply to win the argument or establish metaphysical truth (Allen, 1964, 149). On the subject of philosophical "testing" more generally, note that if Socrates sometimes seems alone in the dialogues, or to be talking to himself, it would seem to be in part explained by a desire to hold himself to an absolute standard of openness to testing and refutation, going beyond what most other people are willing to face. That openness has to be won, I maintain, through the philosophical training that is offered in the *Parmenides*.

2. Parmenides repeats the word "separate" (χωρίς) frequently enough to draw attention to it as the precise subject of his concern. Parmenides' objections will focus on the elements of participation (forms and things) in such a way that obtrusively imposes the notions of spatial proximity and distance on this notion of separation between forms and things. Ultimately, it is the theme of proximity and distance that thus will be the focus in this section, both insofar as we want to uncover the eidetic structure of the proximity and distance between two spatio-temporal participants, and insofar as we want to reject the model of spatial proximity and distance between form and participant for a model that does not invoke these terms at all.

3. Parmenides is referring to the objects of perceptual experience, and this expression, "the others," will have significant import in the hypotheses.

4. Commentators generally agree that the purpose of the part/whole model of participation is to show that certain types of separation between forms and participants imply inappropriate ways of construing each side of the separation, most importantly that forms are understood on the model of things. In the *Metaphysics*, Aristotle says that if the ideas and things by us are taken to be "separate," universally predicated substances are of the same sort as individuals (*Metaphysics* XIII 1086b10–11, cited in Allen, 1983, 114). Reginald Allen refers to these puzzles as the "dilemma of participation" (Allen, 1983, 128–145). Francis Cornford characterizes this objection as resting on "a gross and material sense" of part and whole (Cornford, 1939, 85, cited in Harte, 2002, 70). Allen takes this part/wholes objection to be fundamental to everything that follows in the *Parmenides* (Allen, 1983, 128) and beyond that in other dialogues as well. For example, Socrates raises the dilemma in the *Philebus*, where he says that it becomes a matter of dispute "whether one ought to suppose that there are any such unities truly in existence. Then again, how they are supposed to be: whether each one of them is always one and the same, admitting neither of generation nor of destruction; and whether it remains most definitely one and the same, even though it is afterwards found again among the things that come to be and are unlimited, so that it finds itself as one and the same in one and many things at the same time" (Frede tr., *Philebus*, 15b). As Miller notes and Allen emphasizes, the part/whole structure that frames this

set of objections and appears consistently throughout the *Parmenides* need not apply only to sensible particulars. Unlike Miller, however, Allen takes the part/whole relationship to extend beyond "material" wholes or sensible particulars in the *Parmenides*, and he pursues the possibility of a more general or abstract conception of the distinction. Miller notes Allen's point and takes it seriously, but Miller takes the part/whole model in the context of the *Parmenides* as applying to sensible particulars exclusively; the concept always refers to a spatial whole of spatial parts (Miller, *Plato's Parmenides*, 208n. 20, and Allen, "Unity and Infinity: *Parmenides* 142b–145a," *Review of Metaphysics*, vol. 27 [1974]:724). Miller suggests that the choice of this model is intended to point out to Socrates the absurdity of treating the forms as sensible particulars, that is, as singular beings with composite structure. Harte points out the consistency with which forms are treated as being present in their participants at various points in the Platonic dialogues (Harte, 2002, 64–73), which is a specific example of what she calls the "pluralizing parts principle" (Harte, 2002, 53) and is closely related to what McCabe calls "natural inherence" (McCabe, 1994, 29–37, also cited in Harte, 2002, 70). That principle, as Harte later defines it in relation to the hypotheses, is that a whole is identical to its parts, i.e., composition is identity. In my analysis, the distinction between identity and composition will not be properly addressed until H3.

5. Miller and Sayre agree that there are certain "material" phenomena that are closer to the part/whole relationship appropriate to the forms in their simplicity. Miller describes the image of a day as a simple whole that resists decomposition into separate parts and has a more promising, even "inspired," structure of composition rooted less in sensibles and bearing slightly greater kinship to the simplicity of the forms (Miller, 1986, 49).

6. Socrates' response to this translation is "perhaps" (ἴσως), indicating that he does not see it as fitting but that he does not have a precise account for its falsity.

7. Hermann Sinaiko calls the model crude (Sinaiko, *Love, Knowledge, and Discourse in Plato: Dialogue and Dialectic in Phaedrus, Republic, Parmenides* [Chicago: University of Chicago Press, 1965, 202]). A certain crudeness is the point, i.e., Parmenides is showing to Socrates the limitations of a certain obvious model of accounting for intelligibility in order to educate him beyond the assumptions of a particular stage of education. The logical–linguistic analysis inaugurated by Vlastos, by contrast, contends that Plato held a metaphysical theory with disastrous implications for his account of phenomena, and were Plato able to see the "true logical outcome" of the things he was saying, he would have been forced into a retraction of that theory (Vlastos, 1954, 254). Meinwald believes that Vlastos is right when he says that the "third man argument" is a "record of honest perplexity," but whereas Vlastos believes this is a record of Plato's own confusion writing the *Parmenides*, Meinwald contends that the second part of the dialogue will demonstrate that Plato understood more than he reveals in this passage (Meinwald, 1991, 10). I am in the camp that sees the hypotheses as provocations to deeper thinking about the nature of intelligibility and as intended to extend and radicalize the account of participation.

8. It is at least clear that Socrates' example of the day, in spite of its potential virtues, is in fact an image, and as an image it apparently is not well enough established to secure Socrates against a radical transformation of it into the image of a sail. Miller compellingly suggests that the image of the day is both true and untrue. Insofar as it is an example of a simple unity, the example is true, but insofar as the example is an image rooted in and dependent upon sense experience and an image of what is in some sense a whole divisible into parts, the example is untrue. Parmenides is primarily interested in helping Socrates to free his account from its dependency on sense experience (Miller, 1986, 49–50).

9. Forms of τὰ παρ' ἡμῖν and ἐν ἡμῖν occur 18 times between 133c5 and 135e1, the "greatest puzzle" objection. The sense of immanence that characterizes participants is strong, albeit not yet reflectively precise. It is clear at least that there are certain parameters that inescapably determine the things with which we are most familiar.

10. In the *Theaetetus*, Socrates distinguishes these first two accounts of identity, bringing the young Theaetetus to wonder and undergo what Socrates calls the "beginning of philosophy" (155d2–5). Socrates first proposes the following: "We say surely that six dice, if you apply four to them, are more than the four and one and a half times as much, and if you apply twelve, they're less than half as much, and it's insupportable to speak in a different way" (*Theaetetus*, 154c1–5). Socrates then asks, "is it possible that anything become bigger or more in a different way than by increase?" (*Theaetetus*, 154c8–9). The dice become larger and smaller without having increased or changed at all with respect to themselves: they have gone from being more to less relative to four dice and then relative to twelve dice.

11. I am reading the ἕν as predicative in the opening sentence (οἶμαί σε ἐκ τοῦ τοιοῦδε ἓν ἕκαστον εἶδος οἴεσθαι εἶναι, 132a1).

12. Sayre distinguishes the conclusion of this discussion from the closely related conclusion of the "second third man" argument by pointing out that the focus here is not on an unlimited becoming of ever new forms but, rather, on the way each of the forms appears as "no longer one, but indefinitely multitudinous" (Sayre, *Parmenides' Lesson: Translation and Explication of Plato's Parmenides* [South Bend: University of Notre Dame Press, 1996, 82]). Sayre specifically avoids the language of infinite regress and claims that the account fails because it leaves the forms in the same state as sensibles prior to participation.

13. It is unclear from the text whether the condition that things are "composed of thoughts" (ἐκ νοημάτων) is intended to hold in the second case in which things "are thoughts" (νοήματα ὄντα), since Parmenides has dropped the "of" (ἐκ) qualification.

14. More broadly, there is no fully indeterminate object. Nothing can be or be intelligible unless it is determined in some specific way, as for instance the way an indefinite magnitude is determined by the intelligibly determinate aspects of greater and smaller. The great and the small are contradictory ideas that circumscribe the *apeiron*, which is itself distinct from what they are. What we call *apeiron* would not show up, as it were, unless it were delimited by these ideas. In order for the indefinite amount to show up, it must be measured by and be subject to the forms by which it shows up as large, as small, etc.

15. Like the lovers of sights from *Republic* 5 mentioned in Chapter 1, the "third man regress" requires that we imagine that the sameness and largeness, and so on, of the forms will be found in some place.

16. For instance, inarticulate but true insight guides bifurcatory division in the *Sophist*, continuously guiding discursively precise divisions to produce the definition to which the sophist, or more successfully the angler, is subject. The form, at once guiding and subjected to division, is double. Like individual ones, it is both a simple unity and the complex multiplicity through which that simple unity is articulated.

17. M. L. Gill and P. Ryan, eds., *Plato: Parmenides* (Indianapolis: Hackett, 1996).

18. Malcolm Schofield has argued, effectively in one respect, that the "form" in question here is the specific form of likeness. Schofield principally argues that the relevant aspect in which the participant and its paradigm are being addressed in this argument is as "likes," which does not rely on the premise of self-predication of forms insofar as the shared property of being "likes" is derived from the claims that the participants are copies of the paradigm and that copy and original are reciprocally "like" one another (Malcolm

Schofield, "Likeness and Likenesses in the *Parmenides*," in Gill and McCabe [1996], 49–77). McCabe similarly asserts that the target is not self-predication but self-identity. Irrespective of the being-X of a form, the relation of form to participant is governed by likeness and the reciprocity of the relationship between things that are in any respect "like" one another (McCabe, 1994, 88). Thus, if participants are like forms, forms can be like participants not by sharing a common property but by virtue of the axiomatic symmetry of the likeness relationship. In spite of its appeal and importance to the dialogue as a whole, there are two difficulties with this reading. First, we would appear to be granting with the likeness regress that it is only the form of likeness that is subject to regress, which would seem to grant that all other forms are appropriately incommensurate with things, but that implication seems at least unconfirmed by anything Parmenides says. Second, the same reason for accepting likeness as the explanatory principle that would account for the shared characteristic of X in the participant and X in the form cannot function without the X character itself that is the basis for the likeness. In other words, it might not be so easy to discard the self-predication premise. Insofar as likeness is always of a certain sort or in a certain respect, it will always be just as easy, and perhaps more natural, to read Parmenides as saying that it is the form X that explains the likeness between the shared or common characters. I do not think that a single form governs the relationship between forms and particulars, but neither do I think that this issue can be settled in our reading of this text. The chief point with which I agree, along with Schofield and McCabe, is that this regress dispenses with the self-predication premise. I believe that the property of being-like a copy is assigned to the form by the axiom that likeness is reciprocal, that is, likes are like what is like them (132d5–7). That is, the form need not be like in order to have likeness. This distinction, between being like and having likeness, will be explored in H5 (cf. 161b2).

19. Sayre agrees with Allen that there is nothing vicious about the regress in itself; simply to count implies an infinite number, that is, all of number, as suggested by the early parts of the Second Hypothesis. Sayre claims that the problem with these results is that participation and resemblance are left unexplained (Sayre, 1996, 88).

20. The point might even have been stronger, if we believe this characterization of slavery by military victory. There is reason to believe that it was widely known for the very reasons expressed here that the institution of slavery could not be justified on at least some of the most important principles of Athenian democracy. It was also known that as an essential aspect of the Athenian economy, there was little that could be done to unravel the institution of slavery. The contingency of the master/slave relationship would be amplified by its violence.

21. Miller, "A More 'Exact Grasp' of the Soul?: Tripartition in the *Republic* and Dialectic in the *Philebus*," in *Truth: Studies of a Robust Presence*, ed. Pritzl (Catholic University of America Press, 2010). Miller studies in 55c–59d of the *Philebus* the type of exactness (ἀκρίβεια) Socrates has in mind and what it might tell us about the "finest view possible" of the soul, announced in conjunction with the "longer path" at *Republic* 435c–d, where Socrates reveals his misgivings about the tripartition of the soul. At 504b–c Socrates says that the incomplete is not a measure for anything, and Glaucon replies that many often let it be so out of complacency. At 533a Socrates clarifies that the exactness of the proposed method will lead them from "seeing an image of dialectic" to "seeing the truth." At *Philebus* 55c–59d, Socrates marks out a continuum, moving toward greater degrees of exactness, with pure mathematics situated at an advanced stage. The most exact, he says, is "the

power of dialectic," and its subject matter is "that which really [is] and is by nature forever the same in every way" (Miller, 2010, τὸ ὂν καὶ τὸ ὄντως καὶ τὸ κατὰ ταὐτὸν ἀεὶ πεφυκὸς πάντως, 58a2–3). The privileging of dialectic represents a shift in subject matter to "those 'things' that are always in the same condition and in like manner hold themselves free of any admixture" (τὰ ἀεὶ κατὰ τὰ αὐτὰ ὡσαύτως ἀμεικτότατα ἔχοντα), from "[that which] is as akin to those 'things' as possible" (ἐκείνων ὅτι μάλιστά ἐστι συγγενές, Miller, 2010, 46, 59c3–5). Miller's thesis, in my view correct, is that the increase in exactness does not leave behind the imprecision of embodied soul, what he calls "the empirical," but draws it out: to achieve the "exactness" of dialectical knowledge of the forms is not to leave the empirical behind; rather, it is to disclose in its own terms the eidetic and mathematical order that lies at the heart of the empirical (Miller, 2010, 47).

22. The counter-thrust to philosophical transformation also, I contend, occurs at later stages of the process. Even the "philosopher" who has been freed of the cave and has seen the forms in the world outside the cave resists returning to the cave where the educational course finds completion. But that is a more involved discussion best saved for another occasion. See Ömer Orhan Aygün, "The Apology in Light of the Cave" in John Russon and Patricia Fagan, eds., *Reexamining Socrates in the Apology* (Evanston, Ill.: Northwestern University Press, 2009), 250–70.

23. It has been argued that Socrates is not a "philosopher" in the *Republic* sense of the term. I think these interpretations are based on specific understanding of the nature of dialectic and its relationship of dialectic to knowledge of the Good. Objections to the view that Socrates is, in the *Republic*, what he identifies as a "philosopher" are raised on the grounds that in the *Republic* Socrates does not claim to "know" the good, and he claims that philosophers will rule in the cave with *knowledge* of the good. This objection does not adequately appreciate that the good, insofar as it is "beyond being" (ἐπέκεινα τῆς οὐσίας, 509b9), cannot be an object of *epistēmē* because it is not subject to the combinations and divisions that the "is" of true knowledge makes possible. In the course of the Book 7 discussion, Socrates often says that the philosopher will "see" the good, and he says that the philosopher will grasp the good "by *noēsis*" (e.g., 532b1) and will "contemplate" what is best in things with what is best in the soul (532c5–6), but we cannot identify any of these with knowledge in the sense of *epistēmē*. At 534b–c, Socrates comes closest to the assertion that the good will be an object of knowledge when he says that the dialectician will be able "to define it in account and separate the idea of the Good apart from all others" (διορίσασθαι τῷ λόγῳ ἀπὸ τῶν ἄλλων πάντων ἀφελὼν τὴν τοῦ ἀγαθοῦ ἰδέαν τῷ λόγῳ, 534b7–c1) and, having done so, will put that account through every test. If the account comes through that test on its feet, Socrates will not deny that this person "knows" (*eidenai*, 534c4) the good; otherwise this person will be said to grasp a phantom of the good by opinion and not *epistēmē*. I take this to mean not that knowledge of the Good is possible strictly speaking but rather that a noetic grasp of the Good is possible, a grasp that demands to be tested and strengthened through dialogue. Thus, when Socrates says he does not "know" the Good, we should not take him to be saying that he is not a philosopher. Rather, he is simply acknowledging the proper limitations of philosophical knowledge of the Good: he can only say how it appears (*phainesthai*) to him and let the conversation with others decide if that appearance is strong enough to stand for them as knowledge.

24. See the introduction to the present chapter.

25. Scolnicov takes Parmenides to be applauding Socrates for not allowing "inquiry" (ἐπισκοπεῖν, 135e2) to wander among visible things (Samuel Scolnicov, *Plato's Parmenides*

[University of California Press, 2003, 75]), and McCabe takes Parmenides to be requiring an abstract discussion of the sort that might, but need not, lead to the positing of forms (McCabe, "Unity in the Parmenides," in *Form and Argument in Late Plato* [Oxford: Clarendon Press, 1996, 17, 19]). Gill takes "visibles" to be wandering between opposites (Gill, 1996, 139). I think that the indeterminacy of the referents and therefore arguments of the hypotheses point us in the direction of abstraction, and with McCabe I think we are required to maximize especially at first the non-specificity of this abstraction.

26. I am translating in parallel with Socrates' earlier restatement of Zeno's hypothesis, "If beings are many" (εἰ πολλά ἐστι τὰ ὄντα, 127e1–2) in the sense of "if there are many." The Greek also would allow us to translate this hypothesis in a more straightforwardly predicative sense: "if [it] is many" (cf. note 21, Chapter 1, above). It seems that consistency across several related translation questions demands that we refuse the predicative sense here (as elsewhere). Most importantly, our decision here will bear on the way we translate the First Hypothesis, which could be translated "if it is one" (εἰ ἕν ἐστιν, 137c4). I will reserve the full discussion of this vexed problem of translation until later, but looking ahead, translating the First Hypothesis this way would violate the methodological instructions Parmenides has offered here: that we hypothesize "if X is" and "if X is not" (135e9–136a2). This point is a major contributor to Meinwald's decision to translate the hypotheses as "if the One is" and "if the One is not" (Meinwald, 1991, discussion concluding on 44–45). I agree with her approach primarily for the sake of consistency and coherence, but I take the definite article to be relative, translating the First Hypothesis "if [a] one is." We will have opportunity to examine these issues in more detail later.

27. There is an interpretive question here whether the "in relation to itself and others" qualification will specify distinct hypotheses, i.e., one hypothesis for "in relation to itself" and another hypothesis for "in relation to others," or whether the qualification "in relation to itself and others" should be taken to apply as a whole to each and every hypothesis. Sayre and Meinwald choose the latter route, according to which there are four distinct hypotheses: "X is, in relation to itself," "X is, in relation to others," "X is not, in relation to itself, and "X is not, in relation to others." However, the latter reading seems stronger, given that the relationship to same and other is an explicit and frequent concern in all hypotheses.

28. Isn't the question here what results if "it," the one itself, is one or is not one? Gill translates with this interpretation in mind: "if it is one" and "if it is not one." But this translation and interpretive direction, following Meinwald, are strained in several respects. First and most proximately, this reading would violate the manner of hypothesis that Parmenides proposed when he laid out the method, saying "if X is" and "if X is not." In addition, this is not what they go on to examine in the hypotheses; it is only the first hypothesis that Gill reads as "if it is one," and the second is translated to read "if one is." That reading is designed to undercut the apparent contradiction between the first and second hypotheses, but undercutting that contradiction would be out of place within the paired sets of apparently contradictory hypotheses in H3-H4, H5-H6, and H7-H8.

29. I take the "one itself" in a weak sense: a one, whatever one it is, just insofar as it is one, is going to be hypothesized "if it is" and "if it is not," in relation to itself and the others. We will work on clarifying the further specifications of "one" that are demanded by the individual hypotheses. Someone might object that Plato took the historical Parmenides to have hypothesized "the one itself" with strong and specific theoretical commitments attached to it. But, on the one hand, it would be an odd reading of Parmenides' poem to read it as having "the one itself" as its subject, since Parmenides focuses more on the "is" than

on unity or the sense of the "is" as one. On the other hand, were someone to object that this is what Plato nonetheless believed, that view would seem to be at odds with Zeno's testimony in the *Parmenides*. Zeno describes himself as choosing not to publish a work defending Parmenides' monism against pluralists; it would seem that this Zeno is aware that taking Parmenides to be a monist may be naïve. Furthermore, Zeno in the guise of the "Eleatic Palamedes" in the *Phaedrus* is not a committed anti-pluralist as much as a master of contradiction, which suggests that the affinity between Parmenides and Zeno is not based on a shared belief in monism.

30. To be clear, we can focus on determinate intelligibility without thereby hypothesizing forms. The study of the perceptible "one itself" for instance is a study of the way the object of perception is a "one" that is subject to and characterized by opposites.

31. One of the most naked forms of sophistical aggression can be found in Plato's *Euthydemus*, where the absolute indulgence of the power of words to signify is embraced without restraint in such argument as the one in which it is proven that "your father is a dog" because (a) the dog is a father, and (b) you have a father.

Chapter 3

1. Earlier Parmenides promised to be "hypothesizing concerning the one itself" (περὶ τοῦ ἑνὸς αὐτοῦ ὑποθέμενος, 137b2–4). As mentioned, I have decided to take the qualification in a theoretically weak sense as referring not to a specific type of one but to the *per se* character of an individual *qua* one. Thus, I am leaving the specific character of this one open by translating the hypothesis as "[a] one, if it is." Furthermore, the "one" hypothesized is often referred to in the course of H1 as "the one" (τὸ ἕν). I take the force of the definite article in these cases to be demonstrative, that is, "that" one that we hypothesized. I am in agreement with McCabe, who stresses the abstract character of the exercises, both in relation to the dramatic framing of the *Parmenides* and in terms of its argumentation. McCabe takes the subject of the hypotheses to be the abstract aspects of individuation, and she suggests that in spite of appearances we should distance ourselves from the notion that we are talking about forms: "[Parmenides] stipulates an abstract discussion, such as might lead to the postulation of the Forms. . . . The argument that follows is an abstract thought experiment, free of ontological commitment" (McCabe, 1996, 19). McCabe then clarifies that we are talking about various aspects of individuals as such: "That is, the 'one' which is the subject of all the arguments may be understood to be any individual, abstractly conceived. The arguments that follow in the first hypothesis consider what will follow from supposing there to be some individual; the arguments of the second hypothesis consider what will follow from denying that there is some individual. In each case, the individual is viewed in two different ways: on the generous view, the individual is defined in terms of its properties; on the austere view, the individual is seen to be what it is in isolation from any properties it might have" (ibid., 24). I acknowledge that many of the same consequences as those listed in H1 would follow if we were to assume certain distinct objects of analysis. For example, if the subject of H1 were a transcendent one, many of the same consequences would follow as from taking the subject to be any individual considered under in its aspect of being one. I will abbreviate "the First Hypothesis" as H1, "the Second Hypothesis" as H2, and so on for the sake of clarity and simplification. On the subject of the hypothesis "the one itself" see note 37 to Chapter 1 above.

2. Two important clarifications are in order. Constance Meinwald reads the Hypotheses as grouped first into "if One is" and "if One is not" (Meinwald emends 137b4 to allow the

hypothesis to be taken to be existential in some sense or other). Meinwald then within each side finds a second division between "in relation to self" (*per se*) and "in relation to other" (*per accidens*) (Meinwald, *Plato's Parmenides* [Oxford, 1991]). However, there are significant and necessary uses of the specifications "in relation to itself" and "in relation to other" within each hypothesis. For instance, the distinction between self-relation and other-relation is also critical to the discussions of sameness/otherness, measure, contact, and temporality in both H1 and H2. Meinwald's reading seems unable to account for the apparently systematic shift between self and other within individual hypotheses. McCabe differentiates H1 and H2 as positive and negative movements (McCabe, 1996, 17–18). In my view McCabe takes too formal an approach to the dialectic in this particular respect, but she is I think essentially correct to highlight not the relation of self and other, as does Meinwald, but the guiding perspective according to which the attributions are being made of the one and from which the consequences are being drawn. Second, Meinwald, Gill, Hermann, and Chrysakopoulou take H1 to be about the being-one of the one rather than the being of the one. Gill prefers the translation "if it is one" and adds a footnote in which she mentions that the Greek can also be read "if one is" (Gill, 1996, 144). Hermann and Chrysakopoulou acknowledge the range of meanings to which the Greek offers itself, but they decide with Gill in favor of "if it is one," arguing for the predicative sense of "one" as opposed to an existential sense. I agree in principle with the reasons they give, and this might be the right translation. However, we could equally well translate εἴτε ἕν ἐστιν εἴτε μὴ ἕν as "whether [a] one is or [a] one is not," taking an implied *esti* with *hen*. This translation would better fit Parmenides' earlier framing of the hypotheses. Also note that the opening comments in H2 should not be used to decide our interpretation of H1 because, as it seems to me, the contrast between the being of the one-that-is and the being one of the one-that-is respond to the self-undermining conclusion reached at the end of H1. On my reading, the being one of the one is the first attribution derived from the hypothesis "if one is," that is, if one is, it is one and not many.

3. Allen prefers to translate *hen* as "unity." Meinwald, Turnbull, Gill, and Chrysakopoulou translate it as "one." I take it that the lack of a definite article in the main statement of the hypothesis "if one is" commits us to the translation "if [a] one is." Subsequent inclusion of the definite article, therefore, should be translated as specifying the one that was hypothesized, that is, "that" one, rather than referring suddenly the "the" [one and only] one.

4. I will be referring to the so-called exercises in the second part of the dialogue as "hypotheses," yet nothing I say hinges on this designation. I see reasons why someone would want to call them "deductions." I choose not to do so because I think that gives the impression of greater purposiveness to these eight accounts than they are explicitly granted in the text.

5. See Kosman, 1994, for a discussion of the Aristotelian conception of the all and the relationship between the accounts of the First Mover and the Unmoved Mover (Aryeh Kosman, "Aristotle's Prime Mover," in *Self-Motion: From Aristotle to Newton*, ed. Gill and Lennox [Princeton University Press: Princeton, 1994, 135–54]).

6. Closely related to the unity of any form, "the one itself," or the idea of unity, would be the unique idea in which all other ones, beginning with the forms, participate. This idea, however, cannot be what the "one itself" (αὐτὸ τὸ ἕν) refers to in H1, nor can it be the subject of that hypothesis for the straightforward reason that it is not mentioned in the First Hypothesis; it is not mentioned until 144e6 of the Second Hypothesis. At the same time, however, many of the characteristics of the "one itself" will be identical to the

characteristics any individual has just insofar as it is one, and these characteristics will also be consistent with what any form would be *qua* one. I will take the subject of H1 to be any individual just insofar as it is one, but I want to acknowledge that many of the same consequences can be drawn from other subjects, so it will require special patience on the part of the reader before all the evidence for this reading can be presented.

7. As mentioned above (n. 80), McCabe takes the problem of individuation to be basic in Platonic ontology. Distinguishing Plato's concerns from Aristotle's, McCabe situates the focus of the hypotheses in the question what makes a one *one*-something: "Aristotle sees the key to individuation in specifying the 'something'—for sorts individuate. Plato, I shall argue, is more interested in 'one': he supposes that any one will be a something, and that any something a one. In doing so, as I shall argue, Plato offers a radical alternative to the Aristotelian view" (McCabe, 1991, 18). In one respect, this view is consistent with Proclus's very similar abstract view of individuation in his interpretation of Zeno's first hypothesis: "Let us assume not merely sensible pluralities [τὰ αἰσθητά], nor merely intelligible ones [τὰ νοητά], but all things simply [πάντα ἁπλῶς] that are called 'many'" (Proclus II.725; 1987, 103) (cf. Sanday, "Eleatic Metaphysics in Plato's *Parmenides*," *Journal of Speculative Philosophy*). At the same time, Proclus believes the "one" of the first hypothesis to be a transcendent first principle and separate from garden variety individuals by virtue of ontological priority as a first principle (and he identifies this one with the one of the monistic interpretation of the historical Parmenides), so Proclus does not interpret the hypotheses to be concerned primarily with individuation. What I am identifying with the one in H1, however, seems to correspond to what Proclus calls "immanent form." Analyzing Socrates' response to Zeno in the Parmenides, Proclus writes, "If we go above the many immanent forms to monads of a different sort, existing of themselves and transcendently, he [Socrates] wonders how unity of species can be seen also in them, and if so what is its source and cause" (Proclus, II.728; 1987, 105). Miller, in his book on the *Parmenides* at least, identifies the one of H1 with form (see Miller, 1986, chapter IV, "Hypotheses I , II , and IIa: Form, the Participant Thing, and Their Relation [137c—157b]").

8. I take it to be a real question whether any collection of individual unrelated ones can count as a "whole." At this point in H1 I think we are not able to decide, but in H3 we will draw a sharp distinction between one-whole and one-of-many, a distinction that cannot be coherently drawn without the type of normative structure and indefinite multitudes that will not be introduced until then.

9. In this respect, my reading is in line with Proclus. I am looking here for a condition or cause by which what are other than the one are eidetically ordered. I take this cause to be transcendent, but neither the cause nor its transcendence are properly grasped until after the analysis of the "instant" in H2a.

10. The analysis of the one here takes a turn that has been a source of conflicting interpretations for commentators and a cause of debate. Some commentators have argued that because the discussion of the one here turns to things that are spatially determinate, Parmenides must have had in mind the characters of spatio-temporal ones all along, which were being denied to the one at each step. There is good reason to think that the context of this discussion, because of the earlier discussion with Socrates and the introduction here of spatiality, calls for us to read part/whole complexity as spatially determinate. I agree that we should have spatial complexity in mind, and that we might well take part/whole complexity to be spatial. However, it seems that we might also take complexity on

its own here to include but not be limited to spatial complexity. Doing so allows us to see the secondary aim of H1 more clearly, that is, the normativity governing each of the instances of complexity as opposed to the object that, through normative ordering, is being constituted. To be clear, when I refer to normativity, I do not have in mind the kinds of substantial form that differentiate one sort of things from another but the normativity that structures spatiality and bodies generally.

11. In this early stage of analysis, all that need be implied by the concept of participation is that a one, in its being the sort of thing it is, is subject to those characters or structures in which it is said to participate. For example, if something is "in space," it participates in circular and straight, insofar as these characters, or structures, are the necessary and exhaustive types into which shape as such can be divided.

12. I am tempted to connect this to Aquinas's notion of "aliquid" (*de Veritate*, I.1). However, notice that the "one that is not" is distinguished from "something" (τινός) in H5 at 160e2–7. I will argue that it is necessary for the one-that-is-not [in time and space] partake of "something" and other grammatical categories that constitute it as an object of discursive knowing. This participatory relation will help establish, however, that the one-that-is-not is prior to (not identical with) its status as an object of discursive knowing.

13. See also Gregory Recco, *Athens Victorious* (Lanham, Md.: Lexington Books, 2007), chapter 1.

14. Parmenides hinted at the dynamism implied here earlier in the discussion of being-in, specifically with the notion that the container "touches" the contained, where the container is "doing" (ποιήσειν) and the contained is "suffering" (πείσεσθαι) contact.

15. I do not think the terms of relative impossibility or necessity imply a failure to grasp the notion of logical necessity. They seem instead to point to impossibilities (or necessities) that rest on other more basic impossibilities.

16. The interesting twist on this account is the degree to which this metaphysical interpretive framework draws on a set of assumptions familiar to us from Zeno's so-called paradoxes of motion. Parmenides describes linear motion in the same basic style as Zeno: that something in motion can only be at one point at a given time, and it must in order to move occupy all the points between the beginning and end of its motion at one time. The only apparent shift here is that Parmenides does not locate his object at one point in space but at many, stretched across a span of different parts, each of which moving across the limit from outside to inside at a particular time. Time is construed as punctilious. In order to move, each part of the whole must either be in or out of something into which it is moving at any given time. At the beginning presumably it is completely outside that place, and at the end of the measured time it is completely inside. Parmenides argues that the one cannot move because it cannot have parts, and it cannot be in any place at any time. See my article "Eleatic Metaphysics in Plato's *Parmenides*: Zeno's Puzzle of Plurality," *Journal of Speculative Philosophy*, 23 (2009): 208–226.

17. On the same metaphysical assumptions, perhaps, as the example of the place of the world in the *Phaedo*, where the normatively empty space of the materialists requires "a more powerful Atlas" to hold the earth in place, because wherever it stands, it is there without reason, answering to no measure.

18. The formulation "proper to other-than-another alone" might imply that being-other is irreducibly many, i.e., other-than-another rather than simply "otherness." Insofar as we will go on to become more clear about the simplicity of form and the multiplicity of what are subject to forms (i.e., the "others"), this formulation strikes me as reinforcing the

interpretation that in H1 we are dealing not with a form-like one but with the aspects of being-one, being-same, etc., that are immanent to singular and complex ones.

19. There are of course other "ones" that would yield the same consequence. For instance, if we were talking about a simple and unique one, it would not "by itself" be other than another. But interpretive circumspection demands that we not shift between distinct referents or ontological levels unless required to do so. We are not here required to shift away from a one that is subject to being-one.

20. See H5 161b7–8 for discussion of the likeness the one must have with respect to itself if it is going to be the subject of hypothesis and *logos*.

21. See Francisco Gonzalez, *Dialectic and Dialogue* (Evanston, Ill.: Northwestern University Press, 1998) for a detailed and expansive analysis of the distinction between propositional and non-propositional knowledge in the Platonic corpus.

22. Note that Parmenides has just proven that the one cannot be like or unlike itself or another, and he is here referring to the one as being of a certain sort (τοιοῦτον). "Furthermore, being of that sort (τοιοῦτόν γε ὄν), [a one] will neither be equal nor unequal to itself or another" (140b6–7). We should wonder whether these claims are in tension with each other. While being of a certain sort does not imply that the one is a single member of a class, since it may be of such a sort that it is not like anything else, being of a sort treats the one as a determinate object of inquiry and knowledge, making it sortable in comparison to things of other sorts. Calling the one by any name, even "one," and attributing characteristics to it, even negatively, draws it out into comparison with others.

23. ἄρ᾽ οὖν οὐδὲ ἐν χρόνῳ τὸ παράπαν δύναιτο ἂν εἶναι τὸ ἕν, εἰ τοιοῦτον εἴη;

24. Miller reads the contradictory conclusion of H1 as issuing from Aristoteles' identification of being with spatio-temporal being in this passage. Miller sees the conclusion of H1 as steered by Aristoteles' "fundamentally preemptive assumption that being as such, or every sense in which a being 'is,' is temporally determined . . . Aristotle assumes that the sort of being proper to things-being that, in association with becoming, is either past, present, or future is universal. More particularly, he fails to recognize the difference between the "is" of time present and the tenseless "is" of what transcends temporal determination. . . . [These objections] resolve both contradictions in I, it transforms them into specifications of the One's transcendence of the order of things. Aristotle is justified in denying *not* being as such but only temporally determinate being, being in time, to the One. Thus the basic contradiction—if a One is, it is not—turns into the revelation that this One, if it is, has timeless being!" (Miller, 1986, chapter IV, B.1 "Within I: The Specificity of the Negation of Being; Timeless Being," 90). Whereas Miller sees a positive account of the timeless one emerging from the negative portrait in H1, he stresses the contrast of ontological types, temporal and atemporal being. I believe that timeless being has repeatedly been stressed throughout H1, and that this final flourish is the crescendo of that process.

Chapter 4

1. Thus, H2 will be a more detailed elaboration of the "many" analyzed in the negative portrait of H1. But we should notice that this many is structured at every turn by oneness. It will become more explicit in H3 and H7 (and through *reductio* arguments in H4 and H8) that there cannot be a many that is not directly or indirectly dependent on oneness.

2. Gill takes νῦν δὲ to imply another time, i.e., H1 was one hypothesis and H2 is now another. "Now" can also be taken in the sense of focusing attention, e.g., "But look

here . . ." Allen, Whitaker, and the Loeb edition all translate, against Gill, in the latter sense. Gill follows Meinwald (along with Hermann & Chrysakopoulou) in reading H1 as hypothesizing the "one" in relation to itself and H2 as hypothesizing the "one" in relation to other, with which I disagree for reasons articulated above. I am in agreement with Schofield, for whom the ἕν in the contrasting formulation is not predicative but simply a linguistic substitution meant to show that ἕν and ἐστιν signify different things (Malcolm Schofield, "A Neglected Regress Argument in the *Parmenides*," *Classical Quarterly*, NS 23 [1973]:31). Other interpretations take the H2 hypothesis to differentiate a putatively predicate sense of "one" in H1 from a subject sense of "one" in H2 (Gill, 1996, 65–68; cited in Harte, 2002, 75n. 49). I think Schofield's approach correctly avoids relying on the distinction between predicative and existential senses of "is." From the nineteenth century until recently, the concept of being was sharply divided into its predicative and existential senses, tracing back to J. S. Mill and adopted by Vlastos, Meinwald, and Gill (cf. G. Vlastos, "A Metaphysical Paradox," in *Platonic Studies* [Princeton University Press, 1973]). Meinwald suggests that we consider the "is" of H1 as predicative, i.e., as having the function of joining and dividing intelligible terms in, e.g., "statesmanship is theoretical" or "the one is one." Conversely, "is" predicates existence of a particular being; for instance in H2, the hypothesis would be "one exists." This is the reading adopted by Gill & Ryan (1996) and Hermann and Chrysakopoulou (2007), who render the opening passage of H2 as "the being of the one would exist" (ἡ οὐσία τοῦ ἑνὸς εἴη ἄν, 142b7). G. E. L. Owen, Charles Kahn, and Lesley Brown have challenged this dichotomy. Owen focuses on the priority of predicative "is" and denies any concern with the existential "is" in Plato's *Sophist*, arguing that "to be" is always "to be of some sort" for Plato. Owen thereby retains the dichotomy, by affirming one side, even while undermining it. Kahn challenges the dichotomy more directly by focusing on the fundamental predicative structure of apparently bare existential uses of *einai*, which he argues has tacitly locative-durative force and should be heard in the context of complete specifications of the subject's being in the world (Kahn, *The Verb 'Be' in Ancient Greek* [Dordrecht: Reidel, 1973]; reprinted Indianapolis: Hackett, 2003]). See also Kahn's "A Return to 'Be' and the Concept of Being," in *Essays on Being*, Oxford University Press, 2009: 136–137.

3. ἆρα οἷόν τε αὐτὸ εἶναι μέν, οὐσίας δὲ μὴ μετέχειν; Turnbull notes that Parmenides three times rather easily uses the idea of participation as if the relationship had not been drawn into question earlier in the first part of the dialogue (Robert G. Turnbull, *The Parmenides and Plato's Late Philosophy* [Toronto: University of Toronto Press, 1998], 73). I take it that Parmenides is not specifying how participation happens but merely noticing something, *viz.*, that the "what" something is, the "one," must partake in multiplicity in order to be said, be known, and be perceived among other things. This is not a precise use of the term here, for as we can see he is speaking loosely about the way multiplicity is necessarily a part of being spoken, but what part exactly it is has not been decided (any more than the "one" initially hypothesized in H1 was initially determined with precision).

4. Lesley Brown, working primarily on the *Sophist*, has argued that Plato's primary concern is with what is most basic, which is a question distinct from, although not unrelated to, the concern with which types of existence are the most basic in the Stranger's initial survey of views on the meaning of being. Arguing along lines opened up by G. E. L. Owen and Charles Kahn, Brown distinguishes between complete and incomplete uses of *einai* to point out that predicative statements such as "one is one" draw on a fundamental sense of being. She reads Plato as able to infer from "one is" that "one is one," and conversely that

the statement "one is one" has "weakly existential force" in the sense that the sentence "one is one" implies that one is in some sense real. In her example, Brown draws an analogy with usages of the sort (a) Jane is teaching English, indicating the incomplete usage, and (b) Jane is teaching, indicating the complete use. Transitive sentences of form (a) are the basis upon which intransitive sentences of form (b) have their sense. To say "one is," then, is to say "one exists" and is tacitly consistent with saying "what" one is. We might say that the *esti* ("it is") is inseparable from *ti esti* ("what it is"). Existence is therefore a subordinate sense of *einai* nested in a more comprehensive and complete sense of *einai* that articulates the object in this or that specific way of being (Lesley Brown, "Being in the *Sophist*: A Syntactical Inquiry," in *Plato 1*, ed. Fine [Oxford University Press: 1999], 456). G. E. L. Owen shares with Vlastos et al. faith in the "commonplace" distinction drawn between predicative and existential *einai*, but Owen allows a greater continuity in the distinction by claiming that complete, i.e., existential, uses of *einai* are also predicative, and he therefore denies that the incomplete uses of *einai* in the *Sophist* have existential force (G. E. L. Owen, "Plato on Not-Being," in *Plato* 1: *Metaphysics and Epistemology*, ed. G. Vlastos [Garden City, N.Y.: Doubleday, 1971], 223–67, reprinted in Fine, 1999). Owen does not, however, go as far as Brown to establish a deeper continuity between predicative and existential uses, as Brown points out, because privileging the predicative use and taking existential uses to be "elliptical incomplete" uses does not adequately appreciate the weakly existential force of the incomplete use. Harte proposes, citing Brown, that the distinction between the hypotheses "one is" and "one is one" is not as great as it might seem, since there is what we might call a "weakly existential" force in what we have come to call the "existential is" (Harte, 2002, 75).

5. By unearthing the tacitly locative force and, more generally, predicative structure of Greek *einai*, Charles Kahn has shown, contra Mill, that it is not the metaphysical questions that lack coherence but the notion of "existence" divorced from predicative structure (Kahn, 2009, 142). Kahn draws effectively on Heidegger's notion of being as being-in-the-world to help make the case that the Greek sense of "is" refers primarily and fundamentally to a referential totality, i.e., being is being-there within a larger structured whole. The primary and authoritative question, then, would seem to be the metaphysical question, and H2 is the leg of that larger project in which the locative, durative, and predicatively structured "is" is taken up as such.

6. Note that at 144e8–145b6 Parmenides uses part/whole complexity to refer to a spatial whole of (spatial) parts without marking any deviation from this earlier argument. While there is no intrinsic reason to construe part/whole complexity as spatial—indeed it is construed as explicitly eidetic in the *Sophist* and *Statesman*—there is a contextual reason for Parmenides to steer clear of doing so in the Hypotheses. Parmenides derives shape from part/whole complexity at 145a ff. If it were not the case that part/whole complexity were spatially determinate from the beginning of H2, the account would be incoherent (see Miller, 1986, 49n20, esp. 97n30). Parmenides is consistent later on: in H5, when discussing what we might term "eidetic complexity," he does not invoke a part/whole model to discuss the composition of an idea. As Harte notes, it is established in H3 that part/whole complexity depends on participation in the one, and if it were the case that the one "is not," as premised in H5, then there can be no part/whole complexity (Harte, 2002, 135). I appreciate Harte's precision, but I disagree with her conclusion. The participation is possible, indeed is only possible, in the one that is not [in space and time], as I will detail in Chapter 5, "H5–H6—Veridical Predication."

7. The Greek will not require, nor rule out, placing an indefinite article before "whole" to make it a single whole. But the focus here seems clearly on the divisibility of the one, not its iterability.

8. There is a clear similarity between the divisibility of the one-that-is and the discussion of the being, oneness, and difference of the one-that-is "grasped in thought" (διάνοιᾳ λαβεῖν). Both discussions study the one-that-is under the lens of reflective analysis, picking out its conceptual structure and deriving implications from that analysis. However, in the first argument Parmenides reads properties off the one-that-is as a given, and in the second, reflective analysis identifies the sources from which the one-that-is is constituted.

9. It might be more appropriate in this ambiguous context of analyzing the categorial structures of individual beings to translate "becoming two" (ἀνάγκη δύ' ἀεὶ γιγνόμενον) as "proves to be two," along with Gill.

10. οὐκοῦν ἄπειρον ἂν τὸ πλῆθος οὕτω τὸ ἓν ὂν εἴη; (143a2). Note that there is in principle no definite starting point for dividing the one-that-is. We might be tempted to think of a concrete spatially extended individual, but we would I think be misled by the definite limits of organized bodies. There is no definition of the original one-that-is, and there is no integrity of its parts. The substantial form that would give the one-that-is definite integrity, and organize its parts, is not presented in this account. What is presented in the one-that-is is only the possibility of an integrated whole, not a sufficient condition for such integration. Perhaps we could say that there is a one-being without the "joints" at which it would be properly cut "according to nature," as Socrates remarks in the *Phaedrus* (διατέμνειν κατ' ἄρθρα ᾗ πέφυκεν 265e1–2). The reason for this is, simply, that there is no defining nature (for that, we must wait for H3), only the facilitating nature that enables a spatial whole-of-parts to be present as an aggregate.

11. In Miller's view, this mention and again at the conclusion of the account (144e3–4) and in the summation (144e5) is the only reference to the form of Unity, the Hypotheses are about "the One" not the form of Unity—the One refers to the instantiation of Unity, i.e., a unit (UT 604). The "one" mentioned in H1 is a form taken up under its aspect of being one. I agree in the sense that the function of the form of unity can be provided for the things that partake in that form without the form of unity being the explicit object under consideration. Thus, it can be the case that the unifying function of the form of unity can be present in the parts of the whole, as the way two parentheses attract each other, or in any idea that guides inquiry into its nature, without the inquiry needing to be explicitly about the form of unity. Here, however, it is the form of unity that is explicitly marked out as "the one itself" (αὐτὸ τὸ ἕν). Note that Turnbull translates τὸ αὐτὸ τοῦτο as: "this itself" will be exhibited as one; Gill translates as: "this same thing" will also appear to be many; Allen: "this very thing" will appear many as well (Allen, 1983).

12. Note that the sense of being (οὐσία) here must differ from the sense that it assumed in the passage from 142c–d quoted above. It was implicit above that "something is" implies "something is divisible" and therefore combinable, just as it also implied that something both is and is-one. Here, by contrast, being (οὐσία) does not imply any of these things. A form "is" in a different way than the ones identified above.

13. This therefore carries forward arguments from 139c–d in H1, where it was argued that it was not by being one that the one is other.

14. Notice that Parmenides lists "odd times even" and "even times odd," which are distinct things if we consider the Pythagorean array of units, e.g., (a) three across and two

deep, as opposed to (b) two across and three deep. The potentially interesting point here is that the distinction between these two draws attention to the geometry of arithmetic and toward its indexical situatedness.

15. See Burnyeat, "Platonism and Mathematics: A Prelude to Discussion," in *Mathematics and Metaphysics in Aristotle*, ed. A. Graeser (Stuttgart, 1987).

16. Jacob Klein, *Greek Mathematics and the Origin of Algebra*, tr. Eva Brann, Cambridge, Mass.: MIT Press, 1968. Reprinted Mineola, N.Y.: Dover Publications, 1992.

17. This is an important point for establishing that the object of analysis in H2 is constant, and that therefore the levels of abstraction through which we move are only separable from one another in thought. In being, they belong together as aspects of the one-that-is.

18. ἀλλ᾽ εἴπερ γε οἶμαι ἔστιν, ἀνάγκη αὐτὸ ἀεί, ἕωσπερ ἂν ᾖ, ἕν γέ τι εἶναι, μηδὲν δὲ ἀδύνατον.

19. The qualification "neither greater nor smaller" of course differs from the earlier account of participation by wholes and parts. Here we focus on participation by parts, and we are asked to consider each part as "present in" the individual to which it is distributed without communicating anything other than unity to that individual.

20. οὐ μόνον ἄρα τὸ ὂν ἓν πολλά ἐστιν, ἀλλὰ καὶ αὐτὸ τὸ ἓν ὑπὸ τοῦ ὄντος διανενεμημένον πολλὰ ἀνάγκη εἶναι. As Harte points out, μεριστόν can mean "divided" or "divisible," but the arguments throughout the dialogue have assumed that "divisible" implies "divided." Harte claims that the distinction between divisible and divided is not recognized in what she (following Allen) calls the "Dilemma of Participation" (Harte, 2002, 79). According to Harte, the hypotheses begin their departure from this conception when part/whole relations are established as primitive alongside identity relations (ibid., 121). It seems to me that attention to the distinction between divisible and divided becomes clear after the new metaphysics, introduced in H3, of one and *perata*. Harte has a similar view but does not take it as far (ibid., 123ff.). She believes Plato to be laying out the framework for a new account of complexity in the Parmenides without fully turning to that new account.

21. ἆρα οὖν ἓν ὂν πολλαχοῦ ἅμα ὅλον ἐστί; τοῦτο ἄθρει. (144c–d).

22. Note that this is the first time Parmenides has used *moria* rather than *merē* to refer to parts.

23. I take the καὶ μὴν to signal a new beginning of account.

24. The transition between the two Greek terms Parmenides uses for "parts" (*merē* and *moria*) cannot, I think, be conclusively decided. However, it may be that the notion of parts "unlimited in multitude" differs from a definite number of definite parts. Parmenides uses both senses of part, for instance the former when referring to the dividing up of being and the latter when referring to the divisions of "the one itself." Although it would be difficult to say conclusively whether the distinction in the Greek terms between *merē* and *moria* corresponds to a distinction between limited and unlimited parts, this distinction has been employed and should be kept in mind when deciding the issue.

25. Miller uses this argument, along with other indications, to show that from the beginning of H2 part/whole complexity has implied spatiality, and that the indefinite combination and division discussed above refer to a basic aggregate character of spatiotemporal presence (Miller, 1991, Chapter IV, esp. 96ff.). Miller's reading is more plausible, I think, than others, like Allen's (1983, 239), which see a division between the earlier and later uses of limit and must, therefore, conclude that Parmenides just suddenly assumes

the thesis that "being" means being in space without marking it. I agree with Miller's larger project, which is to underscore the radical gap between H1 and H2, between forms and participants, in order to later use this sharp metaphysical division to argue for the intimate relationship between forms and things. For example, note that Miller treats the "others" of H3 as a composite of limit and unlimited, for which the one of H1 is the limit-providing, incomposite, term, and the one of H2 is the result of constitutive participation. His reading places sufficient stress on the metaphysical dichotomy between forms and participants to yield a transformed view of the spatio-temporal one, in which limit and the unlimited are central. However, in his reading of this section of the text, Miller argues that "Parmenides cannot derive a spatial sense of limitedness from a non-spatial sense of wholeness" (Miller, 1991, n. 25, n. 30, 244–47), and Miller uses this to conclude that the "one" of H2 must have been a spatio-temporal one all along. This seems to me to place too much stress on the future results of the hypothesis and, in so doing, overlooks the metaphysically ambiguous status of limit as something that is "of" space and time but not "in" them, an important category for this hypothesis.

26. καὶ μὴν τά γε πάντα μέρη τὰ αὑτοῦ τὸ ἕν ἐστι, καὶ οὔτε τι πλέον οὔτε ἔλαττον ἢ πάντα.

27. In my view, these claims are all relative to the premise of the hypothesis itself, i.e., that we are talking about a "one" that is complex and individual. Such a "one" must be in place or it "is not" in the sense of "does not exist." There are other ways in which not-being-in-space-and-time does not imply non-existence (cf. H5).

28. Perhaps the reasoning is that the whole cannot be in a part at the same time as the part is in the whole, for then the whole would be in the whole. The one, for special reasons of participating in part and whole, might be in itself, but the whole cannot be in the whole *qua* whole.

29. I mean to argue that the complexity and singularity of the one-that-is are ontologically convertible. It is not until H3 that a sharp distinction is drawn between complexity and individuality (cf. note 170 below). It is not until Parmenides shows that composition is ontologically distinct from denumerable multiplicity that we have grounds for conceptual differentiation.

30. οὕτω δὴ πεφυκὸς τὸ ἓν ἆρ᾽ οὐκ ἀνάγκη καὶ κινεῖσθαι καὶ ἑστάναι; (145e7–8).

31. That the others are the context in which the being of the one is studied and not themselves the object of study is reflected in the way that they most often appear as the object of prepositions and verbs. When they do appear as the subject of a sentence, they are not the focus, as for example instances in which Parmenides says that the others do not partake of number because they are in every way not-one. The one is very much the context of H1 and H2. I have explained this as a direct result of the absolute character of what-is, i.e., that there is no other, no outside, and therefore no way to get behind it. When we study what is absolutely other than the one, we must study that by going through the one, within its context.

32. Albert Keith Whitaker, *Plato's Parmenides*, Focus Publishing, 1996.

33. I translate ἔχει in conjunction with the preposition πρός as "relates to." This largely rests on the preposition, but for each of the many instances of the various forms of ἔχειν in H2, I would like to preserve in translation the sense of being situated and reaching out toward others as a constitutive, elementary principle of individual being.

34. The "itself" here should not be taken to refer to forms. Parmenides avoids the formulation "*auto to hen*," and he calls the one "itself" in the context of comparing it to itself.

Thus, "itself" in this context is an intensifier meant to refer to the one in respect of its being one, i.e., in the context of part/whole complexity and relation to other ones.

35. οὐκ ἀνάγκη ἤδη ταὐτὸν εἶναι αὐτὸ ἑαυτῷ.

36. οὐχ ἑτέρου ὄντος ἕτερον ἔσται;

37. οὐκοῦν ὅσα μὴ ἕν ἐστιν, ἅπανθ' ἕτερα τοῦ ἑνός, καὶ τὸ ἓν τῶν μὴ ἕν; This is commonly translated as "the things that are not one," but I want to emphasize the discrepancy in the grammar between the plural subject and the astonishingly singular quality they all share (i.e., being not-one).

38. αὐτό τε ταὐτὸν καὶ τὸ ἕτερον ἆρ' οὐκ ἐναντία ἀλλήλοις;

39. ἢ οὖν ἐθελήσει ταὐτὸν ἐν τῷ ἑτέρῳ ἢ τὸ ἕτερον ἐν ταὐτῷ ποτε εἶναι; / οὐκ ἐθελήσει.

40. Parmenides is arguing that same and other "grasped in thought," as discussed in the section "Many Ones: The second argument (143a–144e5)" above, are opposites. But this is not precisely how the "one" and "being" were conceived in Parmenides' derivation. In that derivation, "one" and "being" were grasped on their own, and as so grasped they were not even "different" until they participated in difference, let alone opposites. If "one" and "being" picked out "in thought" needed to participate in "difference" to be distinguished and related to one another, then what is it here that takes the place of "difference" and allows these two ideas to be thought as "opposites"? Perhaps the situation is similar to the prior analysis, discussed above in the section "One Consisting of Many: The first argument (142c–143a)," where "one" and "being" are considered inseparable aspects of the one-that-is, always showing up with each other in the case of any one-that-is. But opposition can be understood without reference to a complex individual. Above "one" and "being" were necessary aspects of the one-that-is, and the necessity of their belonging together was explained with reference to the one-that-is. It seems that the one-that-is need not be a condition for seeing the opposites as opposites. It may be the case, of course, that complex individuals are the condition on which to conceive otherness being "in" the same.

41. ἀνομοιώσει ἄρα τὸ ταὐτόν, ἢ οὐκ ἐναντίον ἔσται τῷ ἑτέρῳ (148b5–6). "To make like" or "to make unlike" is a way to translate ὁμοιόω, but to mitigate the potentially misleading connotations of production here, we should take note that there is no word for "making" in the Greek. We will want to be kept aware that, for instance, at 148e–149a the one is described, counterfactually, as producing (ποιέω) certain results and as "being unwilling" to do things against its nature.

42. Note that the necessity by which the individual refuses to be "two" (149a1) is not explained in H2 but simply assumed as a basis in the hypothesis.

43. οὔκουν, φαμέν, τὰ ἄλλα τοῦ ἑνὸς οὔτε ἕν ἐστιν οὔτε μετέχει αὐτοῦ, εἴπερ ἄλλα ἐστίν.

44. A serious question remains as to how the one is in contact with itself. Contact requires the relationship of one to another, and yet the parts do not stand in relation to the whole as one to another. They stand in relation to each other as one to another, and together they are the "one itself." There are examples of external relationships in which two separate things are joined in a relation similar to whole/part continuity. When Aristotle points out that things in water touch through the medium of water without noticing the water, just as things on the earth touch eather other through air without noticing the air (de Anima, II.11, 423a22–423b1), I take him to be imputing a distinction between something and its medium, e.g., a fish and the water, dissimilar to the distinction between one thing and another that are present to each other in that medium. It is as if it were an

internal distinction between parts within the whole, e.g., of fish in the water, or myself within the air I breathe, that divides in two but does not place in contact. The element in which the fish moves is so close to the fish itself that the fish does not touch it. Similarly, we do not touch the air we breathe, except in the rare occurrence that it becomes an object of attention, and we are only ambiguously touching the earth on which we walk and pivot, rather than that earth on which we "plant" our feet to walk or run being an extension of our bodies. Thus, there are several distinct senses in which "contact" may be thought by us to be structured: (1) as the relationship between one individual and another, (2) as the relationship between an element of motion, such as water, and the integrated whole that moves through it, (3) as the relationship between the parts of a whole. In H2, it seems that there is no basis in place conceptually for making a distinction between essential and inessential types of contact, or we might say for making the distinction between the inessential contact between one body and another and the essential contact between one part of an organized body and another. Parmenides has, I think, invited us to think of the internal composition of a body as distinct from and as equivalent to the contact between two bodies without specifying the relationship between these two types of contact.

45. Miller understands this to be saying: "they could not be opposed to each other" in physical-sensible ones and describes it as a modus ponens proof of the necessity of forms for the constitution of greater and smaller (1995, 609; cf. Miller, 1986).

46. The concept of *plēthos* (πλῆθος), which in Greek refers to a great number or quantity or mass, here provides us with the notion of indeterminate mass, i.e., indeterminate multitude and magnitude. It will prove key to the analysis that we think about the ways in which *plēthos* is structured. As of now we have been given the initial account of a continuum framed on either end by excess/deficiency of internally related terms.

47. We might expect the idea of measure might be further developed to include the notion of a proper measure, i.e., an exact amount or number called for and capable of being regulated according to a purpose. However, for now, we are only focused on the possibility that any one-that-is can enter into a numerically precise ratio with another.

48. οὐσίας φαμὲν μετέχειν τὸ ἕν, διὸ ἔστιν; 143a4–5.

49. εἶναι μέν που αὐτῷ ὑπάρχει, εἴπερ ἓν ἔστιν, 151e6–7.

50. τὸ δὲ εἶναι ἄλλο τί ἐστιν ἢ μέθεξις οὐσίας μετὰ χρόνου τοῦ παρόντος, 151e7–8.

51. μετέχει μὲν ἄρα χρόνου, εἴπερ καὶ τοῦ εἶναι. / πάνυ γε, 152a2–3.

52. In the background, we can hear Parmenides' earlier claim about the destruction of the power of dialectic (cf. pp. 45 and 71) (135b9–c2). In this section of H2, we are asked to see that if the very structure of spatio-temporal particularity were not rooted in ideas that are always the same, there would be in general nothing toward which to turn in our experience and understanding of things.

53. ἆρ' οὖν μεμνήμεθα ὅτι νεωτέρου γιγνομένου τὸ πρεσβύτερον πρεσβύτερον γίγνεται; (152a5–7). This seems to be one of the only explicit references in H2 to conclusions reached, or points agreed upon, in H1.

54. The translation of φαίνεται as "it is evident" represents an interpretive choice. The translation could also be a more hesitant "or so it appears," depending on how one understands the nature of Aristoteles' participation in the conversation at this point.

55. I take these occurrences of αὐτὸ τὸ ἓν at 153c3–4 and 153d1–2 to refer not to the form of unity but to be using an intensive *auto* to sharpen the distinction between a one

that comes to be in time and a one that comes to be complete at the end of a process of other ones (i.e., parts) coming to be.

56. Greg Recco makes this point with respect to the distinction between the arms-waving and spinning-top examples in *Republic* 4 (Greg Recco, *Athens Victorious: Democracy in Plato's Republic* [Lexington Books, 2007], chapter 1).

Chapter 5

1. ἕν τε ὂν καὶ πολλὰ καὶ μήτε ἓν μήτε πολλὰ καὶ μετέχον χρόνου, 155e4–5.

2. It may sound somewhat surprising that Parmenides refers to the one of H2 as a "one" that is "neither one nor many" given that the "one" is exempt from such a wide range of attributions in H1 and explicitly characterized there as being "not many" and "not one." Furthermore, the characterization at 156c6–7 of the one as "neither in motion nor at rest" (μήτε κινεῖσθαι μήτε ἑστάναι), so outside of time, suggests a parallel at the level of grammatical structure with the characterization of the object of study as "neither one nor many" (μήτε ἓν μήτε πολλά, 155e5) and suggests that Parmenides is referring to a one that is outside of time, as in H1. But there are a few reasons to reject this reading. (1) In H1 Parmenides calls the one "not many" insofar as it is "one" and not, as here, insofar as it is neither one nor many. (2) Also in H1 Parmenides says that the one "is not one" as a consequence of the claim that it "is not," with "is" construed narrowly as spatio-temporal existence. But in H2a Parmenides does not say that the object of study does not partake of time, which, if indeed he were pointing back to the one of H1, would seem to be an arbitrary omission. These considerations point to the interpretation that the qualification "neither one nor many" picks out the complementary aspects of the one-that-is in H2 as "fully integrated one" (not many) and "in every way many" (not one) in the sameness and other analysis of H2. I credit Mitchell Miller with pointing out that the phrase "neither one nor many" is introduced by what we might consider an epexegetic καί (155e4), implying that it is not so much a new characteristic as it is a clarification of the sense in which the one is "both one and many" and "subject to time." "One" and "what are not one" (*ta me hen*) are considered in H2a distinct phases in the history of the "one" as it combines from "what is not one" into an integrated individual and later decomposes from an integrated individual into "what is not one."

3. Notice that he does not say "partaking in the one" or "partaking in unity." He certainly could have chosen this language, familiar from Socrates' account of participation earlier in the dialogue.

4. The use of αὖ at 155e5–7 (ὅτι μὲν ἔστιν ἕν, οὐσίας μετέχειν ποτέ, ὅτι δ' οὐκ ἔστι [sc. ἕν], μὴ μετέχειν αὖ ποτε οὐσίας;) signals the distinctively contradictory character of the one and many in H2a. The same term (αὖ) is not used in the context of H2, where the language is always rather one of the different respects in which the one-that-is permits itself to be characterized.

5. As if to explain the being of contradictories in time, Parmenides introduces a version of the principle of non-contradiction. The one-that-is is subject to constraints governed by the principle of non-contradiction. The statement of that principle in H2a is a pared down version of the statement that appears in *Republic* 4. In H2a the principle is missing the two qualifications of (1) "with respect to the same [part of itself]" (κατὰ ταὐτόν), and (2) "in relation to the same [object]" (πρὸς ταὐτόν), and simply asserts that the same thing cannot do or undergo opposites at the same time (436b8–c1). The one-that-is partakes of being when it is one, and it does not partake in being when it is not one—i.e.,

many—which it must be at another time. The purpose of emphasizing contradictories in the one-that-is is to reveal the power of the presumption of sameness that underlies the recognition of change.

6. These points about the priority of sameness to difference are made especially clear in Miller (1986) 115–121.

7. We might consider translating "ἄτοπος" here as "out of place" in order to bring out the joke that the instant does not spatio-temporally exist. Credit for this insight is due to I-Kai Jeng.

8. If the "one" that is in the instant were to have parts or be individual, it would be subject to the attributes of the "one" in H2 and would thereby be in time.

9. Parmenides did not use the definite article, leaving us free to translate "if [a] one is."

10. McCabe maintains throughout the hypotheses the view that the dialectical exercise remains "commitment-free" in relation to the ontological commitments of the first part of the dialogue, i.e., free of commitment to form (McCabe, 1996, 20). It seems to me that the implications the hypotheses hold for participation and the first part of the dialogue begin in H3 to become so apparent as to be undeniable, and that therefore hypotheses 3–8 should be considered in light of a very specific set of ontological commitments. I think the repeated reference to participation that we see in H3 makes this point unavoidable.

11. Participation could be thought to allow mutually incompatible contradictories to be reconciled within the one-that-is by, for instance, being distributed to different parts of the spatial whole, but the language of contraries and the context of temporal change is not invoked in H3. Cf. again Recco's description of the spinning top in *Athens Victorious*, chapter 1.

12. One difficulty for my interpretation is that Parmenides seems to privilege complexity over singularity when he says that if these others (which I am taking to be a plurality) do not have parts they would be entirely one. Later in H3 we will discover that these complex others are indeed also one *qua* many individuals ("Things different from the one, I suppose, would be many, for if things other than the one were neither one nor more than one, they would be nothing"; Τὰ δ' ἕτερα τοῦ ἑνὸς πολλά που ἂν εἴη · εἰ γὰρ μήτε ἓν μήτε ἑνὸς πλείω εἴη τἆλλα τοῦ ἑνός, οὐδὲν ἂν εἴη, 158b2–4). I take the oneness of what are other than the one to refer not only to their complexity but also to their singularity as individual ones among many others. What seems to be an initial privileging of complexity over singularity is merely a part of a process of differentiating denumerable multiplicity from complexity. On this point, I am in agreement with Harte, for whom the key move in this section is to establish a basis for rejecting the claim that composition is "ontologically innocent" and to distinguish a one that is "both one and many, both the whole and the parts," from a one that is "composed of many" (ἐκ πολλῶν) (Harte, 2002, 129). In other words, H3 shows us that not every many implies part/whole complexity even if it is the case that each many must be conceived in light of a limit or a one that gathers individuals such that they can be seen as being together.

13. Allen (1983, 267), Gill (1996, 87–9), and Harte (2002, 126) term this a many taken "distributively" rather than taken "collectively."

14. Similarly, if the university were each of its buildings, and I failed to be in any, I would thereby fail to be in what we are calling "the university."

15. Harte, referencing Gill (1996, 89), suggests that the argument may be logically consistent with the prior claim that a mere aggregate cannot be treated as an "all" of which the part is a part. She writes, "If, then, the argument imagines a many which not only cannot

be taken collectively as one, but whole members cannot themselves be assumed to be one, the attempt to draw a distinction between one of the many and the rest begins to look incoherent" (Harte, 2002, 127). I agree with Harte, insofar as I understand her point, that the ability to distinguish between one and other numerically distinct ones requires that we presuppose some one to which they all belong and in the context of which they can be distinguished. However, Harte does not directly address the sense in which part/whole complexity must be presupposed by numerical multiplicity. To be many ones implies a principle that gathers ones together into a field of indefinite number. Whole, by contrast, would imply a definite limit. Placement within an indefinite number of others need not be a specifically ordered relation; it can be aggregate being-with others that allows there to be a mere many. I take it that this minimal degree of participation in the one that is required for a field of indefinite many is what H7 describes as "apparent" unity. My view is that the H7 notion of minimal participation in the one occurs here in H3 for the first time. Harte uses H7 to discuss what a "bare plurality" might look like, and she concludes that such a thought is incoherent (Harte, 2002, 136). I am suggesting that the participation in unity that any plurality requires in order to be coherent entails participation in a limiting whole in which the many parts are minimally gathered.

16. Gail Fine ("Knowledge and Logos in the *Theaetetus*," *Philosophical Review* 88, 1979), Myles Burnyeat (*The Theaetetus of Plato* [Hackett Publishing, 1990]), and John McDowell (*Plato's Theaetetus* [Oxford: Clarendon Press, 1973]) remark that this (157c–e) contradicts the identification of whole with aggregate of its parts at *Theaetetus* 204a (noted in Miller, "Unity and Logos: A Reading of *Theaetetus* 201c–210a, *Ancient Philosophy* 12 [1]: 93). Harte agrees that a new metaphysics, initially introduced at 146b204, is extended here, and that the mark of the new account consists in distinguishing complexity from distinctness and identity (i.e., what I have been calling denumerable multiplicity). In her discussion she emphasizes the ordered composition and completeness implied by the new account of complexity. However, she objects that the μιᾶς τινὸς ἰδέας at 157d8 should not be connected with the "middle-period discussion of forms." Her reason is that here the "form" is explicitly something composite, and the "forms" elsewhere are incomposite (Harte, 2002, 132n.25). My view is that here we see re-introduced to the conversation the necessary condition earlier identified by Socrates that the forms must be one, but now what has changed is that the sense of the "oneness" of the forms has been specified as simplicity prior to the structure of participants. Harte seems to identify the "single look" with the structure of the participant, which in my view is posterior to the form "of which" the parts and whole participate. I think what Harte identifies as the structure is what we should now understand Parmenides to be calling the "whole" transformed by an account of participation. Structure will be as essential to organizing the whole as to determining the parts, and therefore the structuring principle would seem to be something distinct from the whole and its parts (Harte, 2002, 161). The "one form" requires, for its instantiation, an internally complex whole with ordered parts. I am calling this indebtedness of the whole-of-parts to its prior one-form the normativity expressed in and through the compositional receptivity of the others to their ordering principle. Harte also refers to normativity but denies that it is operative in the *Parmenides*: "Plato's less abstract discussions of composition, outside the *Parmenides*, do indeed suggest that there is a normative aspect to his account of composition" (Harte, 2002, 130).

17. As noted, I am taking one-part and one-whole to refer interchangeably to the complexity of the singular one and to the singularity of the complex one.

18. Gill and Chrysakopoulou insert "with each other" to qualify manner of the others' communing. Nothing in the Greek makes such a specification, and inserting it suggests that the subject of the communing is a set of numerically distinct ones, which in my view is incorrect.

19. Harte notes the parallel between the use of "something else" (ἕτερόν τι) that comes to be in the multitude here and Aristotle's use of "something else" to refer to nature and principle of an organized whole, *Metaphysics* VII.17, 1041b17, 19 (Harte, 2002, 133, 137n37). Her larger point is that composition involves structure.

20. There is no independent causality explicitly attributed to the *plēthē* in these passages. However, they seem to have the power of resisting the imposition of limit, which is perhaps what enables them to give rise to appearances and apparent limits in H7.

21. Cf. Harte (2002), 130, 134–135.

22. Outside the limits of the inquiry in the *Parmenides*, this might point in the direction of the *chōra*. However, as long as we are involved in the specifically mathematical-dialectical inquiry of the *Parmenides*, the non-entity imagined as the completely destructured *plēthē* is simply an absurd positing. Cf. the footnote below.

23. In the First Hypothesis (H1) the "one" showed itself to "not be" in the sense of being exempt from all multiplicity, including the structures required for being, being known, being perceived, and being spoken, which led Aristoteles to a *reductio* conclusion requiring a new beginning. But, from our point of view, the *reductio* reflected more on Aristoteles' way of conceiving being in terms of individual perceptible objects than it did on the object of analysis. Indeed, Aristoteles' own response to Parmenides in that exchange pointed us, in spite of his limited understanding, in the direction of the major theme of the different ways in which being is construed in H1–H4. On this point, and in taking the One of H5 to refer to the aspect of unity of any form, I am generally in agreement with Miller (cf. Miller, "Unwritten Teachings in Plato's *Parmenides*," *The Review of Metaphysics*, 48.3, 1995). In H5, the one identified and studied in H1 returns, but we are correcting the error of thinking that the one, because it is exempt from multiplicity, does not at all exist (i.e., in this case, does not have being).

24. The questions engendered by the analysis in H5 are more thoroughly investigated in other dialogues (such as the *Theaetetus* and *Sophist*, but also the *Statesman* and *Philebus*) than any other elements in the *Parmenides*. The discussion of the Five Kinds in the *Sophist*, specifically the importance in that discussion of motion and rest, and the *Theaetetus'* discussion of the order of components that are joined to the object of knowledge and the marks that differentiate the object of knowledge from others, are just two of the most important places where the themes initiated in H5 receive the attention they require.

25. The shift from the hypothesis "if one is not" to what this hypothesis says (λέγειν) or is about (περί) mirrors previous moves (a) from thoughts in souls to thoughts of something that is (ὄν, 132c1), which is some one character (μίαν τινὰ οὖσαν ἰδέαν, 132c4) always the same over all (ἀεὶ ὂν τὸ αὐτὸ ἐπὶ πᾶσιν, 132c6–7), and (b) from many unlike things to the otherness we invoke in each when we call it out (προσαγορεύειν) and "always speak of the same" (ταὐτὸν καὶ λέγειν ἀεί, 147d6).

26. There are abundant references in H5 to the one as something spoken. Parmenides begins H5 by talking about what the Hypothesis says. The hypothesis "if one is not" differs from the *hypothesis* that "[a] not-one is not." He compares this to the way that *saying* (λέγειν) "large is not" differs from saying "small is not"; in each case someone would be

saying (λέγοι) something different (160c2–4). Parmenides says the one must partake of "something" and be like itself, otherwise we would not be talking about something in particular, and the hypothesis would be about something else. Lastly Parmenides says that it must partake of Being in some way because when we say "the one is not" we claim to be speaking truly, but "if true things, then it is clear that we say they are beings" (εἰ δὲ ἀληθῆ, δῆλον ὅτι ὄντα αὐτὰ λέγομεν, 161e5–6). Cf. the discussion just to come of what the hypothesis is "about" (περί, 161a3).

27. Literally, "is to it," using the dative of possession.

28. Parmenides is systematically taking care with his use of the terms "is," "has," and "partakes in" or "is said to be." Here difference is joined to the One with the predicate adjective in the dative case, i.e., "is to it."

29. τὰ δὲ μὴ ἴσα οὐκ ἄνισα; (161c7–8). The distinction to be drawn between being "unequal" and being "not equal" is interpreted by particular commentators as the distinction between ontological commensurates (i.e., things that are both subject to relative magnitude) and ontological incommensurates (i.e., things that are not both subject to relative magnitude) (cf. Miller, 1986, 143–146, and Allen, 1983, 282).

30. Parmenides says that whatever has largeness and smallness has equality between the two: ὅτῳ ἄρα ἔστι μέγεθος καὶ σμικρότης, ἔστι καὶ ἰσότης αὐτῷ μεταξὺ τούτοιν οὖσα (161d7–8).

31. Parmenides never says that the "others" are greater or smaller than the "one."

32. The "right measure" in the continuum of greater and lesser refers to the points of attraction where spatio-temporal being gets it right, as it were, i.e., where the right note, the right moment, the right measure, the right pause, and many others, show the way within the indeterminate multiplicity. Cf. the *Statesman* account of "due measure."

33. Note that we are here reaching the point where the *Timaeus* discussion of *chōra* seems most at odds with the discussion of materiality in the *Parmenides*. The *Parmenides* analysis suggests a formal explanation of materiality from participation in greater/smaller with respect to the "one," by which the *perata* have something to structure. This account reflects the mathematical abstraction required for dialectic. In my view, the *Timaeus* returns to the conception of life from mathematical abstraction, and in this context the unknowability of the material source is granted place (cf. the analysis of the way *chōra* eludes intelligibility in the chapter "The Χώρα," in John Sallis's *Chorology*, Indiana University Press, 1999, 91–124).

34. This would correspond most closely to what Parmenides had in mind when he said that without Socrates' account of forms, one would destroy the power of dialectic. The section on the bond is critical for establishing the possibility of philosophical inquiry into particular forms. Forms are simple and unique ones that nonetheless partake of other forms that are truly said of them and are divided from forms that are not in their definition. Most importantly, this section on the bonds of being and not-being will explain the possibility of bifurcatory division, e.g., in the *Sophist*, and related methods by which knowledge is achieved.

35. It is an unavoidable error that we use "things" to translate ὄντα and ἀληθῆ. We are not talking about spatio-temporal things but about "ones" of the sort that have "being" only insofar as they are determinate and intelligible. As I mentioned above, I take these ones to be consistent with forms.

36. Moments such as these are scattered throughout the hypotheses and are key to understanding what it is that Parmenides is calling us to see (141e, 145e, 151a, 152a,

159b-c, 161c, 162b ff., 163c ff., 166a), i.e., that there must be a kind of being that cannot be reduced to spatio-temporal determinacy.

37. The Oxford edition and Shorey delete this negative. Gill follows the 1923 Budé edition by Diès (cf. Gill, 1996, 170n29).

38. The concept of bond in H5 bears a similarity to the related concept of limit in H3, with the obvious distinction that the bond here pertains to the distinction between the "others" and the "one" to which they are subject. We therefore have construed the one-that-is-not in terms of the relationship between *eidos* (i.e., the one-that-is-not) and the others (i.e., the spatio-temporal ones-that-are), or in terms of an eidetic complex and a parallel *plēthic* complex. Of course, there is no mention in this section of the "others," and I have construed this to mean that Parmenides is referring neither to the *plēthē* nor to the continuum of possible determinations that resolve the *plēthē* into ratios of greater/smaller but rather to the ontological difference between the one and the others.

39. τό γε μὴν ἀκίνητον ἀνάγκη ἡσυχίαν ἄγειν, τὸ δὲ ἡσυχάζον ἑστάναι (162e1–2).

40. I have mentioned that this is the point of furthest advance in the larger metaphysical project that Plato only initiates in the *Parmenides*. Notice, however, that the Stranger for whatever reason seems to avoid explicit use of "is" and "is not," bonds of being and not-being, when placing statesmanship in various categories, asking what statesmanship should be characterized "as," and wondering whether it is "more" this or that (credit to I-Kai Jeng for this point). It may also be worth noting, given that we are pointing toward the entirety of what I am characterizing as the Platonic metaphysical project, that this is also the point at which a striking divergence can be seen occurring between Platonism, Hegelianism, and Heideggerianism. The Hegelian and Heideggerian reading of ideas at this point would emphasize, in the priority of the idea with respect to discursivity, a transcendence that exceeded and disrupted the discursivity to which it was subject as an object of *epistēmē*. Heidegger might emphasize the non-propositional simplicity of the idea, the concealment under which the idea therefore irretrievably stands, and therefore the insurmountable distortion, even violence, to which the idea is subject when brought into speech. Hegel might mark out this transcendence of the idea not for the violence of interpretation but for the way it names the project of a systematic account of the different ways in which the one can be specified (*viz.*, as idea taken under the aspect of its unity, as mathematical unit, as spatio-temporal individual, in some sense analogically as the *plēthē* in which those individuals are set). The specifically Platonic approach to things is, in my view, to treat the ideas as present to intuition in a way that is at least partially comprehended by the structures of discursivity. Whereas the notion that the inexhaustible excess of intelligibility preserves itself within a kind of concealment and withdrawal is not missing from Platonic philosophy (cf. the characterization of the Good in the *Republic*), I caution against locating that theme here and in the related metaphysical studies in other dialogues because doing so will obscure the degree to which these dialogues consider scientific knowing to be possible.

41. It is necessary to place the word "object" in parentheses here because the "subject" of these elucidating bonds of being and not-being is not, strictly speaking, an object except through the very participatory relations that are here being analyzed.

42. In the *Phaedo* we are introduced to the idea that things strive for the relevant forms from which they receive limit and definite identity (74e9–75a3). The animation of the inanimate that this word "striving" implies is not inapplicable to the context of the *Parmenides*, but it would take some work to translate that concept into the context of the

Hypotheses, where the perfection bestowed by the forms through an imposed limit has a more categorial cast and is therefore less animative (cf. Russon, 2000, discussed above in Chapter 1, "Maturing into Scientific Philosophy").

43. The unlimited multitude (ἄπειρός πλήθει) contrasts with the *apeiron* first imagined in H2, which was presented as consisting of already fashioned ones. Here the nature of the unlimited is successfully detached from the normativity that presupposes integrated units subject to number. The integrity of any part/whole composition in H2 was in fact arbitrarily determined, implying all the observations of H7, but that very arbitrary character was concealed along with the normative source of unity not revealed until we reach H3 and H5.

44. It is for this reason that study of the nature of spato-temporal individuals will show that we, mortal inquirers into the nature of being, gather compositional elements into unity of *logos* and understanding only ever at the risk and danger of falsely identifying *doxa* for noetic insight.

45. Οὐδ' ἄρα δόξα τοῦ μὴ ὄντος παρὰ τοῖς ἄλλοις ἐστὶν οὐδέ τι φάντασμα, οὐδὲ δοξάζεται οὐδαμῇ οὐδαμῶς τὸ μὴ ὂν ἐπὶ τῶν ἄλλων.

Conclusion

1. It seems reasonable to conclude that the traditional use of the terms "*eidos*" and "*noein*" prior to Socrates and Plato to refer to the quasi-perceptual grasp we have of the intelligibility of objects in its spatio-temporal presence is not only the background against which Plato introduces the turning of the soul from becoming to being. It is also the specific point of strong resistance that he must break through in order to introduce the notion of form. An excellent example of the powerful allure held by imagistic thinking is Socrates' willingness to switch back and forth between "equality" (ἰσότης) and the "equals themselves" (αὐτὰ τὰ ἴσα, 74c1) in the *Phaedo*, or between "likeness" (ὁμοιότης, 129a1) and the "likes themselves" (αὐτὰ τὰ ὅμοιά, 129b1) in the *Parmenides*. Notice that the very old and the very young Socrates speak in the same patterns. The initiate's extreme difficulty of breaking through the belief that explanatory principles are present to us in space and time requires that the expert and teacher remain sensitive to this error while conducting students along the path of education. The ambiguity of "*eidos*" allows passage from things present in space and time to categorial forms, i.e., forms that do not gather continua to specific limits but that structure the very possibility of a normatively structured thing. Categorial ones are forms that instantiate themselves through other forms, and the problem of the Hypotheses is primarily how form participates in form, and which forms specifically must the "one" participate in, if it is to instantiate itself as a "one-that-is." The type of thinking required by Plato in the *Parmenides* would seem to offer strong evidence that Plato cannot agree with the claim Aristotle makes in *De anima* 3.7 that "the soul never thinks without an image" (3.7, 431a16–17).

2. H2 and the Hypotheses in general do the same kind of work that Aristotle undertakes in the *Categories*, but Plato is doing that work from the perspective of answering the demand to wonder about the unity and systematic relation between the terms that structure those categories, such as the dyad of greater/smaller that structures indefinite magnitude.

3. Note that the "bond of being" binds what-is to its being, which at first referred to its openness as an object of knowledge and inquiry to further determination through its differentiae. However, through the idea of the *onta* that are said of the one-that-is-not,

the "bond" takes on the role of a more articulate metaphor, extending what-is (i.e., the one-that-is-not) to various other ones through which it is rendered explicit as an object of discursive knowledge. I do not think the *Parmenides* elaborates the account of the truth of the one-that-is-not—that job is taken up in the *Sophist*—but neither does the *Parmenides* rule out this further elaboration.

BIBLIOGRAPHY

Works of Plato

Euthyphro. J. Burnet, *Platonis opera*, vol. 1. Oxford: Clarendon Press, 1900 (rpt. 1967): St I.2a–16a.

Parmenides. J. Burnet, *Platonis opera*, vol. 2. Oxford: Clarendon Press, 1901 (rpt. 1967): St III.126a–166c.

Phaedo. J. Burnet, *Platonis opera*, vol. 1. Oxford: Clarendon Press, 1900 (rpt. 1967): St I.57a–118a.

Philebus. J. Burnet, *Platonis opera*, vol. 2. Oxford: Clarendon Press, 1901 (rpt. 1967): St II.11a–67b.

Republic. S. R. Slings, ed., *Platonis Rempublicam*. Oxford: Oxford Classical Texts, 2003.

Translations of Plato

Parmenides. Translated by H. N. Fowler. Plato in Twelve Volumes, vol. 9. Cambridge, Mass.: Harvard University Press, 1925.

The Parmenides and Plato's Late Philosophy. Translated by R. G. Turnbull. Toronto: University of Toronto Press, 1998.

Phaedo. Translated by E. Brann, P. Kalkavage, and E. Salem. Newburyport, Mass.: Focus Publishing/R. Pullins Company, 1998.

Philebus. Translated by S. Benardete. Chicago: University of Chicago Press, 1993.

Plato: Parmenides. Edited by M. L. Gill and P. Ryan. Indianapolis: Hackett, 1996.

Plato's Parmenides. Translated by R. E. Allen, rev. ed. New Haven: Yale University Press, 1997.

Plato's Parmenides. Translated by A. K. Whitaker. Newburyport, Mass.: Focus Publishing, 1996.

Plato's Parmenides: Text, Translation, and Introductory Essay. Translated by A. Hermann and S. Chrysakopoulou. Las Vegas: Parmenides Publishing, 2010.

Republic. Translated by A. Bloom. New York: Basic Books, 1968

Republic. Translated by A. Bloom. 2nd ed. New York: Basic Books, 1991.

Republic. Edited by Ferrari, Translated by Tom Griffith. Cambridge University Press, 2000.

The Tragedy and Comedy of Life: Plato's Philebus. Translated by S. Benardete. Chicago: University of Chicago Press, 2009.

Interpretations

Allen, R. E. "The Interpretation of Plato's *Parmenides*: Zeno's Paradox and the Theory of the Forms." *Journal of the History of Philosophy* 2.2 (1964): 143–155.

———. *Plato's Parmenides*, revised edition. New Haven: Yale University Press, 1997.

———. "Unity and Infinity: *Parmenides* 142b–145a." *Review of Metaphysics* 27.4 (1974): 697–725.

Bailey, D. T. J. "The Third Man Argument." *Philosophy Compass* 4 (2009): 666–681.

Baracchi, C. "Measure, Excess, and the All: *To Agathon* in Plato and Aristotle," in a volume in preparation with the working title *Companion to Ancient Philosophy* edited by S. Kirkland and E. Sanday.

Benardete, S. *The Rhetoric of Morality and Philosophy*. University of Chicago Press, 1991.

Brown, L. "Being in the *Sophist*: A Syntactical Inquiry." In *Plato* 1, edited by G. Fine. Oxford: Oxford University Press, 1999.

———. "Negation and Not-Being: Dark Matter in the *Sophist*." Forthcoming.

———. "The *Sophist* on Statements, Predication and Falsehood." In *The Oxford Handbook of Plato*, edited by G. Fine, 437–462. Oxford: Oxford University Press, 2008.

Burnyeat, M. *The Theaetetus of Plato*. Indianapolis: Hackett Publishing, 1973.

Chen, C. H. "On the *Parmenides* of Plato." *Classical Quarterly* 38 (1944): 101–114.

Cherniss, H. *Aristotle's Criticism of Plato and the Academy*. Baltimore: Johns Hopkins Press, 1944.

———. "Parmenides and the *Parmenides* of Plato." *American Journal of Philology* 53 (1932): 122–138.

———. "Some War-Time Publications Concerning Plato I," *American Journal of Philology* 68.2 (1947): 113–146.

———. "The Relation of the *Timaeus* to Plato's Later Dialogues." *American Journal of Philology* 78 (1957): 225–266.

Cherubin, R. "Inquiry and What Is: Eleatics and Monisms." *Epoché* 8.1 (2003).

Cohen, S. M. "The Logic of the Third Man." *Philosophical Review* 80 (1971): 448–475.

Cornford, F. M. *Plato and Parmenides*. London: Routledge and Kegan Paul, 1939.

Crombie, I. M. *An Examination of Plato's Doctrines*. 2 vols. London: Routledge and Kegan Paul, 1962–63.

Curd, P. "*Parmenides* 131C-132B: Unity and Participation," *History of Philosophy Quarterly* 3 (1986): 125–136.

Damschen, G. "Grenzen des Gesprächs über Ideen. Die Formen des Wissens und die Notwendigkeit der Ideen in Platons 'Parmenides.'" In *Platon und Aristoteles—sub ratione veritatis. Festschrift für Wolfgang Wieland zum 70. Geburtstag*, edited by G. Damschen, R. Enskat, and A. G. Vigo, 31–75. Vandenhoeck & Ruprecht: Göttingen, 2003.

Desjardins, R. *The Rational Enterprise: Logos in Plato's Theaetetus*. Albany: SUNY Press, 1990.

Devereaux, D. "Separation and Immanence in Plato's Theory of Forms." *Oxford Studies in Ancient Philosophy* 12 (1994): 63–90.

Evans, N. *Civic Rites: Democracy and Religion in Ancient Athens*. Berkeley, Los Angeles, London: University of California Press, 2010.

Fine, G. "Immanence." *Oxford Studies in Ancient Philosophy* 4 (1986): 71–97.

———. "Knowledge and Logos in the *Theaetetus*," *Philosophical Review* 88 (1979): 366–397.

———. *On Ideas: Aristotle's Criticism of Plato's Theory of Forms*. Oxford: Clarendon Press, 1993.

———. (ed.) *The Oxford Handbook to Plato*. New York, Oxford: Oxford University Press, 2008.

Forrester, J. W. "Arguments an Able Man Could Refute: *Parmenides* 133b–134e." *Phronesis* 19 (1974): 233–237.

Frances, B. "Plato's Response to the Third Man Argument in the Paradoxical Exercise of the *Parmenides*." *Ancient Philosophy* 16 (1996): 47–64.

Fujisawa, N. "Echein, Metechein, and Idioms of 'Paradeigmatism' in Plato's Theory of Forms." *Phronesis* 19 (1974): 30–58.

Geach, P. "The Third Man Again," *Philosophical Review* 65 (1956): 72–82.

Gentzler, J. "Forms, Individuals, and Individuation: Mary Margaret McCabe's 'Plato's Individuals.'*Apeiron* 29, no. 2 (1996): 163–181.

Gerson, L. "Plato on Identity, Sameness, and Difference." *Review of Metaphysics* 58, no. 2 (1996): 305–332.

Gill, C., and M. M. McCabe, eds. *Form and Argument in Late Plato*. Oxford: Clarendon Press, 1996.

Gill, M. L. "Introduction," in Plato: *Parmenides*, Gill and Ryan, 1–116, 1996.

———. "Method and Metaphysics in Plato's *Sophist* and *Statesman*." In *The Stanford Encyclopedia of Philosophy*, edited by E. N. Zalta, 2005. http://plato.stanford.edu/entries/plato-sophstate/

Glazebrook, T. "Zeno against Mathematical Physics." *Journal of the History of Ideas* 62, no. 2 (2001): 193–210.

Goldstein, L., and P. Mannick "The Form of the Third Man Argument." *Apeiron* 12 (1978): 6–13.

Gonzalez, F. *Dialectic and Dialogue: Plato's Practice of Philosophical Inquiry*. Evanston, Ill.: Northwestern University Press, 1998.

———. "Plato's Dialectic of Forms." In *Plato's Forms*, edited by W. Welton, 31–83. Lanham, Md.: Lexington Books, 2002.

Harte, V. *Plato on Parts and Wholes: The Metaphysics of Structure*. New York: Oxford University Press, 2002.

Hathaway, R. F. "The Second 'Third Man.'" In *Patterns in Plato's Thought*, edited by J. M. E. Moravcsik, 78–100. Dordrecht: Reidel, 1973.

Havlicek, A., and F. Karfik. *Plato's Parmenides: Proceedings of the Fourth Symposium Platonicum Pragense*. Prague: OIKOYMENH Publishers, 2005.

Hermann, A. *Plato's Parmenides: Introductory Essay*. Las Vegas: Parmenides Publishing, 2010.

Hopkins, P. "Zeno's boêtheia tôi logôi: Thought Problems about Problems for Thought." *Epoché* 11:1 (2006).

Hunt, D. "How (not) to Exempt Platonic Forms from *Parmenides*'s Third Man." *Phronesis* 42 (1997): 1–20.

Irwin, T. *Plato: Gorgias*. Oxford: Oxford University Press, 1979.

Kahn, C. "Drama and Dialectic in Plato's *Gorgias*." *Oxford Studies in Ancient Philosophy* 1 (1983): 75–121.

———. "A Return to 'Be' and the Concept of Being." In *Essays on Being*. Oxford University Press, 2009.

———. *The Verb "Be" in Ancient Greek*. Dordrecht: Reidel, 1973. Reprinted Indianapolis: Hackett, 2003.

Klein, J. *Greek Mathematics and the Origin of Algebra*. Translated by Eva Brann. Cambridge, Mass.: MIT Press, 1968. Reprinted by Dover Publications, Mineola, N.Y., 1992.

Kraut, R., ed. *The Cambridge Companion to Plato*. Cambridge: Cambridge University Press, 1992.

Lee, E. N. "Plato on Negation and Not-Being in the *Sophist*." *Philosophical Review* 3, no. 81, (1972): 267–304.

———. "Reason and Rotation: Circular Movement as the Model of Mind (*Nous*) in Later Plato." In *Facets of Plato's Philosophy*, 70–102. Edited by W. H. Werkmeister. Assen: Van Gorcum, 1976.

———. "The Second 'Third Man': An Interpretation." In Moravcsik, *Patterns in Plato's Thought*. Dordrecht: Reidel, 101–122, 1973.

Lewis, F. "Parmenides on Separation and the Knowability of the Forms: Plato's *Parmenides* 133A ff." *Philosophical Studies* 35 (1979): 105–127.

Malcolm, J. *Plato on the Self-Predication of Forms: Early and Middle Dialogues*. Oxford: Clarendon Press, 1991.

Mann, W. E. "The Third Man=The Man Who Never Was." *American Philosophical Quarterly* 16 (1979): 167–176.

Mates, B. "Identity and Predication in Plato," *Phronesis* 24 (1979): 211–229.

Matthews, G. *Plato's Epistemology and Related Logical Problems*. London: Faber, 1972.

McCabe, M. M. *Plato's Individuals*. Princeton: Princeton University Press, 1994.

———. "Unity in Plato's *Parmenides*: The Unity of the *Parmenides*." In *Form and Argument in Late Plato*, ed. C. Gill and M. M. McCabe, 135–151. Oxford: Clarendon Press, 1996.

McDowell, John. *Plato's Theaetetus*. Oxford: Clarendon Press, 1990.

McPherran, M. L. "Socratic Epagoge and Socratic Induction." *Journal of the History of Philosophy* 45 (2007): 347–364.

Meinwald, C. C. "Good-bye to the Third Man." In *The Cambridge Companion to Plato*, edited by R. Kraut, 365–396. Cambridge: Cambridge University Press, 1992.

———. 1991. *Plato's Parmenides*. New York: Oxford University Press.

Miller, M. "Ambiguity and Transport: Reflections on the Proem to Parmenides' Poem." *Oxford Studies in Ancient Philosophy* 30 (2006): 1–47.

———. "Aporia and Conversion: A Critical Discussion of R. E. Allen's 'Plato's Parmenides.'" *The Review of Metaphysics* 41, no. 2 (Dec. 1987): 355–368.

———. "Figure, Ratio, Form: Plato's Five Mathematical Studies." In *Recognition, Remembrance and Reality: New Essays on Plato's Epistemology and Metaphysics*, edited by M. McPherran. *Apeiron* 32, 4 (Dec. 1999): 73–88.

———. "A More 'Exact Grasp' of the Soul?: Tripartition in the *Republic* and Dialectic in the *Philebus*." In *Truth: Studies of a Robust Presence*, edited by K. Pritzl. Washington, D. C.: Catholic University of America Press, 2010.

———. *Plato's Parmenides: The Conversion of the Soul*. Princeton: Princeton University Press, 1986. Reprinted University Park: Pennsylvania State University Press, 1991.

———. "Unity and Logos: A Reading of *Theaetetus* 201c–210a." *Ancient Philosophy* 12, no. 1 (1992).

———. "Unwritten Teachings in Plato's *Parmenides*." *The Review of Metaphysics* 48.3 (1995).

Mohr, R. "Forms as Individuals." *Illinois Classical Studies* II (1986): 113–128.

Moravcsik, J. M. E., ed. *Patterns in Plato's Thought*. Dordrecht: Reidel, 1973.

———. "The 'Third Man' Argument and Plato's Theory of Forms." *Phronesis* 8 (1963): 50–62.

Mourelatos, A. *The Route of Parmenides*. Princeton: Princeton University Press, 1970.

Munn, M. *The School of History: Athens in the Age of Socrates*. Berkeley: University of California Press, 2000.

Nehamas, A. "Self-Predication and Plato's Theory of Forms." *American Philosophical Quarterly* 16, no. 2 (April 1979).

Neils, J. *Goddess and Polis. The Panathenaic Festival in Ancient Athens*. Hanover: Hood Museum of Art, 1992.

Nichols, Jr., J. "The Rhetoric of Justice in Plato's *Gorgias*." In *Plato: Gorgias*. Ithaca: Cornell University Press, 1998.

Owen, G. E. L. "The Place of the *Timaeus* in Plato's Dialogues." *Classical Quarterly* N.S. 3 (1953): 79–95.

———. "Plato on Not-Being." In *Plato* 1: *Metaphysics and Epistemology*, edited by G. Vlastos, 223–67. Garden City, N.Y.: Doubleday: 1971. Reprinted in *Logic, Science, and Dialectic*, edited by G. E. L. Owen and M. C. Nussbaum, 104–37. London: Duckworth/Ithaca, N.Y.: Cornell University Press, 1986. Reprinted in *Plato* 1: *Metaphysics and Epistemology*, edited by G. Fine, 416–54. Oxford: Oxford University Press, 1999.

Palmer, J. *Plato's Reception of Parmenides*. Oxford: Oxford University Press, 1999.

Panagiotou, S. "The Day and Sail Analogies in Plato's *Parmenides*." *Phoenix* 41 (1987): 10–24.

Patterson, R. "Forms, Fallacies, and the Functions of Plato's *Parmenides*." *Apeiron* 32 (1999): 89–106.

———. *Image and Reality in Plato's Metaphysics*. Indianapolis: Hackett Publishing, 1985.

Peck, A. L. "Plato's *Parmenides*: Some Suggestions for Its Interpretation." *Classical Quarterly* 3/3 (1953): 126–150.

———. "Plato Versus Parmenides." *Philosophical Review* 71 (1962): 159–184.

Pelletier, F. J., and E. N. Zalta. "How to Say Goodbye to the Third Man." *Noûs* 34 (2000): 165–202.

Penner, T. *The Ascent from Nominalism: Some Existence Arguments in Plato's Middle Dialogues*. Dordrecht and Boston: Reidel, 1987.

Peterson, S. "The Greatest Difficulty for Plato's Theory of Forms: The Unknowability Argument of *Parmenides* 133c–134c." *Archiv für Geschichte der Philosophie*, 63 (1981): 1–16.

———. "The Language Game in Plato's *Parmenides*." *Ancient Philosophy* 20 (2000): 19–51.

———. "New Rounds of the Exercise in Plato's *Parmenides*." *Modern Schoolman* 80 (2003): 245–278.

———. "The Parmenides." In G. Fine, ed., *The Oxford Handbook to Plato*. New York, Oxford: Oxford University Press, 2008: 383–410.

———. "Plato's *Parmenides*: A Principle of Interpretation and Seven Arguments." *Journal of the History of Philosophy* 34 (1996): 167–192.

———. "A Reasonable Self-Predication Premise for the Third Man Argument." *Philosophical Review* 82 (1973): 451–470.

Pickering, F. R. "Plato's "Third Man" Arguments." *Mind* 90 (1981): 263–269.

Prior, W. J. *Unity and Development in Plato's Metaphysics*. London: Croom Helm, 1985.

Recco, G. *Athens Victorious: Democracy in Plato's Republic*. Lanham, Md.: Lexington Books, 2007.

Rickless, S. C. "How Parmenides Saved the Theory of Forms." *Philosophical Review* 107 (1998): 501–554.

———. *Plato's Forms in Transition: A Reading of the Parmenides.* Cambridge: Cambridge University Press, 2007.

Runciman, W. G. "Plato's *Parmenides.*" *Harvard Studies in Classical Philology* 64 (1959): 89–120.

Russon, J. 2000. "We Sense that They Strive." In *Retracing the Platonic Text,* edited by J. Russon and J. Sallis. Evanston, Ill.: Northwestern University Press: 70–84.

Ryle, G. "Plato's *Parmenides.*" *Mind* 48 (1939): 129–151 and 302–325.

Sallis, J. *Chorology.* Bloomington: Indiana University Press, 1999.

Sanday, E. C. "Eleatic Metaphysics in Plato's *Parmenides*: Zeno's Puzzle of Plurality." *Journal of Speculative Philosophy* 23 (2009): 208–226.

Sayre, K. M. *Parmenides' Lesson: Translation and Explication of Plato's Parmenides.* South Bend: University of Notre Dame Press, 1996.

———. *Plato's Analytic Method.* University of Chicago Press, 1969.

Scaltsas, T. "The Logic of the Dilemma of Participation and of the Third Man Argument." *Apeiron* 22 (1989): 67–90.

———. "A Necessary Falsehood in the Third Man Argument." *Phronesis* 37 (1992): 216–232.

Schipper, E. W. *Forms in Plato's Later Dialogues.* The Hague: Martinus Nijhoff, 1965.

Schofield, M. "The Antinomies of Plato's Parmenides." *Classical Quarterly* 27.1 (1977), 139–158.

———. "Likeness and Likenesses in the *Parmenides.*" In *Form and Argument in Late Plato,* edited by C. Gill and M. M. McCabe, 49–77. Oxford: Clarendon Press, 1996.

———. "A Neglected Regress Argument in the Parmenides." *Classical Quarterly* NS 23 (1973): 29–44.

———. "Plato on Unity and Sameness." *Classical Quarterly* NS 24.1 (May 1974), 33–45.

Schweizer, P. "Self-Predication and the Third Man." *Erkenntnis* 40 (1994): 21–42.

Scolnicov, S. *Plato's Parmenides.* Berkeley: University of California Press, 2003.

Sellars, W. "Vlastos and 'The Third Man.'" *Philosophical Review* 64 (1955): 405–437.

Sharvy, R. "Plato's Causal Logic and the Third Man Argument." *Noûs* 20 (1986): 507–530.

Shiner, R. *Knowledge and Reality in Plato's Philebus.* Assen: van Gorcum, 1974.

Silverman, A. *The Dialectic of Essence.* Princeton: Princeton University Press, 2002.

Sinaiko, H. *Love, Knowledge, and Discourse in Plato: Dialogue and Dialectic in Phaedrus, Republic, Parmenides.* University of Chicago Press, 1965.

Solmsen, F. "The Tradition about Zeno of Elea Reexamined." *Phronesis* 16 (1971).

Spellman, L. "Patterns and Copies: The Second Version of the Third Man." *Pacific Philosophical Quarterly* 64 (1983): 165–175.

Sprague, R. K. "Parmenides' Sail and Dionysodorus' Ox." *Phronesis* 12 (1967): 91–98.

Strang, C. "Plato and the Third Man." *Proceedings of the Aristotelian Society* (Supplementary Volume) 37 (1963): 147–164.

Stauffer, D. *The Unity of Plato's Gorgias: Rhetoric, Justice, and the Philosophic Life.* Cambridge: Cambridge University Press, 2006.

Taylor, A. E. *Plato: The Man and His Work.* London: Methuen, 1926.

Teloh, H. *The Development of Plato's Metaphysics.* University Park: Pennsylvania State University Press, 1981.

Teloh, H., and D. J. Louzecky. "Plato's Third Man Argument." *Phronesis* 17 (1972): 80–94.

Vlastos, G. "Addenda to the Third Man Argument: A Reply to Professor Sellars." *Philosophical Review* 64 (1955): 438–448.

———. "A Metaphysical Paradox." In *Platonic Studies*. Princeton: Princeton University Press, 1973.

———. "Plato's Testimony Concerning Zeno of Elea." *The Journal of Hellenic Studies* 95 (1975): 136–162.

———. "Plato's 'Third Man' Argument (*Parm*, 132a1–b2): Text and Logic." *Philosophical Quarterly* 19 (1969): 289–301.

———. "Postscript to the Third Man: A Reply to Mr. Geach." *Philosophical Review* 65 (1956): 83–94.

———. "The Third Man Argument in the *Parmenides*." *Philosophical Review* 64 (1954): 319–349.

Waterlow, S. "The Third Man's Contribution to Plato's Paradigmatism." *Mind* 91 (1982): 339–357.

Weingartner, R. A. *The Unity of the Platonic Dialogue*. New York: Bobbs-Merrill, 1973.

White, F. C. "Plato's Middle Dialogues and the Independence of Particulars." *Philosophical Quarterly* 27:108 (1977): 193–213.

———. "Problems of Particulars in Plato's Later Dialogues." *Apeiron* 16:1 (1982): 53–62.

Wieland, W. *Platon und die Formen des Wissens*. Göttingen, 1982.

Yi, B., and E. Bae. "The Problem of Knowing the Forms in Plato's *Parmenides*." *History of Philosophy Quarterly* 15 (1998): 271–283.

INDEX